Praise for Jailbreaking the Goddess

"A deep examination of the limitations of the triple Goddess form … and how that form is an inaccurate reflection for modern day feminist activists and ritualists. Lasara Firefox Allen delves deep into the ways in which colonialist language has shaped our experience of the Divine Feminine for centuries and she meets a need that has risen in the feminist spiritual movement for years."

—Suzanne Sterling, founder of Voice of Change,
co-founder of Off The Mat, Into the World

"Moving beyond our feminine biology as a definition of who we are, and how we relate to the Divine Feminine, Lasara Firefox Allen creates a whole new template more suitable for women today, redefining femininity as innocent, powerful, generative, creative, wise, and all of it reverent. Every student of feminism and feminist theology should read this book. It is a game-changer."

—Anodea Judith, PhD, author *Wheels of Life* and *The Global Heart Awakens*

"Lasara has brought us the goddesses who speak across time and space, who invite us to be inclusive and intersectional in our worship, who demand that we are open and honest about who we are in this world and in our bodies. They remind us that the survival of our species, of all species of life, requires that we create diverse, complex, dynamic communities. Audre Lorde said that we can learn to mother ourselves and this book gives us more tools and voices to do just that."

—Mai'a Williams, journalist, teacher, activist, editor of *Revolutionary Mothering*

"Lasara Firefox Allen includes complex and important elements in the process of this book, leaving the audience empowered to think beyond the previous construction of woman. Bringing in the layers that we embody and embracing that in our spiritual paths allow for a celebration of self; and in celebrating the wholeness of woman, we are also liberated by the space for self-determination."

—Crystal Blanton, MSW, editor of *Bringing Race to the Table*

"Allen suggests that all who are called by the Goddess chart their own course and unlocks the Goddess' potential as a revolutionary force, untethered by biology. She asks all seekers to engage in a potent practice of respect, work, self and other as aspects of the collective divine which, taken together, can birth more than a new approach to the Goddess, but a new world entirely."

—Darcy Totten and Jasper James, Activism Articulated

"Lasara Firefox Allen has liberated the goddess from every possible stereotype: race, reproductive status, age, sexual preference—even gender identity. *Jailbreaking the Goddess* provides countless possibilities for everyone to meet and engage with archetypal feminine power on their own terms. I love this book!"

—Barbara Carrellas, author of *Urban Tantra*

"For nearly fifty years I have been the consort of a most extraordinary Woman/Priestess/ Goddess. Never in those fifty years (or in our childhood years that preceded them) has her divine and infinite person-hood ever allowed itself to be limited and taken captive by the simplistic classic model of maid, mother, and crone. Lasara Firefox Allen's Fivefold Goddess model identifies and describes the Mysteries of Modern Woman, and comes dangerously close to allowing me to at least hear Her sphinx's riddle."

—Lon Milo DuQuette, author of *Low Magick*

"*Jailbreaking The Goddess* is a delicious tool for dismantling (and reimagining) the way we think about women's spirituality and power. [The] fivefold goddess model honors the divine nature in all women, regardless of age, ability, sexual orientation, gender identity, race, and economic status. This is an exciting, smart, and practical approach to liberating the mind, body, and spirit."

—Laurie Lovekraft, Reclaiming Witch, priestess, and *Huffington Post* columnist

"Lasara is a dynamic and powerful woman who shows us that revolution starts within. This radical new way of looking at the divine feminine injects a much-needed freshness into Goddess spirituality!"

—Sharon Knight, musician and priestess

"Yes and more yes to this new model, which moves us out of the expectation of conformation to outdated cultural norms. One of the things I love most about this book is how it allows for other forms to exist within it (and you!). It's an opening of possibility for all women to re-divine all parts of ourselves."

—Jenya T. Beachy, teacher, blogger, and author of the forthcoming *The Secret Country of Yourself*

"A fantastic and sorely needed contribution to feminist spirituality discourse. It breaks open the tired tropes of maiden, mother, crone and makes more space for the variety of lived experiences of anyone who relates to the female experience."

—Niki Whiting, MA, co-founder of Many Gods West

"In Allen's vision the goddess is young and old, creative and wise, and above all strong. This is a Goddess who can map onto our own journeys at any part of our life. Allen's gentle, fierce, and wise work guides us through the process of rebuilding our sense of ourselves as holy through relationship to these new faces of the Goddess."

—Brandy Williams, author of *For the Love of the Gods* and *The Woman Magician*

"Lasara Firefox Allen has created what may well be the definitive guide to feminist spirituality… The depth of Lasara's passion, knowledge, and skill allows her to reveal and reframe the fundaments of magick in a way that will have a lasting impact within the field of magick and throughout the wider culture."

—Philip H. Farber, author of *Brain Magick*

"*Jailbreaking the Goddess* is challenging, unabashed and wild, yet thoughtful and articulate. I found pieces of myself and my personal Goddess journey that have never been illuminated by any other text. Lasara Firefox Allen has truly broken the Goddess out of an antiquated jail. The world needs this freed Goddess. This book is part of that liberation."

—Courtney Weber, author of *Brigid: History, Mystery, and Magick*

"Reading *Jailbreaking the Goddess* is a view into a world that but rarely exposes itself to the likes of me. The magic is classic, but updated to self-rooted authority, and the politics are heart-felt, leading to a vision of societal transformation centered on the Woman of Power, Wisdom, and Compassion."

—Sam Webster, PhD, MDiv, Executive Director of the Pantheon Foundation

"*Jailbreaking the Goddess* is one of those rare Pagan books that will still be talked about in fifty years; it's that groundbreaking. Lasara puts the tired trope of maiden/mother/crone to bed and replaces it with a Goddess who is living, vital, and more accurately represents the women of today."

—Jason Mankey, editor of the Patheos Pagan channel and author of *The Witch's Athame*

"Whilst honoring the roots of Goddess worship, Lasara has successfully opened up avenues of exploration for anyone who identifies with worship of the feminal divine in clear and loving guidance towards a stronger community of men, women, and all in between."

—Xochiquetzal Duti Odinsdottir, HPs/x, Wayfarer Tradition

Jailbreaking
the
Goddess

About the Author

Lasara Firefox Allen is an author, coach, educator, and activist. A family-traditions Witch, Lasara is a second generation ordained Pagan clergy member with ordinations from multiple traditions and religious organizations. Lasara's first book, *Sexy Witch* (Llewellyn Worldwide, 2005) is available in four languages and is distributed internationally. *Jailbreaking the Goddess: A Radical Revisioning of Feminist Spirituality*, will be her second book with Llewellyn. Lasara regularly offers online courses, in-person workshops, and retreats on a range of topics: feminism, bodily sovereignty, sexuality, relationships, parenting/family dynamics, media literacy, body positivity, magick, and spirituality. Married to the love of her life and mothering two amazing kids, Lasara lives in the wilds of northern California.

To Write to the Author

If you wish to contact the author or would like more information about this book, please write to the author in care of Llewellyn Worldwide Ltd. and we will forward your request. The authors and publisher appreciate hearing from you and learning of your enjoyment of this book and how it has helped you. Llewellyn Worldwide Ltd. cannot guarantee that every letter written to the author can be answered, but all will be forwarded. Please write to:

Lasara Firefox Allen
℅ Llewellyn Worldwide
2143 Wooddale Drive
Woodbury, MN 55125-2989

Please enclose a self-addressed stamped envelope for reply,
or $1.00 to cover costs. If outside the USA, enclose
an international postal reply coupon.

Lasara Firefox Allen

Foreword by Ariel Gore

Jailbreaking
the
Goddess

A Radical Revisioning of
Feminist Spirituality

Llewellyn Publications

Woodbury, Minnesota

FIRST EDITION
First Printing, 2016

The meditative approaches in this book are not a substitute for psychotherapy or counseling, nor are they a substitute for medical treatment. They are intended to provide clients with information about their inner workings that can add another helpful dimension to treatment with a trained medical or mental health professional, as their circumstances may warrant.

Book design by Bob Gaul
Cover design by Lisa Novak
Cover image by www.iStockphoto.com/12725130©flyparade
Interior art by Llewellyn Art Department

Llewellyn Publications is a registered trademark of Llewellyn Worldwide Ltd.

Library of Congress Cataloging-in-Publication Data
Names: FireFox, LaSara, author.
Title: Jailbreaking the goddess : a radical revisioning of feminist
    spirituality / Lasara Firefox Allen ; foreword by Ariel Gore.
Description: First Edition. | Woodbury : Llewellyn Worldwide, Ltd, 2016.
Identifiers: LCCN 2015049779 (print) | LCCN 2016013036 (ebook) | ISBN
    9780738747972 | ISBN 9780738748900
Subjects: LCSH: Goddess religion.
Classification: LCC BL473.5.F57 2016 (print) | LCC BL473.5 (ebook) | DDC
    201/.43—dc23
LC record available at http://lccn.loc.gov/2015049779

Llewellyn Publications
A Division of Llewellyn Worldwide Ltd.
2143 Wooddale Drive
Woodbury, MN 55125-2989
www.llewellyn.com

Printed in the United States of America

Jailbreaking the Goddess is dedicated in memoriam to two strong and amazing women who passed on during the time in which this book was coming into form: Shannon Williams and Morning Glory Zell-Ravenheart. Each loved the goddess in her own way. Each was the goddess in her own way. May they rise again in power.

It is also dedicated to all the ones who walked this wild path before me, my foremothers and comrades of blood, thought, and spirit: my mom, Marylyn Motherbear Scott; Starhawk, Macha Aline O'Brien, Rosa De Anda. And to the visionaries, creatrixes, and harbingers of our collective liberation: bell hooks, Luce Irigaray, Trihn T. Minh-Ha, Arundhati Roy, Maya Angelou, Gyatri Spivak, Julia de Borgos, Dorothy Pitman Hughes, Gloria Steinem, Leslie Marmon Silko, Audre Lorde, Paula Gunn Allen, Amina Wadud, Wilma Mankiller, Sylvia Rivera, Assata Shakur, and innumerable others. Thank you.

And to my children, Aurora and Sol.

And to future generations. We will find our way together.

Contents

Foreword

– by Rosa De Anda –

In *Jailbreaking the Goddess: A Radical Revisioning of Feminist Spirituality*, Lasara Firefox Allen elevates us to living life as an incantation, mastering our full power as sacred magical beings and as women; born not for others but living life for ourselves. This book is pivotal in deconstructing the patriarchal myth of the Virgin, Mother, and Crone.

Lasara's writing honors the feminal essence in every living being. Her words challenge and change how we perceive and feel about ourselves as women, liberating us from the patriarchal synonymous construct of females as child bearers and/or females as comfort givers for the sole pleasure of men.

This scripture is a recipe for a sacred revolution and evolution of assigned or reassigned feminine power.

This creative blueprint is a roadmap with essential keys that will awaken and assert all of our senses as magical tools working with nature, as prayers to the universe, invoking the elements as working allies for directed and guided transformation. Regardless of class, language, or skin color, we are all part of this natural world and speak the language of Nature— and through this language we are all nurtured. We all have the power to commune with the natural world around us. This book invites us to be the director, teacher, and the student of our lives not separate from but with the same magical powers as our natural world commands around us.

This rare book deconstructs oppressive language and gender bias, and it breaks cultural and ethnic linguistic barriers. Through the author's inventive morphology, she has liberated us from the dogma of patriarchal verbal consequence. The author has abandoned the language of the oppressor, breaking away from a proscribed male-dominated communication norm historically used to define and control a woman's life. She gives us praxis; the practicum application on how to activate and create a magical life filled with beauty and limitless vision through the practice of ritual and/or new ways of thinking. We become the student and master of our own life interchangeably as needed.

This doctrine is a new code. A new way of communication which can be used with any other existing spiritual practice you may have. Whether your current beliefs are Christian, Buddhist, Muslim, Hindu, atheist, agnostic, Wiccan, or any other spiritual combination—this mighty book holds the knowledge to end xenophobia and make you a stronger, freer you. In Lasara's words, "As we decolonize language, we decolonize thought. This is a challenging process. It will require rethinking, withholding judgment, and pulling up whole aggregations of thought by the roots." *Jailbreaking the Goddess* is a resounding cry to end xenophobia and claim your life as your own in a DIY application. This book will inspire women to claim sovereignty and move foreword collectively, learning to live life for ourselves and with one another.

This book can easily be part of the course work in our college and university campuses, covens, women's and men's study groups, or in the hands of intrepid individuals searching for knowledge and discipline to break our restraints. This fiercely inspired body of work is art, theory, and passion. Genius.

Foreword

— by Ariel Gore —

The first time I met Lasara, my shoes didn't match. We had connected through my zine, *Hip Mama*, and decided to meet up at a park in Oakland to talk shop and to let our kids play. In those days it felt important to reach out to other moms who were "weird like me." We were both weird like that.

I'm not sure how the mismatched shoes happened. I was probably just tired and distracted—I was a single mom and working writer running a business.

When I noticed the shoes, I laughed. Lasara said, "It's all good," like she was some old hippie. She didn't care. There were more important things to focus on, and sometimes people put on the wrong shoes.

She was talking about women and ownership of our own bodies; about motherhood and feminism. These were the 90s and a new wave of Christian right men were declaring feminism dead—again. But we were feminists. And we weren't buying in to the latest obituaries.

Lasara was angry in a good way—the way that ignites into activism. She talked about her spiritual point of view at a time when a lot of feminists we knew shied away from religious topics for good and righteous reasons. "The personal is political," we all said. But Lasara understood that the spiritual was political too.

I was of course familiar with the goddess movement—what 1990s feminist could avoid it?—and I'd found value in it. I'd grown up in a 1970s progressive agnostic-Christian church myself where my father, an ex-communicated but still practicing Roman Catholic priest, used male and female pronouns interchangeably when he referred to God and performed gay weddings every weekend. Still, I knew a lot of women and men had been traumatized and continued to suffer under the singular vision of an angry white male god in the sky.

Yet the goddess movement seemed to hang onto threads of patriarchy. I got that the notion of a maiden-mother-crone goddess acknowledged the female—and that was something—but here I was in the "mother" phase and as much as I worshipped pregnant bellies, it did feel a bit at odds with my own maternal feminism that sought to acknowledge the complexity of real life. I was a proud mama, but I rejected the idea that my sexuality was behind me, my wisdom elusive, and my roles as an ambitious artist and ass-kicking bread-winner were seen as side hobbies.

In *Jailbreaking the Goddess*, Lasara addresses all these questions and more, opening up a conversation about the intersections of feminism, spirituality, and women's real lives. The book offers a starting point for a feminist spirituality that decenters assumptions and makes room for authentic enquiry into issues of sex and gender, race, ethnicity, nationality, and class.

Whether or not you believe in the Goddess (or even gods as a whole), *Jailbreaking the Goddess* offers an opportunity to break free. Jailbreaking the goddess out of her patriarchal trappings won't change everything. It won't end patriarchy. But a sovereign goddess will change the spiritual lives of some. And that change will ripple outward.

Lasara doesn't care if your shoes don't match. Ultimately this is a come-as-you-are kind of a gathering, a deeply engaging and ever-welcoming conversation on a park bench about our own sovereignty.

Part 1

A Radical Revisioning
of Feminist Spirituality

1

Starting Where We Stand

Jailbreaking the Goddess: A Radical Revisioning of Feminist Spirituality is a guide to deconstructing feminist spirituality. It is part magickal incantation, part intersectional feminist manifesta, part liberationist book of shadows, and part how-to guide for the cocreation of our collective emancipation. We are breathing into a space in which we will conspire to build a more intersectional, vibrant, socially evolved feminist spirituality.

A revolutionary reconceptualization of the feminal divine, *Jailbreaking the Goddess* offers a dynamic, inclusive model for experience of our divine nature. In these pages you will find a new format for experience and worship of the divine through an archetypal system that welcomes, includes, honors, and offers representation to all women seeking a home in a shared concept and vision of the feminal divine.

Breaking away from limitations embedded in the hyperfocus on procreative capacity and function modeled by the Maiden, Mother, and Crone trinity, we deconstruct the threads of patriarchal conditioning. We are more than our biology. In the contemporary awareness of—and awakening to—the myriad forms of womanhood, we reweave and refashion our understandings of our divine nature.

*While the concept of intersectionality was already taking form in the 1960s in the multiracial feminist and Black womanist movements, the term **intersectionality theory** wasn't coined until 1986. Kimberlé Crenshaw, a scholar and professor specializing in the field of critical race* *theory, originally used the term to define the differences in racialized experiences of womanhood.*

Intersectionality is a method of feminist theory that studies intersections between systems of oppression and domination. Awareness of complex relationships between gender, sexuality, race, ethnicity, nationality, and class is the edge of the rising wave with which we—as feminists, as women, as those who worship the feminal as a facet of the divine—must rise up. This will not happen by forcing old thoughts into new forms; it will only happen by reaching out, asking questions, and listening for answers we may not have expected.

Intersectional concepts allow us to have a conversation about feminism, spirituality, and feminist spirituality that recognizes that the center is always shifting, and the margin is shifting too.

In deconstructing our ideas of goddess spirituality, we will also by necessity deconstruct our identities as women and as carriers of the divine thread of womanhood. This will mean pulling apart the fabric of identity and being. It will mean dismantling concepts of womanness, ethnic and racial identity, age, and education. It will mean acknowledging privilege and positionality. It will mean examining structures of power, authority, and relationship.

I enter into that process with you right now by acknowledging my position and privilege; I am a white woman who is deeply dedicated to the concept and the practice of intersectional feminism. I recognize the privilege I hold and have made a commitment to using that privilege as a tool for dismantling the system within which it exists.

In *Jailbreaking the Goddess* I have invested deeply in creating a book that will be accessible and appealing to Pagans, polytheists, and goddess worshippers and feminists of all ethnicities, races, classes, ages, sexualities, and genders. I have sought out participation and engagement from a wide community in bringing this book into being. The voice on these pages is not mine alone; it has been shaped by many other voices and by the voice of this work itself.

The process of self-examination goes on. The content and conversation is new and rugged and wild. All I can be sure about is that it is the place we are starting from right now. Together.

We work to dismantle the system from the inside because we are all inside the system, and the system is inside us. Together we will bring it down. As we deconstruct, we will see new forms emerging from the liminal spaces where magick takes shape.

The processes and concepts offered in this book will help our spiritual realities to change and shift, in order to allow us to shift in rhythm with them and to become who we are reaching to be collectively and individually.

> *Journaling questions and actions included throughout this book give you the opportunity to use the material to go deeper into your process. Use them all, use some, or use none! It's your process. Do it however it works for you.*
>
> *JOURNAL: What does feminist spirituality mean to you?*
>
> *ACTION: Notice the shifting intersections of power and dominance in your world. How do they influence interactions? Apply this to your ideas about feminism and spirituality.*

The Path from Here—A Basic Overview

Reading this book will be a journey of divine-self-exploration. It will offer opportunities for new ways to see yourself in the feminal divine, to see the divine feminal in you, and to see her in the world.

In part 1 we deconstruct some standing thoughts, and explore the faces and phases of the fivefold model. In addition to breaking down and reevaluating aspects of the feminal divine, you will find lists of deities who relate to each aspect, relevant holidays and celebrations, some correspondences, mini-bios of some real-life women who embody these different aspects, and invocations.

Each chapter on her five faces begins with a sigil. You may integrate this sigil into your ritual work, your devotional art, your spell casting, your magickal wheel, and your contemplations.

In part 2 we move deeper into integration and application. You will learn practices for decolonizing your magick, building magickal community, deepening your relationship with the Goddess and goddesses, and grounding your relationship with the land you are on. You will be brought into conscious magickal conspiracy.

You will be given tools that will help you update the formats and interactive processes of your coven or spiritual circle or group. You will learn some advanced magickal techniques, be given the opportunity to reclaim the power of your magickal tools, and learn some fundamental elements that will help you create effective, consensual rites of passage. You will have the opportunity to develop—and, should you choose to, perform—rituals for her five faces.

In the appendix you will find basics of ritual design and other elements that will help if you are new to magickal practice. After that I have included a list for further reading. It includes some of the books that helped me to get to and through some of the concepts presented in this book.

Throughout, you will be invited to craft, write, build, play, draw, sing, create, and co-create this germinal relational reality into being.

Making It Up As We Go

As the author of this book, I am the first to admit I am making it up as I go. I encourage you to do the same.

Not only am I making things up, I'm also shaping old stories to fit new molds. I'm taking used cloth and in true riot goddess/punk rock/DIY fashion, I'm cutting it to pieces and repurposing it.

> *You make it up too! Trust yourself. Trust your magick. If a **correspondence** or a **story** or a **belief** doesn't work for you, create or find one that does.*

Create new ways out of old ways. And when I say "old ways" throughout these pages I may be referring to traditions, the ways of women, the old stories, or even simply "the way things have been." I am not saying that I believe there was some static, monolithic, prehistory Way That Things Were. I do not believe there ever was such, regardless of how far back in our evolutionary prehistory we could go; a belief in a monolithic prehistory society is by nature overly simple, ethnocentric, and ultimately exclusionary.

The work we are doing here is as far from reconstructionism as you can get. I am not interested in arguing the true roots of lineages, proving or disproving that the goddess/es ever reigned supreme, or in rebuilding old temples or rites. I am not even as interested in the factual accuracy of the stories we tell as much as I am interested in the overall veracity.

Even more than that, I am working to create the space for new stories. To this end I will use old words in new, creative ways. I will use incorrect pronouns. I will even combine wildly disparate theological and sociological theories, practices, and beliefs. I will use terms you may not have heard many times before reading them here, but will come to know well—and maybe even love. Words like *femina*, *feminal*, and *feminality*. Words like *intersectionality* and *decolonization*. Words like *sapience* and *rewilding*.

Truly, we have a lot of good material to work with. We're going to have to get creative, get our hands dirty, make a mess, and see what's on the other side of letting it all go.

Creation is an act requiring one part will, one part chance, one part faith, and one part straight up love. Look at this new world we are creating, this new aeon, where women are whole and holy unto ourselves.

> JOURNAL: What elements are you already deconstructing? What do you hope to repurpose?
>
> ACTION: Create a piece of artwork; a collage, drawing, painting, or even an assorted collection of items perhaps held in a vessel, that includes elements of what you are already awakening to. It may also include elements of what you hope to achieve in this journey of self and cultural examination. If you created an altar, you can place this piece or collection there.

The Fivefold Goddess Model

The fivefold model for the goddess offered within these pages is an entirely new system, one that takes into account the diversity and flexibility of the lived experiences of women. The archetypal system offered here is creative, complex, organic, and allows a fluid, cyclical flow deeply rooted in the diverse and multivalent experiences of womanhood.

This divine system is not built from relics or ashes of historical times or patriarchal models. It is created with honor for the divine nature of all women, and it comes forth from the flexibility of female creative expression and the vastly varied experiences of living as a woman.

In this system, goddesses are self-defined and self-defining. In conceptualizing a system for the feminal divine built with personal agency at the core, we usher into being a new aeon where we as women may discover, uncover, and create representations upon which to model our own expression of self-actualization. By recognizing her agency, we bring it forth in ourselves, and for one another.

The names used in these pages for the five faces of the goddess are in Latin. While some of the terms may have familiarity for you, the hope is that by using Latin terms instead of English or another more contemporary language you start with more of a *tabula rasa*—a blank slate.

This archetypal system is right now being born in us and through us and will evolve as we do. It is a model designed for evolution.

These are her five faces:

- *Femella* (/feˈmel.la/, or *feh MEHL lah*) means *girl*. She is the primal child, the divine child.

- *Potens* (/po.teːns/, *POH tehns*) means *able (to), potent, mighty, strong, powerful*. She is the woman of strength, full of potential and power, bursting forth.

- *Creatrix* (/kreˈaː.triks/, *kree A triks*) means *female creator*. She is the creator, the mother, the maker, the author.

- *Sapientia* (/sa.piˈen.ti.a/, *sah pee EN tee uh*) means *wisdom, discernment, memory, forethought, intellect, perfection of character, a science*. She is the wise woman, master of her craft, teacher, leader, woman of science and art.

- *Antiqua* (/anˈtiː.kʷua/, *AHN tee kwa*) means *old, ancient, aged, time-honored, simple, venerable, traditional, essential*. She is the old woman, the dreamer, the storyteller, the witch at the gate.

All of her faces have degrees of flexibility. In this model we are working from the awareness that in a lifespan of possibly 73.5 (global average lifespan for women according to the World Health Organization) to 87.6 years (highest average lifespan for women in 2013; Andorra) or more, a woman will go through many cycles of beginning, potential, creation, mastery, and reaching out to her community for support in cycles of death and rebirth.

In each of the chapters on these five faces of the goddess, you will find a section titled "In the Linear and Nonlinear." This section is devoted to conceptualizing the ways in which our process of growth and development is sometimes linear in progression, sometimes spiraling, sometimes circular, and always spherical.

A woman may be experiencing the Potens archetype in a love relationship and Sapientia in her family at the same time. She may be sitting in Antiqua as she holds deathwatch over a loved one while inhabiting Creatrix in her work. She may be casting about in a range of childlike emotions and impulses in her Femella as she experiences a parent's passing.

The fivefold model recognizes that women's rites of passage are complex and that they may best be revealed as a self-defined and self-defining processes. These rites are not static. This model recognizes that while some rites of passage may be rooted in biology or procreative capacity, a vast many are not.

> JOURNAL: What thoughts do you have so far about this five-fold model for the feminal divine?
>
> ACTION: Think back through your years and recognize some self-defined and self-defining moments in your personal history.

Seeing Our Face in Her Faces

In each of the chapters that address her five archetypal faces I have included a number of deities as examples of her aspects. I don't know all of these goddesses intimately, but I have done my best to offer a glimpse of a wide variety of goddesses from a number of religions, countries, and cultures.

There is a vast wealth of woman-power that has been handed down in diverse cultures. There are goddesses who are in some cases still worshipped to this day who have carried the thread of that power forward generation by generation. In other cases, the goddesses who were the source and receptive cauldron of woman-power were nearly wiped away by colonization. In all cases, these goddesses represent part of our collective story as women.

In Paganism and in many branches of goddess spirituality the focus has been primarily on white European goddesses, but we all deserve to see our face in her faces. I have reached out and attempted to pull in accurate information on goddesses from many cultures as examples of the five faces.

Some of these goddesses you may know better—or differently—than I do. You may have heard different stories about (or from) her than the ones I tell. And the story she tells here may be one you haven't heard yet. And I have surely gotten some stuff wrong; it's a challenge to learn about goddesses whose stories have been all but obliterated by colonization and suppression.

Each of these goddesses carries her culture forward. Each of us has a responsibility to her culture should we choose a goddess as our own or should we be chosen by her.

Honoring or Appropriation?

Appropriation is a deep issue. It is a force for wounding that is actively happening right now. We will go more deeply into the concepts in the second half of this book, but it is important to offer the concept up front so it can be in the air as we work our way through the pages.

Cultural appropriation happens when dominant culture "borrows" something from the culture of a minority group without the consent or input of that group. It is a form of cultural theft or exploitation.

Cultural appropriation is an issue that needs to be addressed on a deep and incisive level; we each need to take responsibility for decolonizing our spiritual process and development. This includes looking at where we are committing spiritual appropriation by taking or using cultural practices (or deities) without consent.

That said, as a community, movement, and culture we also need to be thinking, feeling, and talking our way through the sticky topics of ethnological ownership, racial essentialism, and the very dangerous concept of racial purity. Prohibitions on worshiping gods from outside your own traditions can end up in a very ugly place. An example of this is the attempt of white supremacy groups to take over the American Heathen movement.

The reality of it is that most of us do not come from one ethnographical group. Most of us are a confluence of varied bloodlines. When we also take into consideration relationship with the land where we live and the spirits and gods rooted there, and the stories we were raised on, the complexity of our spiritual lives begins to make itself visible.

As you read about the goddesses in these pages, as you research others, and as you are called by them to worship, it is important to create a process by which you can make sure you are honoring a god *and* her people.

If a particular goddess speaks to you as one of her five faces and you're not sure if she is for you (or if you are for her), the first bit of advice is to sit with her for a while. A good long while. Like maybe a year, or a year and a day. In that time, perhaps you hold sacred silence, and allow yourself to tend to the messages she is bringing to you. Learn her stories. Study her, and be in sacred conversation with her.

Remember that she lives within a framework in the religion and culture that she comes from; she does not exist in a vacuum.

Cultural appropriation reinforces casual racism, and a sense of ease in taking things for our own just because we are attracted to them. In this, it is easy—unconscious, even—to pick up the parts we like and leave behind what we perceive to be the less desirable parts. Be careful you are not doing this with a goddess, or with that goddess's people.

If, after your time of silent reflection and relationship investment, she is still devoted to you and you to her, then it is time to give your relationship due diligence.

You will learn what I mean by that in part 2, where we will examine skills and tools you can draw on in creating relationships with goddesses and on building relationship and co-alition with a goddess's people.

> JOURNAL: What are your thoughts about spiritual appropriation?
>
> ACTION: Research the roots of a tradition you observe or a magickal tool you use. Once you have traced it back to its beginning, evaluate whether you are practicing in a way that honors its origins, or whether this practice was appropriated along the way.

Colonization and Decolonization

Colonization is pervasive. Indigenous people, ways, lands, and nations the world over are being colonized actively and violently as you read this page. Colonization is conducted by many means: political, military, corporate, media.

It is essential that we fight colonization. While the goal of decolonization is our collective liberation and liberation of the Earth herself, the work of it will often be different for white people than it will be for people of color.

For racialized and Indigenous people, decolonization means reclaiming territories, lands, traditions, languages, stories, gods, and spiritual and magickal technologies. It means reclaiming ways of being and actively addressing wounding and the effects of transgenerational trauma. It means rooting out the lateral effects of colonization.

In a video clip calling for a healing ceremony in recognition of and mourning for the genocide of Native American peoples, Ohlone activist Kanyon Sayers-Roods says about the Indigenous community, "We need to heal. We carry the grief. We carry the oppression. We carry the suppression. Sometimes in our pain, we lash out, and it turns into a form of lateral oppression. The psyche of the oppressed takes on the characteristics of the oppressor. It's a form of colonization. It's an adopted method that we have learned in order to survive."

For white people it means that we must *stop colonizing*. It means paying attention when someone says that you are practicing their tradition without consciousness, relational awareness, or consent. It means taking seriously the topic of appropriation. It means not casually "god collecting," or cherry picking from the spiritual systems and cosmologies of cultures other than our own.

Decolonization requires that we all examine our actions and reactions, our judgments, the way we share space (or don't share it), our communal responsibilities, and even our ways of being in our bodies. The very fiber of our socialized selves was woven within the framework of colonization.

Decolonizing our spiritual realities means incisively examining our spirituality as we practice it now, and taking responsibility if we have unwittingly adopted practices, gods, or technologies that are not ours to take. It also means researching our own ancestors, and the stories of their—and our—colonization. It means searching for and retrieving our forgotten gods, cosmologies, and magickal technologies. And it means supporting our friends, comrades, and community members in the fight against further colonization.

There is some concern that using the term "decolonize" in contexts other than land- or territory-related conversation will weaken the term, will render it metaphor. The active colonization of Indigenous cultures and lands is a continuation of the desecration of the Earth. The global Indigenous rights movement is part of our collective story right now.

If we choose to honor the Earth and respect the sovereignty of spiritual and magickal traditions of cultures that have not been dominated by colonizer culture, if we hold sacred the lives of our Indigenous neighbors, comrades, and family, then it is essential that we take up the fight of moving colonizers out of occupied territories. In order to do this, we must recognize the fact that we are all colonized people. That the history of colonization is a shared wound. Our scars are older and have been turned, in many cases, to callous; the place where we say, "This is the way humanity is. Conquest and colonization is what we were designed for." This is colonialist reasoning and rationale.

We have been brainwashed. Your people were colonized. Your old stories have probably been lost—in part or in whole—to those who dominated your first people. Your people were assimilated by those who colonized them. What exists in you of your people exists because your first people carried it with them into the colonizing culture. And as your people assimilated whether by force or by desire for peaceful relations, your people joined forces to some extent with the colonizer. And if your story is like most stories, over the generations the history of the colonizer became your history. And your people came to be part of the colonizing force.

Some say that the stronger have always disarmed and overtaken the weaker. This is colonizer rhetoric. In our woman ways we know more about strength and weakness than this tells. Perhaps it is the case that humanity has spent much of its history stealing, raping, and destroying. But even if it is the case, there is no reason it need continue to be the way of things.

I'm using the terms "colonization" and "decolonization" in this book to define the very real process of excavating our ages-old histories that tie us to precolonial awareness. I'm calling upon us to examine how we are participating in colonialist culture. I am inviting us to reclaim our lives, our minds, our struggles—personal and collective, our old stories—the stories of our first people. I am also talking about coming present in our bodily sovereignty. Ultimately, about helping us all find our way to our own personal and cultural sovereignty.

In the work of revolution and evolution, we will dig deep, excavate, observe, and deconstruct. We will sort the hurtful from the generative and reseed the fertile ground with new stories. And as we need to we will find new words, or repurpose old ones in order to do it.

Decolonization happens in fits and starts. We will reclaim the terrain of our stories, bodies, souls, minds, imaginations, and spirits inch by tender inch.

> *JOURNAL: What does colonization mean to you?*
>
> *ACTION: Look into your own cultural story. Who were your first people? To where are your people indigenous? Can you trace your lineage back that far? What about the mythologies and old stories of your family? What is the creation myth of your family line?*

Organic Magick

While the origins of the practices and systems that are mixed together and taken apart in this book are eclectic, the framework offered as a moving-forward-from-here point is called *organic magick*. Based in an intuitive, conscious relationship with nature, the elements, the forces and gods, and with magickal practice, organic magick is in a sense an anti-system, and an anti-tradition.

Organic magick is about undoing as much as it is about doing. The ideology of organic magick is based in deconstructing our ideas about how magick works and investing in the experience of it. Organic magick is about process, not about goals. It is rooted in intuition in place of memorization, experience instead of idea, an awareness of shifting power structures and negotiated authority. Organic magick is designed to encourage magickal growth and evolution on personal and systemic levels.

Organic magick encourages and relies upon grounding into your inner sense of relationship with place and with practice. It's about being present in your spiritual process.

In addition to exploring the new formats for recognition of the feminal divine offered in the fivefold model, we will also work with deprogramming from ethnocentric biases in ritual design, creating intuitive relationships with deity, and building consent in magickal relationships.

One of the ultimate messages of organic magick is this: if you feel unsure about the integrity of an option I've offered, check in with yourself. If it comes down to a choice between applying what's suggested or applying what you feel is accurate, always trust yourself.

Every system was made up by someone along the way. Perhaps that someone was a god, or perhaps it was a magickian, or a witch, or an animal spirit. Perhaps the system was made up a long time ago. Perhaps the system was made up more recently. Perhaps it was made up by the First People, or the Old Ones.

Whoever made the system, whenever they made it, was not more right than you are about where you are standing in this moment. If you are present in your body, your practice, and tuned in with the space you work with, systems will reveal themselves to you. Stay grounded and trust your gut.

When you settle into a thing that works, thank the spirits and their people. If you research what you have learned through this interaction with your present time and space, you may find that the practices or patterns are tied to older energies. You may be able to layer in more levels of knowledge and awareness by researching the messages and teachings that you receive.

If you try something and it doesn't feel right, clean it up and either go back to the way it was before, respectfully and consensually borrow someone else's system for a while, or try something new.

Sunwise Has No Meaning in Space

One of the outcomes of taking a more critical approach to magick, worship, and witchcraft was a natural and essential veering away from some of the assumptions I grew up with. My early magickal education took place within the contemporary eclectic American Pagan movement. Influenced by Wicca, Feri, and ceremonial traditions, my magickal training had a strongly Eurocentric flavor.

In my first book, *Sexy Witch*, I offered ritual structures which had grown from that soil, resulting in a solidly Northern Hemispheric bias in circle design. Eurocentric directional and elemental correspondences lead us to an "east equals air" assumption. It also leads to terms like *deosil* and *widdershins* reiterating that bias.

Deosil is a Scottish Gaelic word that means "right"; to the right, right not wrong, and beneficial (as in, "May things go right for you"). In casting a circle it means "to the right," which is clockwise. In the Northern Hemisphere right, clockwise, and sunwise are synonymous.

However, in the Southern Hemisphere, sunwise is to the left. Down under, a counter-clockwise, left-turning circle is a sunwise casting.

The origin of widdershins is a little more hazy, according to linguists. In Scottish Gaelic, *widdershins*—and a similar word, *widdersonnis* in Lowland Scottish—can mean either "against the sun" or "away from the right." Widdershins may come from the Germanic *weddersinnes*, which means "back from."

In an effort to create more inclusive ritual templates and in order to limit confusion, I have chosen to use the term *sunwise* rather than *deosil* and *opposite sunwise* in place of *widdershins*. Of course much of ritual has no need for those designations, either. If this is the case with your practice or tradition, do your magick how you do!

Liberating the Elements

In addition to the orientation offered for sunwise and opposite sunwise in most of the ritual design sources generally available, there are numerous other biases from which we work. Many of these I have undoubtedly not yet even recognized in my own practices and beliefs; the deconstruction of assumption is an ongoing process. There is always more that can be done…or undone, as the case may be.

In an effort to uproot some basic assumptions of ritual design, instead of using the somewhat standard and thoroughly ethnocentric east/south/west/north directions with elemental attributions, I have chosen to simply refer to the elements themselves. In other words, you will find in this book that air is referred to as air, not as east or whatever direction you may associate with it.

To unpack this concept a bit, if one were to stick with the somewhat standardized format for witchy elemental association that is mentioned above, it doesn't hold accurate in the Southern Hemisphere. As with casting sunwise instead of to the right, some have adapted elemental and directional associations in the Southern Hemisphere to align fire with north—toward the equator, and earth with south—toward the South Pole. In this case, sticking with the "traditional" model offered above, the casting starts at east with air, and moves sunwise (left) to north and fire, then west and water, then south and earth.

Even with adjustments, even within the aggregation of European and American originating traditions, this system is not truly standardized. There are many different ways that elements and directions can be called in, and the number of directions recognized or honored varies from tradition to tradition.

When the actual spatial relationship with the land upon which you perform ritual is taken into the equation, your ceremonial design may shift too. A different elemental/directional association may be more accurate for your purposes, like water in the direction of the creek or ocean, fire over by that wildfire-hollowed tree, air at the opening to the canyon, earth at the stone outcropping.

Taking it a step further, in some traditions the concept of calling in the elements would be taken as impolite. After all, the elements are already present.

Trust your process, trust the land, trust your guides, trust your magick.

Associations and Attributes for Her Five Faces

In my work with the five, these associations are what have come to me. They are not static, and they may or may not align with what you have experienced. Above all, trust yourself.

> JOURNAL: What are some foundations of magickal practice that you are currently reexamining?
>
> ACTION: Question your assumptions about the static nature of belief.

Your Magickal Wheel

The magickal wheel you will create in working with this book is a representational system for *your* magick. It will root your relationship with her five faces and your magick into a two-dimensional representation. This can become a useful map for you as you work your way into and through your relationship with her, with the elements, with your magick, and with your spirituality.

The design of this wheel may be familiar to you from representations of the Year Wheel.

Even your unique wheel may not be static. It is likely to shift and change over time as you come to know her and yourself more deeply. Over time you may see her shift seasons or elements. Feeling into your process, you may want to create more than one version of your wheel. You may start with a basic seasonal wheel and then add colors, drawings, words, and any and all things that will make you feel as though you know her more intimately.

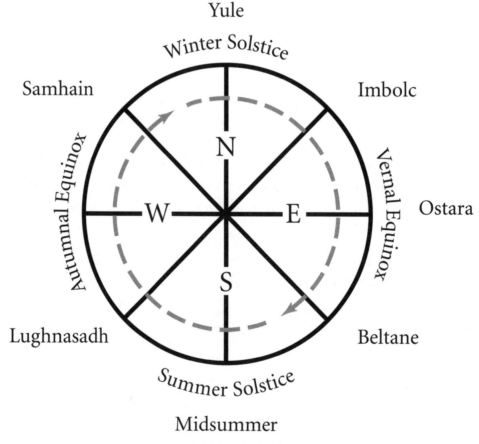

An example of the Wheel of the Year

As you do this act of simple, playful magick, you will feel your spiritual reality putting roots down into the earth, into your heart, into your daily life. You will feel her growing into you, and yourself growing into her. You will see how her face greets the day and holds the nights.

Craft or draw your wheel using whatever media feels best for you: ink, paint, collage, clay, a digital drawing app. Re-create your wheel whenever you feel something shifting. Allow yourself to shift with it.

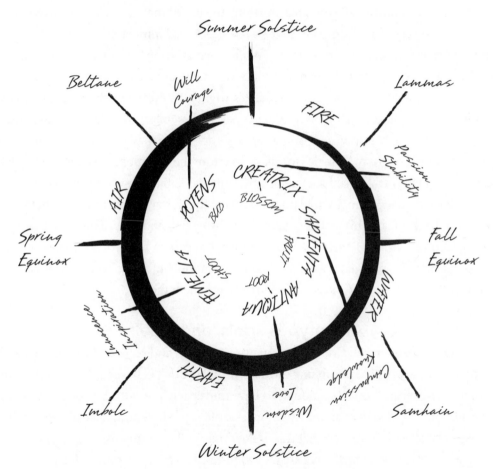

Allow your wheel to change and adapt as needed

Your magickal wheel may include an overlay of seasons, elements, aspects, and attributions.

> JOURNAL: What attributions do you currently associate with the elements? With the seasons?
>
> ACTION: Start creating your magickal wheel.

The Generic, Universal She

The generic *he* or *universal masculine*, meaning the use of masculine language to refer to all subjects—male, female, or otherwise—has been used almost exclusively in English language literature since the mid-1800s. While normative both in literature and in spoken language, generic male language choices are male-centered or *androcentric*.

While the intention of generic language is to include everyone, the actual result is a non-inclusive language structure. The generic male makes "pilot," for example, the standard. However the more common outcome is an assumption of masculinity with generic use and then adding the term "female" to "pilot" to create the variation: a female pilot. Male-centered language makes male the linguistic default and female the exception or variation.

I'm bucking the system! I wrote this book using the universal feminine. In other words, instead of he, him, and his as the default, I used she, her, and hers. This may take some getting used to, even for female-identified people. I'm certain some of the male-identified people reading will experience a bit of discombobulation, but in the end the experience of putting themselves into the shoes of the Other may benefit them.

Archetypes, Idols, and Ideals

My use of the term *archetype* is about structures of myth and recurrent motifs. While the language I use may call to mind Jung's work for some, I don't believe (as Jung posited) that human consciousness is static enough to have universally present ideas or concepts that have been transmitted unchanged since the time of our earliest human ancestors. I believe our consciousness is fluid, and that this, if anything, will be humanity's saving grace.

The archetypes I put forth here are offered in an effort to create some reformatting possibilities to the software of human consciousness; creating new language and new concepts to spread new ideas. In some cases, they may be very *old* ideas.

Our history is a boneyard. Perhaps these seeds will take root in the decomposing matter, the life-giving soil.

> JOURNAL: What questions are you starting with? What is your ideal outcome?
>
> ACTION: Create an altar space that will hold your work of transformation as you read and work through *Jailbreaking the Goddess*.

2

More Than Our Biology

The Threefold Goddess and Why We Need a Shift

The threefold system—that of the maiden, mother, and crone—is common in many traditions of contemporary witchcraft, Paganism, and goddess spirituality. It is arguably the most well-known system of divine female representation in contemporary Paganism. For many Pagans, witches, and goddess worshipers, this threefold model is the first format of personification of the feminal divine with whom they interface. Many of us have felt kinship with her, or have identified as her. The maiden, mother, crone system has felt perhaps natural to us.

However, many of us felt that this model was just a little bit—or a lot—*off*, that we couldn't truly settle into it or that it didn't reflect nor represent us. Feeling into my own discomfort with the model and asking others about their experience of the model, it became clear that the threefold system is embedded with damaging programming on many levels. First, the threefold model in much of its usage is rooted in female biology. The arc of this representation of the power of the goddess is defined by her procreative power and fertility. If we overlay our experience of feminality onto this divine representation, a woman's life trajectory and her sense of self, and of her importance, is defined solely by her uterus.

When a woman's worth is defined by her uterus, her valuation is in her procreative power. When her value is defined by her ability or inability—or willingness or unwillingness—to procreate, her basic worth is based in utility. Rooted in utility, or *usefulness*, her body is a commodity.

When a woman's body is seen as a resource, she does not have the right to full self-determination; she does not have bodily sovereignty.

In the dominant culture, this lack of agency has led to countless instances and kinds of reproductive injustice. From lack of access to reproductive health care to the gross violation of forced sterilization, the common denominator is that women do not have bodily agency.

In adhering to a biology-based model for the feminal divine, we have carried the seed of inequality forward, disguised as worship of the feminine. At the core, the maiden, mother, and crone model for the feminine divine is a patriarchal system rooted in the ideology of ownership and utility. When our utility is our meaning, our bodies are community property.

On a more basic level; in the maiden, mother, and crone archetypal system, mother means woman. If a woman cannot or will not bear children, she may not easily see her face in this goddess.

In some branches of the American goddess traditions, the uterus is seen as the most holy and defining seat of a woman's power and of women's power collectively. In these groups, you are not a woman if you don't have a uterus. Trans women are not welcomed into the circle of women in these communities.

Additionally, when menarche (the first menstrual cycle) is the rite of passage from maiden to mother, we are not only leaving girls and women who cannot bleed out of the equation, we're also putting undue weight on our young children. What we're saying when we couple a rite of passage into womanhood with menarche is basically "old enough to bleed, old enough to breed."

This point of transitional recognition may have made sense at some point in our collective history; girls may have started bleeding later on average, and many bore children earlier than most do now. But the meaning of this rite is something that as women it is our responsibility to take into deeper account.

On another front, women who were not born with uteri, or who do not want to or are unable to bear children, haven't historically been recognized as being fully *woman*—not in the dominant culture or within the model of the maiden/mother/crone.

Women who are childfree by circumstance or design are regularly harassed about their reproductive status. If a woman chooses not to have children she may be called selfish. She will certainly be second-guessed. She will be met with incredulity, if not outright hostility, and told that someday she will surely feel her biological clock ticking.

If a woman is physiologically unable to have children, she may be pitied. And while sterility that hasn't been chosen may be a difficult experience for a woman, her fertility really isn't anyone else's business unless the woman in question has specifically invited questions or support. Yet we are culturally so entrenched in the mindset that a woman's productivity is her purpose that it's rare we even realize how intensely personal—and potentially painful—questions about reproductive capacity and choice are.

Without a thought any one of us might ask a woman, "So, are you going to have kids?" as if it were our right to know. Or even more likely and more potentially insensitively we might ask, "So, *when* are you going to have kids?" In a world that respected women to the point of recognizing that women's bodies (and lives) are our own, these questions would fall away.

Also problematic is the external verification aspect of perceived readiness for feminal rites of passage. When a girl's or woman's transitions and rites of passage are based on externally verified phenomena—the presence or absence of her blood cycle, the appearance or lack thereof of sexual characteristics, pregnancy, or childbirth—her right to self-definition is once again degraded.

Even preceding concerns of fertility, a woman's availability as a sexual commodity may become an issue. In contemporary goddess and Pagan traditions, a girl's or woman's sexuality is often seen as a gift of the gods—but as a gift to whom? In this case also she may be reduced to her utility: sexual utility, procreative utility, community utility. She is an object in this equation, not a subject. She is without agency. Whether sexual or procreative in nature, a woman being measured by her usefulness is a woman who has been stripped of her sovereignty. Put another way, her value is about *doing*, or more accurately in many cases being done *to*, instead of about *being*. She is seen as her service, not for her selfhood.

Some may argue that maidenhood doesn't end when a girl starts bleeding—that it instead ends when a young woman becomes sexually active. In this case, an external element is required for the rite of passage; a woman does not become a woman under her own power but under the power of her lover or the person who "initiates" her.

If this is the argument, what about women who choose not to become sexually interactive, or those for whom sexual desire is not a feature of their internal terrain? And what about the women who were sexualized as girls, not of their own volition? What about the women whose sexual awakening was stolen?

Furthermore, does this idea assume or reinforce a heteronormative frame? If a sexual rite of passage marks the transition from maiden to mother or mother-in-waiting, the procreation-as-destiny model is again reified.

At the other end of the threefold model, we have the dimly defined territory of cronehood. Many women have complex feelings about aging, and there is little place to explore that complexity in a spiritual context when limited by the threefold model. We place much value on youth as a culture. Even in our countercultures cronehood is not given ultimate recognition; it is a vague designation, and what definition is offered is often seen—even by us, the ones doing the aging—through a lens of loss rather than gain. For those who are not mothers, the leap from maidenhood directly to cronehood without even a single intermediary step causes a lack of representation in ritual experience at the very least. And even for those who do mother children, the gap between the end of active mothering and assumed cronehood is an expanse that longs for recognition.

Additionally, cronehood is often defined by what it is *not*; it is not the fertile phase of motherhood nor the innocence and passion of youth. Culturally we are afraid of, alienated from, and even disgusted by aging. Again we return to the core issue: when the divine feminine is defined by biology, she is defined by the expectations, assumptions, and attributions wrapped up in the biological trajectory.

We live what we believe. When our concept of the female divine is rooted in utility, our cultural ideas of woman are also rooted in the same; a woman's body, existence, and life are public property.

JOURNAL: What are your thoughts about the utility of women?

ACTION: Question your assumptions about biology-based transitions.

EXTRA CREDIT: Talk with other women about ways in which they have felt the pressures of assumptions about their bodies, sexuality, or reproductive capacity.

Countering Dominant Culture

Contemporary Paganism and goddess spirituality are a counterculture. More precisely, Paganism and goddess spirituality are many countercultures and subcultures. By definition, all countercultures and subcultures exist within the fabric of the dominant culture. This being the case, all countercultures are built on the same foundational elements as the dominant culture.

Even once we have done a lot of work around deprogramming from the values and morals of the dominant culture, the effects still infiltrate in subtle (and not so subtle)ways. The patriarchal construct we all live within defines much of what we think of as the bedrock of our self-identity, our spiritual beliefs, and our assumptions about life in general.

The stealthy tendrils of patriarchy worm their way into the deepest recesses of our consciousness and thought processes. Patriarchal thoughts, values, and beliefs are so deep in us that we think they come from within. Patriarchal ideologies predict our actions and reactions, our assumptions of normalcy, and the measures by which we evaluate culture and identity.

Genderized language creates relationships between qualities (nurturing, robust, bitchy, weak, powerful) and the binary genders (male and female). When we say that strong is a male or masculine quality and soft is feminine or female quality, we are reinforcing gender-based norms and adherence to them.

What if strong was just strong, soft was just soft, and nurturing was just nurturing?

There are walls erected within the patriarchal system, and they are made of glass. Just like the glass ceiling, we can't see them but they build us into stuck patterns that lead to exclusion, erasure, and subtly enforced adherence to norms of gender identity, sexual identity, cultural identity, and even spiritual identity.

We think we are choosing but the choices were made for us before we had the filters in place to evaluate sufficiently. We have been infected by xenophobia. It lives in us like a virus. We fear and fight against anything different from ourselves. As we awaken to this internal struggle, we ache. We writhe with discomfort.

The antibodies to this illness are acceptance, respect, and an awareness of intersectionality. These keys will lead us ultimately to our collective liberation.

> *JOURNAL: If you identify as a woman, what is it about yourself that informs you that you are a woman? What identifies other people as women to you?*
>
> *ACTION: Examine ways in which you may reinforce the biases of dominant culture.*

Colonized Minds, Colonized Bodies

Our bodies have also been colonized. In dominant culture, white, male, heterosexual, able-bodied, cis-gendered, and Christian are the central measures of normalcy. White male values are normative. White male social markers are normative. Even to ourselves we are the Other. Our bodies are not our own. We see ourselves from the outside.

In some schools of feminist thought, reclaiming the term "Other" is an act of defiance against patriarchal normativity. Sometimes referred to as *difference feminism*, this branch of feminist theory holds that women are different from men. Inherent in difference feminism is the belief that women's ways, contributions, and qualities are devalued in the patriarchal paradigm.

Yet Otherness is difference, and not all difference is equal; some are *more* different than others. And when cultures value normativity often above all else—and many cultures do—Otherness is a liability.

Globally, the bodies of women have been colonized. And, the treatment and mistreatment of the bodies, minds, spirits, and beings of Women of Color necessitate that we take the conversation of Otherness and colonization and sovereignty deeper.

In the structure of domination, the less "normative" a person is the less acceptable they are. The less acceptable a person is, the less valuable they are. The less valuable they are, the more disposable they are. And at that, *valuation* is a dangerous concept. *Valuation* is a word with monetary meaning, and comes from a mindset of external ownership.

Black women in the United States carry the personal and transgenerational trauma of slavery. These are not merely echoes; these are memories from a time recent enough that there are women still alive to talk about it who were born to parents who were slaves. The effects of slavery live in the bodies and psyches of Black women. Memories of children torn from the breast in the slave shacks of a hundred and fifty years ago reverberate.

Not only that, these memories are replicated in contemporary life; from slave yards to jail yards, the cycle of suppression is repeated. According to the National Association for the Advancement of Colored People (NAACP), one out of three Black boys born in the United States in 2014 will spend time in jail or prison if current trends in incarceration continue. Also according to the NAACP, 1 in 100 Black women in America is in prison, and that number is rising.

In the United States, Black people are still treated like property and Black women doubly so. Often exoticized and fetishized, bodies of Black women are marginalized, dehumanized, seen as something less-than. They are imagined as "too" sexual, but are not afforded agency within their own sexual or personal identity.

> *Slavery* is not over. It is still happening around the world. From human trafficking to indentured servitude, slavery has not yet been eradicated.

The horror of the mostly ignored holocaust of Native Americans is a hidden part of American history. Nations, tribes, and peoples were eradicated. Children were stolen from their people and forced to assimilate. They were forbidden their languages, spirituality, and cultural traditions at risk of torture and death.

Native Americans were literally herded onto reservations, and were in almost all cases removed from the lands that hold their origin stories and the bones of their ancestors. What treaties were made with the US government were broken, and are still being broken today.

In Canada, Indigenous women are murdered at a rate of more than 4.5 times higher than all ethnicities combined, according to a 2014 report released by the Royal Canadian Mounted Police (RCMP). The Report of the Special Rapporteur on the rights of Indigenous peoples, James Anaya, to the United Nations (UN), states that more than one in three Native women in the US and Canada will be raped in her lifetime. (For women as a whole in the United States the risk is less than one in five.) And six in ten will be physically assaulted.

On some reservations, the murder rate of Native women is 10 times the national average. According to the report made to the UN, 88 percent of these crimes are committed by non-Natives, over whom tribal police have no jurisdiction.

Sexual Abuse to Prison Pipeline: The Girls' Story is a report created by the Human Rights Project for Girls, Georgetown Law Center on Poverty and Inequality and the Ms. Foundation for Women and was released July, 2015. It states that Native American girls are the most likely of any race or ethnicity to be arrested and incarcerated. And of the girls who are incarcerated, 31% have been sexually abused.

Again we see the real-time results of transgenerational wounding.

Xicana and Latina women, when not erased as a group, are portrayed by mass media as hypersexual, less smart than their white counterparts, and somehow simultaneously sexually promiscuous *and* conservative. And, in the United States they make an average of 0.53 on the white male dollar. Xicana and Latina women are literally treated as worth-*less*.

Trans women face a host of life-threatening factors, from lack of access to health care to increased chances of rape and murder. The *National Transgender Discrimination Survey Report on Health and Healthcare*, conducted in 2010 by the National Center for Transgender Equality and the National Gay and Lesbian Task Force, showed that 28 percent of transgender and gender nonconforming people had experienced discrimination in healthcare settings. Fifty percent reported having to teach their medical providers about trans health care.

Trans and gender nonconforming people surveyed for "Injustice at Every Turn: A Report of the National Transgender Discrimination Study," conducted by the National Gay and Lesbian Task Force and the National Center for Transgender Equality in 2011, were asked about assault at work, in educational settings, at homeless shelters, in interactions with family members and with police, accessing public accommodations, and in jails and prisons. Twenty-six percent of respondents reported having been physically assaulted due to bias regarding gender identity or presentation in one or more of those settings. Ten percent reported sexual assault in the same settings. And intersectionality of course comes into play here; race and ethnicity, gender, and sexual orientation all intersect with increasing levels of risk.

Goddess spirituality communities on the whole have not been inclusive; in Pagan and goddess spirituality communities, trans women are often distinctly excluded from women's circles.

> *Subaltern* means of lower status. Feminist author and academic Gayatri Chokravorty Spivak used the term in her most well-known essay, "Can the Subaltern Speak?" The paper is a foundational work in postcolonialism and postcolonial feminism.

This is a known tactic of colonization: the colonizing force takes one of the subaltern groups and gives them marginally more power than the other oppressed groups. Then those who have been given slightly more power than the others—yet who are also being colonized—do the work of the colonizers for them. We are both colonized and colonizer.

We are fragmented. Divide and conquer; women are telling other women how they must or must not be in order to be goddesses, to be feminists, to be strong, to be women. It is time to recognize, learn about, and seek to understand the complexity of intersectional realities. It is time for recognition of the right of *all women* to our own bodies, stories, lives. Our rights to—and of—self-definition, sovereignty on all levels; and in our Pagan and goddess spirituality communities, our right to a system of feminine divine that embraces all of the faces—and all the bodies—of woman.

JOURNAL: In what ways can you commit to claiming your own sovereignty, and safeguarding the sovereignty of other women?

ACTION: Take action on one or more of those ideas.

The Body of Woman

All of this echoes the dominant culture; women's bodies are not our own. Even when our counterculture teachers, parents, and friends teach us the best they can that we own our bodies, the dominant culture tells us without exception that we do not.

From legislation of reproductive rights to forced sterilization, our basic relationship with the concept of self-ownership is eroded. In our lack of authentic choice about our actual bodies, our personal sovereignty is destroyed again and again.

From lack of diverse representation in media to lack of basic safety on the streets, our insecurities are perpetually magnified. Rape culture reminds us daily that we need to fight for every inch of space, even in our own skin. Fashion requirements, cultural and social expectations, and institutionalized insecurities enforce and reinforce our adherence to "appropriate" gender performance.

This keeps us fighting—instead of relaxing into—our aging process; keeps us adhering to body weight and appearance expectations. And even the preoccupation with liberating ourselves from the petty tyranny of lookism, ageism, and matters of identity keeps us far from the core of the deeper self and the greater liberation of awareness.

The body of woman is an ancient artifact. We are remnants of dead stars and galactic explosions. We have the blood of our mothers' mothers' mothers running in our veins. We have memories and mysteries encoded in our DNA.

JOURNAL: In what ways has your bodily sovereignty been
challenged or eroded?

ACTION: Volunteer for a rape or sexual assault hotline, or a
group that protects trans and queer rights, or a sex workers'
rights group. All women, and all people, have a right to bodily
sovereignty.

Binary Gender Is Colonization

Gender exists on a spectrum, or a grid, or a sphere, or perhaps in a morphic field. Physical and genetic sex exists on a continuum. And sexual expression and orientation exists beside gender, sometimes intersecting with it. In other words, there are vastly more than two genetic sexes, and possibilities of gender expression and identity are literally limitless.

The gender binary, and adherence to assigned gender norms, are colonialist attitudes, and tools of cohesion to colonial domination. Gender identity and gender role flexibility is diverse and complex in Indigenous and ancient cultures worldwide.

In many cultures there are—or were—more than two genders. In India in 2013 a third gender that has existed since well before colonization was finally legally recognized. Though this legal win for other-gendered people was felt worldwide, there are innumerable stories of cultures that have had their multiple gender designations stripped from them by colonizing forces.

The Chukchi people, an Arctic Siberian tribe, recognized seven genders. Many Native American nations recognized "two spirited" people as having genders other than the binary; in Diné culture this variation resulted in the recognition of four genders.

The Bugis, an Indigenous Indonesian ethnic group, recognize three sexes, four genders, and a meta-gender. In parts of Africa women could marry women, and in some cultures a woman who sought a wife could be considered a "female husband."

In many Indigenous tribes and ethnic groups around the world, gender norms were—and are—different from what we consider to be normative. Many cultures had egalitarian distribution of work, wealth, and political and social power and influence. Some were and some are matrilineal, some were matriarchal, some were both, some were neither.

> *JOURNAL: What assumptions do you hold about gender? Do you think gender is a thing that just is?*
>
> *ACTION: Notice how you perform your gender. Notice how others perform theirs.*

Language is a Virus

Language is colonized. Language colonizes. Language spreads ideas. Ideas spread culture.

Standardized language is a tool of colonization and an act of—often enforced—assimilation. Assimilation is a tool of colonization. Our languages have been taken from us. Native, Black, Brown, Indigenous languages have been stolen and systematically destroyed. The languages of the poor, of the country people and hill dwellers and hidden people. The stories that are told and not written are dying with the languages that held them.

Standardized language steals our voices, the meter of our songs, the fluid nature of our stories.

We women are praised when our writing and speaking and storytelling is seen to have relevance outside of being "women's" writing, or queer writing, or feminist writing. We are expected to erase who we are in order to be taken seriously.

The markers of literature tell us our stories are not important artifacts or cultural indices; that the recipes and lullabies and little rituals passed down from one generation to the next are not as important as the battle hymns and litanies of victory and power.

But our languages are the containers of our cultures. They hold the center of our distinct cosmologies and cosmogonies. Our old wives' tales are the whispered bedtime wardings and poetic incantations that carry the secrets of our lineages of flesh and spirit. Passed through generations, our secret spells and superstitions have held the evils of the world at bay.

As we decolonize language, we decolonize our minds. This is a challenging process. It will require rethinking, withholding judgment, and pulling up whole aggregations of thought by the roots.

Language is layered with racist meaning. I chose not to use the words "shadow" or "dark" in reference to negative, unconscious, or subverted aspects of consciousness in this book. On a linguistic level we equate dark with bad and light with good. It's not just language; it's ideology. In examining the impact of my own language, I made the choice to not reinforce the "dark equals bad" mindset.

As you will see in the next chapters, I have used the term "occult" in place of shadow. Occult is a rich word with complex meanings: hidden, occluded, secret, mysterious, and esoteric are a few.

Decolonization requires that we reclaim the ways of our own stories, our own ways of talking. It requires also that we think through and beyond concepts like *inclusivity*. When we say "inclusive," the opposite is also a truth; exclusive. *Inclusivity* is a word offered like a fruitless olive branch. It does not mean what we want it to mean, but it does mean what too often is intended. Extended as an empty gift, when we say *inclusivity* we too often mean "if you will take on my cause, we can fight together." Or "let me tell you what the cause is, and you can join the struggle." When I say, "You are invited," I mean the table is already set in my home and you can come if you like. This may be nice for a dinner party, but it is no way to create a coalition.

There is power in words. As workers of magick, we must believe this if we believe anything.

Occupation is a word inherently traumatizing for anyone who has lived in a region with active conflict. Whether the occupied territories are in Palestine, the territories of the United States or Canada, or Africa, occupation is colonization. Occupation is war. Occupation is one of the steps of genocide. And even knowing this and having spent time in occupied territories, I was part of the Occupy movement. I saw the hope that the movement brought forth for many, and I ignored the obvious: Wall Street already *is* occupied. It has been since 1524.

There has been substantial backlash toward the Occupy movement for the insensitive—at best—word choice. In response to awareness of the colonizer-mentality of the name, some groups have started using the term *decolonize*. This term is also used globally by anti-colonialist movements. Ideally, the name change in the groups who are post-Occupy will also mean that the political focus of the groups includes Indigenous land claims. This is the level of examination we must adhere to; think a word or phrase through before you use it. And when you get it wrong (and we all do get it wrong), change it.

We will not get anywhere by continuously centering the already central and dominant arguments. When we are reaching toward and moving into the question of collaboration and cocreation, we must purge the ideologies that say dominant thought (even feminist dominant thought, or radical dominant thought) is right, and marginal voices are wrong. We must believe other women when they say they are feminists or women or working for liberation. We must even move beyond the reliance on the term *feminism* as the glue for our collaborations. We must respect our sisters enough to move into the space of embracing difference and acknowledging and living into our shared struggles and our shared liberation.

We must stop offering assimilation and instead seek a respectful interchange of ideas. We must step out of our comfort zones and ideologies, and into honest communication about real life and the living of it.

When I say, "May we eat together?" I mean: can we create this thing, you and I, we, us? Can we collaborate, cooperate, cocreate?

We must move out of the process of colonization to find words that mean what we mean; we need to stop saying, "You are invited to participate in my process." Instead we must ask, "What needs to be done? How should we go about it? And can we do it together?"

We must reach straight through good intention and reach toward wholeness, liberation, respect.

JOURNAL: What do you want to help build, or make, with your community of women? Do you want to open yourself to a wider social justice or spiritual community? If so, how will you go about it?

ACTION: Talk to other women about what their lives look like, what their day to day reality consists of, what their concerns are.

New Languages of Woman

The Yanyuwa are an Indigenous people who live on the northeast coast of the continent now known as Australia. The Yanyuwa language has one dialect for men's spoken language and another for women's. Children speak the women's language until puberty, from which point forward the boys live with the men and learn the men's language.

The Yanyuwa are far from alone having different dialects for men and women. There are several documented cases of cultures where women and men have or had radically different dialects, or even whole bodies of words that were only used by men or by women. Consider the case of China's Nüshu script, a written language developed by and for women as a way to communicate. It was handed down generation to generation, mother to daughter. It was written on fans and sewn into wedding dresses and other pieces of clothing.

Spoken Japanese, from traditional dialects to contemporary, is considered a gendered language. Many written languages had, and some have, variations in character use for male and female versions.

In contemporary languages worldwide there are distinct differences in word choice and ways of speaking between women and men. In linguistic theory, there are four main approaches to evaluating communication variations:

- *Deficit:* women's speech is deficient compared to the normative male speech

- *Dominance:* women are dominated by men, and language shows that men are dominant through male-centered language

- *Difference:* a model based in equality that holds that women and men are different subcultures with differing communicative conventions

- *Dynamic:* the intersectionality of language and communication theory! The dynamic approach is not gender-static and takes into account the dynamic elements that go into communicating

All four approaches agree that language conventions are gender-based, and that women have decidedly different ways of using speech than men do.

The language of women is a language with different pauses. It is the language that stops and leaves spaces for other voices. It is the bone-deep rhythm of call-and-response that offers the meter of work and play. It is the starry night chant around the fire circle interspersed with laughter, children's demands, sharing of news, and tears for loved ones who are missing.

It is also the *Stop now!* of women calling for an end to rape and sexual violence. It is the rage and fury of a community mourning its children lost to genocide. It is the wail of grief as another virgin forest gets cleared for cattle ranching. It is the swift, primal snarl, and the pounce-and-tear of the mother lion protecting her young.

Our new languages are old languages revived. They are the reclaiming of feminal power in all its ghastly glory and reverential whispering. They are the coded languages that allow us safety in unknown places and privacy in crowds.

The new languages we choose and shape and share and discover are languages that pull in from the edges and work their way to the center. They are languages that recognize a shifting center or need, and adapt to that which is most pressing. Not so much like in a crisis, but in the way a caregiver is one step ahead of the needs of those in their care who are most vulnerable and how the stronger ones step in as needed. In the way a lull is followed by a rush, and a rush by a lull.

In these new languages we will *will* ourselves to listen to the parts that are hard to hear because the stories need to be told and heard in order to be healed.

JOURNAL: What stories are ready to be told by you?
Are they your stories? The stories of your culture?
Woman stories? Stories in your mother tongue?

ACTION: Pay attention to your language. Notice the words
you use, the rhythms you fall into, whether you are exerting in
a comfortable way or pressuring yourself or others. Allow your
language to open up. Look for the words that truly fit. Give
yourself time and space to say what you really mean.

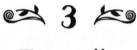

3
Femella

Femella's sigil

Femella—The Child

Femella is *girl*. There is beauty in simplicity.

Femella nestles into the nook of an arm, toothless grin smiling at the breast of her mother. Tiny feet find purchase in cool mud, fingers grasping rocks and leaves. She dances with the breeze, climbs the branch of a tree, rules with a shining crown. She is by turns graceful and rageful; the divine child, the innocent child, the crowned and conquering child. She is timid and brave, curious and stubborn, sunny and wild like a thunderstorm. She is the child clinging to her mother's leg, and the "I am" in the mirror—the first recognition of self as Other. She's the little one learning to walk, the one walking on her own into the dark woods, the child running free in the fields.

41

She is the learning of words, singing of mish-mosh songs, laughing and crying with similar ease. She is the self before judgment, liberated in her innocence.

Instead of biology determining the shift from child to woman, Femella allows the divine child to be unto itself. Instead of the "becoming" aspect implied in the archetype of maiden, Femella just *is*.

As the divine child, Femella is the eternal innocence of childhood. In this case, innocence is not synonymous with some vague purity or virginity; this precious innocence comes from a place in consciousness before those concepts—purity and virginity—even exist.

Innocence in this case is the blamelessness of the toddler who does not know her own strength and power. The child who is not yet aware of the possible ramifications of her actions.

Femella is at once the good-natured self-centeredness and the ultimate and unde-manding generosity of spirit inherent in small children. And she is the trickster nature of the toddler as she runs and hides in the park, playing her surprise game of hide and seek. Yes, she strikes fear into the hearts of the grownups with her childish fearlessness.

Femella is a full-bodied NO! She holds the solid boundary of her awareness of individu-ation. She wants to do it for Herself, do it her way, she must have her sovereignty recognized. She is the joy of strength exercised.

She is the fury of the exhausted toddler who can't find her way to sleep. She is the playful girl dancing to the sound of the wind in the trees. She is the master alchemist making magickal potions out of rainwater and flowers and sweet cakes out of mud.

Faerie queen and storybook princess, and prince, and dragon, and miller. She is the huntsman and the creatures of the wood. She is Little Red Riding Hood *and* the wolf.

JOURNAL: What aspects of Femella so far speak most strongly to you?

ACTION: Tell or write a simple faerie tale with Femella at the center of it.

Her Occult Expression

Femella is self-centered. Sometimes naively, sometimes willfully. Quite obviously, she doesn't know what she doesn't yet know. She may be brash, unsafe, pushy, or have horrible boundaries.

She may throw a tantrum when she doesn't get her way. She may fight, flail, and scream bloody murder. She may pout and slam the door. She may push away, isolate, or even hurl insults.

Femella may be fickle; her interest may wander, as it does in children. She may be unwilling to listen, unwilling to sit still. Unwilling to focus. She may be distracted and distracting.

> *JOURNAL: Do you ever find yourself dropping into a "little girl" state when feeling frustrated, angry, or threatened? If so, what does that look like?*
>
> *ACTION: Notice when your unexamined behaviors mirror Femella's, and engage with the part of you that is not feeling, seen, heard, or safe.*

Her Empowered Expression

Femella in her empowered expression is light, newness, life incarnate. She is the power of the first "I am!" She is fearless in the way little children can be. She is wise as the unbroken are. She is wild and unfettered.

Her emotions are untempered. Her joy is absolute, and her fear is too. She laughs with her whole body. She cries in utter despair. Her empowered expression revels fully in the eternal *now*, fully present in this moment as it is. Nothing is held back as she surrenders to her experience, or rails against it.

She will not hold on to passing hurt, anger, or resentment unless they become commonplace, or are deeply hurtful. She is forgiving and resilient as long as she is unconditionally loved, taken care of, and nurtured.

*At six years of age, **Ruby Bridges** became the national face of school integration. This brave child entered into a new and frightening situation with openness, trust, and a strong will. She and her family endured hardship for the ultimate benefit of all Americans and ultimately, for all people. Bruised but not broken by her childhood experiences, Ruby later founded the Ruby Bridges Foundation to promote celebration of differences.*

In her most fierce expression, Femella is a protector of children in their times of need. She will not sit by and witness bullying, intimidation, or abuse; she is not afraid to throw a swift elbow in the name of safety, or to scream at the top of her lungs for justice. She speaks truth to power. She does what's right because it must be done. She says what needs to be said. She breaks painful secrets out into the light and asks for safety and protection from her community.

In her willingness to reveal the things that are wrong, she gives her community the chance to honor her by protecting her. We do so by protecting all children.

Femella can talk to creatures living and nonliving. She communes with the wee folk and the elfin. She knows the secrets of the untamed places. She believes, and because she believes, she can see.

Knowing the world is hers to discover, she doesn't await permission before tasting what she wants to taste, touching what she wants to touch. In her empowered expression she encounters friends and stranger alike with curiosity, playfulness, and openhearted, unabashed joy.

She is sometimes timid and shy. She may need to be slowly engaged with, or she may just need to be given space for herself. In her empowerment, her boundaries are also stated without fear or shame.

The Radical Brownies is a girls' group similar to the Girl Scouts, but influenced by radical groups like the Black Panthers and the Chican@ group the Brown Berets. Radical Brownies can get "LGBT Ally" and "Black Lives Matter" badges among others. The group organizes social justice activities where the young Radicals have opportunities to make their voices heard and be part of the solution. The Radical Brownies also focuses on body love, self-empowerment, and claiming identity as women and girls of every color. The group was founded in Oakland, California, in 2014 by **Anayvette Martinez** and **Marilyn Hollinquest**, two very radical youth educators.

JOURNAL: What does empowerment feel like to your younger self?

ACTION: Young girls can be fearless forces for change, and in them lies the future of humanity in this time of great change. Do something with the empowerment of Femella in you. Whether it is for the little girl in you, or all the little girls in the world.

EXTRA CREDIT: Watch the documentary **Girl Rising**. Be prepared to learn a lot, to cry, to laugh, to be both heartbroken and inspired.

Her Sexual Expression

Femella is not devoid of a sensual awareness, but her sensual reality is grounded in her body and in the process and experience of being embodied. Her sexual reality is about discovering her own body, playful sensual awakenings, primal sense-based interaction with the world around her, and the playful sensuality of a child.

It is that of the infant nuzzling the breast, the child playing naked in the mud, the toddler finding words for all the parts of her body, the youth learning when, how, and where she wants to explore her more shared sexual awakenings.

Femella sometimes lacks the awareness to create boundaries for herself and often needs to be reminded to respect the physical—and sometimes emotional and mental—boundaries of others. In her natural inclination to self-centeredness, she may forget that the boundaries of others are also sacred.

In a perfect world, we offer protection to Femella as she explores her sensual awareness on her own terms. We create the safe space where a child owns her *yes!* by deeply respecting her *no*. As we honor the divine child, we recognize her experience of her innocence not as devoid of sexuality, but as inviolable in the experience of it. Femella's experience of her sexuality is for herself alone.

> JOURNAL: *In what ways does Femella's sensual and sexual experience of the world speak to you?*
>
> ACTION: *Experience your senses—your sensual awareness—as a sovereign right; one that you own, and can share or not share as you feel moved to. Eat something delicious and savor the taste. Touch a luxurious fabric, or new blades of grass, or the petals of a flower, and feel how the sensation affects your whole body. Smell something that awakens girlhood in you and feel the emotions that arise. Look at something beautiful, something intriguing, something compelling. Feel how the seeing lands in you.*

Femella in the Linear and Nonlinear Trajectories of Womanhood

In the linear, Femella is the child. However, Femella does not refer to one's stage of sexual and/or reproductive development.

As an archetype Femella recognizes and makes room for the fact that each girl is unique in her experience of self, growth, and girlhood. As is each woman.

The flexibility offered in this archetype is that one's own process may determine the appropriate times for rites of passage, either in addition to or instead of a rite of first blood. This allowance of and encouragement toward self-assessment as the basis of one's psychological, emotional, spiritual, and physical movement integrates the understanding that not everyone who is female will have a rite of first blood. Not all women will experience childhood as a person designated female at birth. Not all women bleed.

In the nonlinear sense, Femella is a wonderful archetype to play with throughout our lives. Her curiosity, love, and innocence shakes up old, stuck patterns and allows us to rediscover joy.

Femella is the one who dreams the dreams we grow into.

We are acting from the Femella archetype when we allow ourselves to sink into simple pleasures without overthinking things. Whatever age we might be she offers us access to innocent joy, curiosity, playfulness. In areas of learning, we sink into beginners mind when we sink into Her presence. She may be called present in our lives through bubble-blowing in the forest or at the park, playing hide and seek, climbing trees, or getting muddy in the late spring rains.

> There aren't many examples of the Femella archetype in popular media. This may be dangerous territory, as we haven't learned how to value girls and girlishness very well yet. But the positives of not "acting one's age" (whatever that means) are worth mentioning. Some icons of the positive aspects of holding girlishness at a premium throughout their lives are *Goldie Hawn, Zooey Deschanel,* and *Anne Hathaway.*

*There are also young women and girls in our pop cul-
ture consciousness who are revolutionary examples of
Femella. **Willow Smith** is a Femella divine. In her 2015
song "F Q-C #7," she sings about kid things like jumping
in creeks and climbing trees. Author and revolutionary
mama **Mai'a Williams** brought home to me the power
that Willow and the whole Pinkett Smith family are claiming for Black children in making the space for Willow to
be exactly the girl she is. In dominant culture, Black girls
and other girls of Color are routinely sexualized at inap-
propriate ages, expected to be demure, or grown up, or
strong, or silent, or guarded, or all of the above. While
Willow rocks the fashion world and has been a bit of a
pop sensation since she was eight, she is none of those
things listed above. Her creative spark is joyful, authentic,
expressed, a little capricious, and very open hearted.*

Femella gives us permission to enjoy finger painting, egg dying, and jack o' lantern carv-
ing. She invites us to experience the moment just as it is, rainfall or sunshine. She leads us on
wildflower walks in springtime and invites us to take tea with the faeries and talk to the trees.

Women who did not get to experience girlhood may want to throw a tea party for Femella and invite her to play. Invite her to tell you how to best celebrate her in you.

For those who experienced early childhood trauma, calling Femella in can offer healing on a deep level because Femella can also offer the innocence present in the time before
wounding and the wholeness that exists outside of it. Femella is resilient and forgiving. She
lets go of hurt and reclaims trust again and again. Hers is the merciful heart, glowing with
grace.

*There are magickal and psychological tools that can help you to connect with your child self that exists outside of wounding. Some techniques you might want to consider follow below. The ones I suggest here are based in **neuro-linguistic patterning (NLP)**, because both as a practitioner and a sometimes-client, I love the healing potential of NLP. These techniques are perfectly aligned for this work: timeline regression, communication with parts, hypnosis.*

You can also create a ritual where you invite the eternal innocent (and eternal innocence) to come and tell you how to best access her.

If you need to be held in the heart of the divine child or you need to feel her *as* you, have a tea party, take a young friend to see the latest kids' movie, or even go alone. Lie under the trees and listen to their stories, sing songs that don't have to make sense, tell yourself a bedtime story full of excitement, adventure, and courage. Allow yourself to be afraid of your monsters, and then make friends with them.

Invite the little people in for cake. Sing to the forest creatures. Make a faerie house at your local park. Set treats out for Femella, and let her come to you.

JOURNAL: What are some of the ways in which the archetype of Femella shifts your relationship with your idea of the divine feminine?

ACTION: Draw or paint a picture of Femella. Be PLAYFUL! Offer her your joy of creation. Release attachment to outcome and find a childlike creative flow. Try finger paints or mud painting on freezer paper, crayons, markers. Or do whatever brings Femella forth in you.

The Divine Girl

There are very few goddesses who are portrayed as girls. There are maiden goddesses—I include some in a list below—but many goddesses we think of as maidens are truly becoming-women goddesses.

There are many divine boy gods: Horus, the Christ child, Krishna, and other more obscure, ancient boy child gods. There are very few divine girl child gods.

The lack of a divine girl child points to the ingrained psychology of patriarchal power. As the female is valued primarily for sexual and reproductive usefulness, there has been no room for a divine girl child.

Our relationship with the divine mirrors life as we know it. Cultures that practice atrocities like femicide and infanticide have no room for the deification of the Divine Girl. Cultures that see girls as future mamas, future brides, or future soldiers even, have no room for the worship of the timeless, awe-inducing, comprehensive, complex, unfathomable being-ness of feminal childhood unto itself.

In a world where girls are seen as woman *in potentia*, girls do not have sovereignty. The girl is the woman-child. She is the child-mother. She is the caregiver in training, the invisible martyr (and mater) of her family, the one who gives up her schooling in favor of her brothers', the one who gets fed last, the one who gets sold off, traded away, perpetually devalued.

She is the child who is not asked to succeed but to follow. She is the one who is expected not to thrive but to acquiesce. In the patriarchy, the girl child is born destined for a narrow and arduous road. She is not expected to take to the pickaxe or bulldozer and forge a wider berth. She is not expected to find her own path through the underbrush to open fields. But we know that she *does*. The girl child does find her way into her strong center, and when she does she changes the whole world with her commitment to her own life.

In our spiritual practices and paths we get to choose the ways we observe. As Witches and women of Earth we learn to observe the turning tides; we know how to reroute rivers.

The time to correct this lack in our collective psyche is now.

As we create mythos that venerates the divine girl, we create a reality that raises girls up. By living into a system that honors the divine child as a child; a girl child, and even beyond that a child free of the gendered rules and expectations that culture lays at the feet of even the youngest among us, we create a safe space for all of us to explore the self in a brand new, primal, wild creation of self.

Someday we will be ready for the divine child completely free of gender consideration. Perhaps we will be able to worship the child as that imaginal state where the cells remember themselves into a new and ancient form. Someday we may be able to give this child her/their sovereignty as a sacred being worthy of respect outside of the expectations of girlness or boyness. For now we take this initial step for ourselves, our daughters, sisters, mothers, aunts, nieces, granddaughters of blood and spirit. We claim the divine child as daughter of god, daughter of goddess.

JOURNAL: How will it change things when the world begins to see a version of the Divine Child as a girl?

BONUS JOURNALING: What might the childhood of one of your favorite goddesses have been like? Would she have been carefree, wild, and strong? Would she have been creative, expressive, sensitive? Would she have been a crusader for children's rights? A princess, or a dragon? Would she have been a budding healer, a dancer, an acrobat? Would she have created great works of childish art? Would she have started fires, danced with whirlwinds, led monsters to a rebellion?

Who was this powerful goddess in her infancy? Who was she as she grew into self-awareness? Who was she as she learned to stand on her own? As she began seeing herself as separate from her surroundings, as an individual?

ACTION: Notice when you think of something as "girly" or "like a boy," or even have thoughts of what men or women are like or "should be" like. You don't need to even do anything beyond just noticing. Just notice.

Deities Who May Embody Femella Energy

In this section I have included divine boy gods, because we have so few examples of the divine girl. In these cases, I have used the pronouns *she*, *her*, and *hers* in place of *he*, *him*, and *his*. This may read oddly at first, but it will begin shifting your perception of the attributes given to girls, divine and human.

I am not suggesting you work with the deities this way. The gods might feel offended by that or their people might. I am not trying to appropriate or steal and change these gods for a new use. This is merely a mental exercise to help us break free from gender attachment.

It is my hope that you can allow the use of the female pronoun in place of the male to inform your experience of Femella as a goddess in her own right and as an archetype.

The Christ child is the baby Jesus. As I said earlier, we're crafting a divine girl deity here, so including building blocks that are traditionally considered "boy" is a thing worth considering. The girl deity we are creating can—perhaps *must*—include the attributes of the male divine child. She must, because in the consciousness of the dominant culture boys are strong and girls are sweet. The divine child is beyond gender, and in her liberation from these restrictions she exists as purely powerful, loving, and compassionate.

The Christ child is the miraculous babe, the divine spirit made flesh through intercession and miracle. Much of what makes the Christ child divine in the context of Christianity is not aligned with the values of goddess spirituality; that her divine mother, having been a virgin when the Christ child was born, is "unsullied." In the goddess faiths we don't consider sex as dirty, so virginity is not required—or even desired—as a requirement for cleanliness.

However some of the aspects of the conception, inception, and deliverance of the divine child are lovely and worth integrating into our concept of the divine girl; that she is a child of God/dess. That she is the divine made flesh. That she is love embodied.

Can you see her sitting in the throne of the heart, crowned with a glowing nimbus of light, her sacred heart glowing in her chest, light streaming from her cherubic, little, sacred, healing hands?

Her attributes are grace, mercy, compassion, healing, miracles, the sacred heart, connection to God/dess. Spirit made flesh.

The Ibeji are an orisha from the Yoruba religion. While personified as twins, the Ibeji are one being. They are a personification of the divine child. While there are variations according to lineage, the twins are often known as a girl and a boy. The older twin's name is Kehinde and is often known as a girl. The younger is Taewo and is most often known as a boy.

In rituals where the Ibeji are being honored, children's games are played. Even the grown-ups let loose and play like children in honor of this orisha. The attributes of the Ibeji are playfulness, mischievousness, and curiosity.

Kore means maiden in ancient Greek. In the Eleusinian Mysteries, Kore is the daughter of Demeter. She is the embodiment of the eternal springtime that existed before the scheming of Hades and Zeus brought about the abduction.

Kore is the child without fear. She is birth and rebirth. Her attributes are innocence, newness, growth, adventurousness, simple trust.

Krishna is a god of love. In the divine child representation, she is a protector and a trickster. She saved her people from all sorts of dangers through strength and wiliness. She is beloved of the cowherds. When Krishna played her flute by the riverside, the cowherds, all graceful, beautiful young women, would come running to play and dance with her. Their play is called the *Rasa Lilla*, the dance of divine love.

The child Krishna is the embodiment and representation of play for the sake of play. Her attributes are adventurousness, playfulness, beauty, dance, protection.

Lucia means light. In pre-Christian, northern European myth, she was the female representation of the returning light that comes forth at the darkest time of the year.

Her attributes are hope, joy, generosity, newness, light in the darkness.

Nimue is the flower maiden. She is honored by practitioners of Feri. The Feri tradition is an initiatory lineage of Witchcraft. It is an ecstatic path rooted in the sensual experience of being embodied. In Feri tradition, Nimue is known as the Black Heart of Innocence. She is the divine child, tiny new crescent of moon. She is tender and innocent but when angered is wrathful, acting without hesitation. She can turn from sunshine to storm cloud in the blink of an eye.

Nimue is both dark and light. She is impenetrable, virginal, inviolable. But she exudes a mysterious sexual thrall, confusing to many because she is a child. In Feri, she is an embodiment of the primal state of Being.

Her attributes are innocence, grace, power, primal sexuality, connection to Earth and spirit.

Ra Hoor Khuit is a Thelemic deity. A truly new aeon Western Ceremonial tradition, Thelema was founded by Aleister Crowley in 1904 and has been widely influential in the spread of modern ceremonial magick.

Ra Hoor Khuit is a more wrathful face of the divine child. Armed and dangerous, she wants what she wants and knows how to get it. She is the furious two-year-old but with an arsenal at her disposal. She is the hawk-headed goddess of war.

Ra Hoor Khuit is traditionally considered a male child, but she is also referred to as the crowned and conquering child. She is revolutionary impulse overthrowing old, stuck, broken traditions to make space for the new. This child is the one who destroys the old Worlds, and is the reigning force of the new aeon.

Her attributes are power, strength, sovereignty, fury, destruction, vengeance, new ways born from accomplishment of one's true will, the wreckage of the old, birth of the new aeon.

> JOURNAL: What deities feel the most like Femella to you?
>
> ACTION: Find a story about a goddess you don't know yet from the preceding list, or one from your own lineage, and read it.

Rites of Passage Related to Femella

Rites of passage under the purview of Femella all have to do with the life of the child. Rites to Femella are not rites of transitioning out of childhood. They are rites that recognize the long arc that childhood and child-like innocence encompass.

Childhood birthdays are already designed perfectly as celebrations of Femella. Some other rites that may be considered as falling under her provenance are lost baby teeth, a first haircut, the first night sleeping alone in a big-girl bed, baptism, first communion, or walking to school, going to the park, or crossing the street alone. Many of these are rites of increasing responsibility. As we allow our children (and our child selves) to take on responsibility, they find their way into greater and greater self-awareness and resilience. These step-by-step rites are the gifts of childhood.

Starting school, the beginning of every school year, buying school supplies are all opportunities to honor Femella.

Even after growing into and through the other phases of the fivefold goddess, we may wish to come back to Femella, make offerings, and do a rite to her to invoke the attributes of the divine child in one's life. Anyone can create a rite to Femella and ask the child to bless and heal them. Any person of any age can be given a rite of passage into the innocent and wise knowingness of the divine child.

A menarche/first blood rite could be made as a rite to Femella instead of seeing it as a transition to the next phase of the arc of femininity. In your personal tradition this may or may not feel right, but consider that many girls are not ready to majorly shift identity just because they've started bleeding.

Beginning to bleed in and of itself is a lot of change and can be shocking for some more than others. Some girls don't want blood rites. (See part 2 to find guidelines on creating collaborative, consensual rites of passage.) Further, some who were designated female at birth and begin bleeding are not even female identified. Menarche is a complicated time for most, and for some there will be no amount of external honoring that will change its internal landscape.

For others, a blood rite may be a beautiful thing: it may be a celebration of potential, body changes, a shift in self-image. Yet at eight, nine, ten years old (or even fourteen or fifteen), not all girls are ready to shift away from girlhood.

What if these rites of first blood could be about honoring the girl body instead of being seen and reinforced as an all-too-often premature transition from girl to woman?

A trans girl's ritual of taking her new name could be designed as a rite to Femella. Her first day of publicly wearing "girl" clothes no matter her age could be dedicated to Femella.

> JOURNAL: What rites of passage can you think of that belong to Femella?
>
> ACTION: You may want to create a rite of passage for Femella. See part 2 for information on rites of passage.

Offerings to Femella

In the eclectic Neo-Pagan traditions I came up in, it was not uncommon for Disney figurines, Barbies, and other dolls to end up on altars.

One of the faces of Femella I have done a lot of work with, Kore in her youngest form, in my experience LOVES certain candies.

Femella loves art supplies, stickers, glitter, and Play-Doh. She loves beautiful flowers and sweet heart-shaped vases and candleholders.

She also loves dirt, grass, beautiful crystals, and little creatures and critters. She adores rocks and acorns and tiny frogs. Strawberries, and sparkling pomegranate juice.

Lace, and tulle, and costume jewelry are favorites, as are torn T-shirts and cowboy boots. She loves having her nails painted, and she loves mud squishing between her toes. She loves dancing, and singing, and losing herself completely to her daydreams.

Femella is likely to be drawn to things that make the little girl in you speak up. Sometimes you will hear her *squee* with delight at a thing she wants on her altar. Sometimes she'll let roar a giggle. Sometimes she will let you know with a strong voice, "THAT'S MINE!"

Listen to her, and let her teach you how to honor her.

JOURNAL: What does the little girl in you love? What do the little girls you know love? What offerings does Femella want from you right now?

ACTION: Make an offering to Femella.

BONUS ACTION: Build an altar to Femella. New to magick? See the appendix for help with altar building.

When to Call on Femella

You may want to invite Femella when you are having a hard time asking for the care you need, are looking for ways to engage with your joy, or are needing to be reminded of the simplest of pleasures. Call on her when you:

- Are looking for your inner voice.

- Need to be reminded of the simple joys in life.

- Need to see the simple truth living in this moment.

- Need the sweetness of an afternoon picnic with your stuffed animal friends.

- Are getting ready to take time off from work.

- Want to connect with children in your life.

- Want to rock a princess dress while rock climbing.

- Feel like you need help finding your way to your own secret self.

- Are celebrating your own *birth*day!

Some Days Sacred to Femella

Easter

The Goddess Ostara, or Eostre, belongs in the category of Potens due to her association with fertility. However, the celebration of Easter is definitely a holiday designed to bring joy to the hearts of children.

While Easter is considered a Christian holiday, the elements of celebration at the heart of Easter have clear ties to the seasonal aspect that likely reflects traditions older than Christianity. Bunnies, brightly colored eggs, baby chicks, flowers; all of these are signs of birth and rebirth. The candy is thrown in just to sweeten the deal, putting icing on the Easter-is-for-kids cake.

> *Did you know that the days on which Easter and the religious observations attendant to it are decided by the moon? Easter is celebrated on the first Sunday after the **Paschal (Easter) full moon**; the first full moon after the vernal equinox.*

Spring Equinox

This holiday is observed March 21 in the Northern Hemisphere and September 21 in the Southern Hemisphere, but actually it's movable. In the tradition I came up in, we celebrated spring equinox as the rebirth of Kore. As spring begins, she is reborn with the green growing things bursting out of the cold, wet soil. She is the springtime. She is the green growth. She is the tiny wildflowers blossoming.

International Day of the Girl Child, UN—observed October 11

> *The hashtag **#dayofthegirl** is used to track celebrations and honoring of girls on International Day of the Girl in social media. Join in!*

> *Empowerment of and investment in girls are key in breaking the cycle of discrimination and violence and in promoting and protecting the full and effective enjoyment of their human rights.*
>
> —United Nations Resolution 66/170

On this International Day of the Girl Child, I call on all governments to take action to end all forms of violence against girls in all parts of the world. Together, we must create a world where violence against women and girls is never tolerated and girls are always empowered to reach their full potential.

—Secretary-General Ban Ki-moon

You can find out more at www.DayoftheGirl.org.

International Girls Day, Confidence Coalition—November 14

The hashtag #youcan is used in reference to International Girls Day in social media.

Vision: A world of confident girls and women who embrace the belief that they can achieve anything and consistently exceed their own expectations.

Santa Lucia's Day—December 13

There are many gory Christian stories of Lucia and how she got her sainthood, but those are not the first stories about her. Lucia's name means *light*, and her goddess story is one of the few where the winter night is made less frightening by the coming of a girl child.

In Scandinavia and other northern European countries, the pre-Christian celebration of Yule was dedicated to Lucia. Her feast day landing on December 13 instead of on the actual solstice is a fluke of the battle of calendars; for a time, December 13 fell on solstice.

On Yule, represented by a young girl in white with a wreath of candles upon her head, Lucia led processions of children who brought forth the sacred and powerful light.

Winter Solstice

In the Northern Hemisphere the Winter Solstice lands on December 20, 21, 22, or 23. In the Southern Hemisphere, it is June 20, 21, 22, or 23. The rebirth of the light has been observed by welcoming the newborn sun in the guise of a boy child or baby. Why not Femella?

> JOURNAL: What days would you celebrate as sacred to Femella?
>
> ACTION: Create a Feast Day for Femella.

Seasons Sacred to Femella

In the Wheel of the Year there may be overlap between multiple faces of the five. The best way to create your wheel is to feel your way into it and see what makes the most sense with your already existing formats for worship.

An obvious space for celebration of Femella is springtime, with the new shoots coming from the ground. It may be equally accurate to celebrate Yule or Winter Solstice as sacred to her.

> JOURNAL: What time of year do you associate with the divine child?
>
> ACTION: Begin the process of creating a Magickal Wheel of Attributions graph that incorporates the five faces.

Weather Patterns Associated with Femella

Late winter snow (snowball fights! skiing! snow forts!), sunny spring days, springtime rains (puddle jumping! April showers bring May flowers!), early summer storms (Femella is not always gentle), gusty wind (sometimes it is frustrating to be a kid!), gentle breezes (faerie winds).

Her Time of Day

Femella is present in the first whispers of sunrise. She is the pink blush on a seashell grey sky, a few bright stars still shimmering, sun rising gently and urgently into a new day.

Her Colors

Silver, white, lavender, periwinkle, green, pink.

Animals Sacred to Femella

Baby animals. All of them. Also tiny animals; little frogs, mice, snakes. Butterflies. Moths. Dragonflies. Fireflies.

Plants Sacred to Femella

Ferns, springtime flowers, newly sprouted grass, moss, baby trees.

Suggested Elemental Correspondence for Femella

Many magickal traditions have a correspondence list for the elements. In crafting a magickal circle this is a good graph to have. It is not important that you use the correspondences or associations that I offer, but in the work of building a ritual circle you will want to find the one that works for you.

Some traditions recognize five elements and/or directions, some seven, some eleven, some four. These elemental correspondences may align with different deities, animal spirits, colors, or attributes. Some wrap these different parts together.

Throughout *Jailbreaking the Goddess* we will be working with five directions. I offer two possible associations for each of the five faces. You may come up with other options.

The primary suggested elemental correspondence for Femella is center, where the child is held in the circle and kept safe there by the tribe. Another reason is because children are naturally self-centered. By offering Femella center, her attribute of child-like self-focus is given sacred space.

In some traditions the center represents ancestors and future generations. Others recognize the center as spirit. Your personal lineage may recognize center as having different attributes.

The secondary suggested correspondences for Femella is air. Some traditional correspondences for air are dawn, innovation, newness, light, breath, laughter, song.

Other correspondences are intellect, logic, and communication, making air perhaps more suitable for one of the other faces, as you will find in a later chapter.

From your intuitive center, where do you feel Femella aligning? Does she naturally merge with either of these directions in accordance with your existing beliefs? Or are those willing to move aside to allow Femella to gracefully take center stage?

JOURNAL: *If you already have a magickal practice, how does this elemental correspondence work with your existing magickal practices? If you don't, how does it feel to you internally based on what you know so far?*

ACTION: *Work on your magickal wheel, starting with Femella at the center, or wherever you feel her aligning.*

An Invocation to Femella

Have you seen the child
New as dawn?
She is the Child of God
Child of Goddess

Femella, Divine Child
Sweet and wild
Come play with me

Femella, Little Child
Timid and open
Come cry with me

Femella, Dancing Child
Tender and wicked
Come laugh with me

Femella, Sweet Child
Curl up with me
And let's tell stories about who we will be

Femella, Queen of Wild Things
Let's make friends with our monsters
And rule the moon lit night

Glorious Child
Wake with me
To morning light

Yawn, stretch, sigh,
Greet the day
With blessed newness
You are the radiant light

JOURNAL: *How does this invocation affect you?*

ACTION: *Write your own invocation to Femella.*

4
Potens

Potens' sigil

Potens—Woman of Power

Potens means *powerful*. She is the woman full of potential.

Potens stands solidly in the space she inhabits. She surveys the world around her, anxious to move forward. And so she moves, centered in her own being. She's on her path, the path that only she can find and define.

Her stride sure, heart shining, she is ready for what the days and nights will bring. She hears the call of far away shores, the sweet song of lovers, the rise and fall of voices calling for answers to age-old questions.

She smells unknown flowers, dirt, water, spices on the breeze. She tastes the sweet berries from within the brambles growing just to the side of her sometimes inclement path.

Potens carries a pen and a sword. She knows that both are mighty. She carries her shield with strength and her mirror with grace. She loves and she fights with equal fervor.

Potens is she who goes and she who stands. She is building, mounting energy, the explosion, and the aftermath. She is the picking it all up again and continuing the experiment.

Lovers' furious, sweet, explosive dance as midmorning sun graces the dappled ground and under starry skies. Potens is new love; she is lust; she is learning how her body meets and melds with other bodies, the friction and fascination.

Not afraid to fail, Potens tries this, tries that, and tries again. She finds her way in the world step by powerful step.

Potens is burgeoning strength. She is the energy of bud bursting to blossom, the spark catching flame. She is the energetic, passionate energy that moves forward.

She is the warrior, activist, explorer, student, sacred fool, traveler, lover. She is the art freak, the drama geek, the prima donna; the world is her stage. She is the young queen, the beauty queen, the prom queen. She is the knight who rides her trusty steed along the border. She is the circus girl with a knapsack on her back. She is the street artist, the revolutionary, the homeless, streetwise kid busking on the corner.

Potens is the woman girt with the sword. She is the woman crowned with flowers, laughing in the blossoming orchard. She is the awakening of sexuality, sensuality, passion, power, courage, strength.

> **The Woman Girt with a Sword** is an Honorific of Babalon, a Thelemic Goddess. It also easily applies to all women warriors. Some women girt with swords—or in some cases, spears: Joan of Arc, Boudicca, Lady Triệu, Nakano Takeko, Tomoe Gozen, Colesta, Buffalo Calf Robe. And one Disney character—Mulan.

Potens is inspired by innovation, not tied to tradition. She may be inexperienced, but she is overflowing with passion. She is the wave of the coming generation. She is the One who will change her world; through force, through passion, through art, through fight, through words.

*Harriet Tubman, born **Araminta (Minty) Ross**, was an African-American revolutionary. Tubman was born into slavery around 1822. Early in life she suffered a blow to the head at the hands of a slaver, and suffered lifelong bouts of illness from the head trauma. That didn't stop her from escaping—more than once—from the slavers. After multiple attempts, Tubman found her way to the north. She traveled at night following the North Star in order to avoid being found by bounty hunters.*

After her escape Tubman became a conductor on the Underground Railroad; the same network of secret routes, people and organizations, and safe houses that had helped her find her way to the north.

The path from slavery in the south to freedom in the north was arduous and dangerous, but Tubman made the trek nineteen times. She returned to the south over and over, at great peril to herself, in order to help other slaves find freedom.

In addition to her work as a conductor and abolitionist, she was active as a suffragist. During the American Civil War, Tubman was the first woman to lead an armed assault. She also worked as a scout and spy for the Union.

*In honor of her work, Harriet Tubman was called by the names **Moses** and **General Tubman**.*

She is unrelenting, wild, untamed, untethered. She has broken free of her chains and fights for the freedom of others too. Sometimes she is short of compassion and other times overwhelmed in it. She is righteous anger at the state of things. She is the willingness to risk it all to create a new outcome.

Potens is a different sort of differentiation from the little child seeing herself in the mirror for the first time. Potens is seeing herself as herself, separate from her previous self, separate from the ground of being, springing forth from divine source. Yet she knows that she is connected by relationship, and that she has power to change what she sees around her.

> JOURNAL: What aspects of Potens speak most strongly to you so far?
>
> ACTION: Notice how Potens shows up for you as you read this chapter and in the coming days.

Her Occult Expression

The occult expression of Potens is self-righteousness, blind privilege, self-centeredness—which is much less "charming" in a young person than in a small child. In her occult expression, Potens's anger may burn bridges, sever ties, and burn friends and loved ones. Her self-centeredness may make her act in unconscious ways, or she may come off as uncaring. She may even be ruthless at times.

She is impatient and often blames others rather than seeing her own culpability. Because of this, she may not be a team player much of the time. She may work better on her own, even though there is a loneliness to that.

Potens may feel misunderstood, like she is the only one who *really* knows what's going on, or that she is the only one who hurts or loves or works "*this* hard." There may be an element of self-martyrdom when Potens shows up in her unexamined expression.

In love, her unexamined territory is that of the jealous lover, the spiteful "woman scorned," or a self-indulgent, self-focused, "I get what I want," sentiment that may not take the whole picture into account. She may wreck relationships, break promises or agreements, take risks that are not always worthwhile or caring.

The Mean Girl is an unconscious expression of Potens. She is the Queen Bee, seeing herself as the super star and everyone else as the supporting cast. Her anger may easily come out as lateral aggression, destroying her relationships with the women who could be her circle-mates, sisters, allies, lovers, friends.

Her Empowered Expression

In her empowered expression, Potens commits to self-exploration before seeking to change the world. She lifts up her sisters, fights the righteous fight, and loves with her whole self. In her empowerment, she empowers the world.

As Potens awakens more and more fully to her capacity, her confidence, and her passion, she becomes a greater and greater force of nature.

Asmaa Mahfouz was one of the leaders of the 2011 uprising in Egypt. Mahfouz sparked the demonstrations at Tahrir Square by uploading a video to social media sites calling for the resignation of Hosni Mubarak and his cabinet. In her video she invited others to gather with her at Tahrir Square. Four brave, dedicated, young Egyptians joined Asmaa that day. From there, the number grew. The rising tide of unrest led to an eighteen-day occupation of Tahrir Square, with hundreds of thousands of people calling for governmental reform by mid-February. As of 2015, the revolution is not over. And Asmaa is still fighting on the front lines.

Potens is a force of bold, new, innovative ideas. Her empowered expression brings an openness to new solutions that may have been obstructed before. In her empowered aspect she's not afraid to fail because a failure means she has tried. And Potens is very much about trying and trying again. She is tenacious, optimistic, and bold.

Her empowered expression lives for the journey, not the outcome. She is fearless, directed, and willing to risk comfort in favor of ingenuity.

> JOURNAL: What does the empowerment of Potens feel like in you?
>
> ACTION: Take action on some part of what you notice in feeling the power of Potens.

Her Sexual Expression

She is the young face of infatuation, love, sensual and sexual indulgence and communion. And she is choice embodied; this indulgence may be something she keeps to herself or eschews entirely for other passions.

Regardless of expression, hers is the sparkling promise of early spring growth reaching toward the sun. She is the raw power and transformation of the Beltane fire. She is the randy, wild play of the first heat. Sometimes this is expressed as passion for connection, or for her chosen work, or for her spiritual path. Sometimes it is expressed as sex for sex's sake. Or it may be expressed as self-love and self-worship; she may choose the solitary path of sexual expression and exploration, choosing her self as her own best—or only—lover.

In her sexually interactive expression, she loves the energy that her experience of sexual play and interplay brings. Her sexual range is from the first fiery kiss to the joy and release of orgasm. Her sexual exploration may be about conquest, or it may be about seeking divine union. Or both at once.

Potens is fascinated by sexuality. She may not always be totally comfortable in it and may not always know her own effect, but even her discomfort leads to new ways of knowing herself. Potens plays her edge, plays *the* edge, finding the spaces beyond the boundary sometimes tripping and falling and sometimes easily growing her sense of self into the new territory she has discovered.

She owns her sexual expression and sexual choice as a place of power.

Sacred whores, also known as *sacred prostitutes* or *temple prostitutes*, were priestesses that, according to some scholars, offered rites of sacred sexuality in some ancient cultures. The Ancient Greek term *hierodule* may have meant *sacred prostitute*, and the Hebrew word *qedesha* is often translated as *temple prostitute*. There is controversy between historians as to the veracity of the theory of a widespread practice of temple prostitution, or sacred sexual rites.

In contemporary use, the Sacred Whore is also an honorific title that is used by worshipers in reference to the Goddess Babalon.

In recent years some sex workers—who in some cases are ordained priestesses—have claimed the terms *sacred whore* and *sacred prostitute* as their own. Sacred whores experience and offer the work they do as sex workers as healing work, work of the Goddess, and part of—and in some cases, all of—the work they do in their capacity as priestess.

Some sacred whores ask for donations for their healing services. Others offer their services for free. Some work in a private or shared temple space—which under US law would be considered a house of prostitution.

While this work is currently illegal in most of the US, many sacred whores—and some feminists—are working for the decriminalization of sex work.

In one of her most sexually interactive expressions, Potens is a face of the archetype of the sacred whore. Potens may be an exuberant sexual healer who combines her raw power and her dawning sexuality to create healing in herself, in others, and in the world.

> *JOURNAL: In what ways does Potens's sensual and sexual expression speak to you?*
>
> *ACTION: Feel your sexual power. Notice it. Play with it. Express it.*

Potens in the Linear and Nonlinear Trajectories of Womanhood

Potens is the transition into forward momentum. In the linear aspect of the fivefold system, Potens is visualized as the youth. She is the young woman in high school, finding her own way into an individual sense of self. She is the one leaving home, going into university, going traveling, joining the circus, joining the military, or diving into social justice activism.

In the experience of the five faces, Potens is the embodiment of the point in time when we experience the world for the first time unmediated by the protection of parents, family, or even tribe. She self-defines by standing on her own, sometimes pushing away things that identify her with her child self.

While Potens is represented as a youth just starting out on her own, the flexibility of the fivefold structure acknowledges that this stage is a recurrent one in most women's lives. While it's easy to conjure a sense of this aspect when thinking of—or remembering—getting ready to move out of our family's home or our first time traveling on our own, there is an inherent liberation to recognizing that we touch upon this stage of development again and again in our lifetimes.

> *Hélène de Pourtalès was the first female Olympic Champion, winning gold and silver medals in the sailing division in 1900, the first year women were allowed to compete. She was thirty-three at the time, and her sailing crewmates were her husband and her nephew.*

Adventurers, soldiers, athletes, activists, journalists, or actors may find that Potens is their primarily resonant archetype. Even those who move solidly into the other phases of the fivefold goddess may find that Potens is where they feel most aligned and alive.

> *Ernestine Shepherd* and *Edith Wilma Connor* are American bodybuilders who have both been recognized by Guinness Book of World Records as the oldest female bodybuilder; Shepherd in 2010 and 2011 at 73 and 74 years of age, and Connor in 2012 at 77 years of age. Shepherd started bodybuilding at 56. Connor entered her first bodybuilding competition at 65, and won first place.

> *JOURNAL: What are some of the ways in which the archetype of Potens shifts your relationship with your idea of the divine feminine?*
>
> *ACTION: Create an image of Potens.*

The Maiden

Potens is a very self-possessed archetype. This is a necessary departure from the previously existing archetype of the maiden. In many stories, maiden goddesses are considered the property of their mothers and/or fathers, and then of their lords.

> *Majority world* is the newest term for what was previously known as the developing world, third world, or the global south. The minority world is what was previously known as the first world, or global north. Where previous terms have enshrined and justified colonialist mentality, using the term "minority world" reminds us that the fewest people have the most resources, influence, and power.

As the gods reflect humanity and humanity reflects the gods, we don't have to think very hard to realize that in cultures around the world, girls and women are still considered property. Even in minority world civilizations, the concept of men "letting" their daughters do or not do a thing—down to how they are allowed to dress—is not uncommon.

In this interpretation of the myth of the Demeter/Persephone story I am looking through a contemporary lens. At the time that the myth came into being, there was no concept of self-time, or even true individuation for girls or even for women. These are relevant questions and comments in the quest for sovereignty and liberation.

In the story of Demeter and Kore and her shift to Persephone, Kore/Persephone follows exactly this trajectory. She is in deep relationship with her mother, Demeter, to the point of a pronounced lack of individuation. She is bartered away by Zeus, her father, and given to Hades to square up an old disagreement.

Persephone is abducted by Hades—as had been agreed upon by the men—and then she belongs to him. Though Persephone grows to own her station as queen of the underworld, she transitions to queen and mother because it is forced on her. She comes into her initiation through violation. In the resolution of the myth, she spends half her year as Kore with her mother, and half as Persephone with her lord.

Where is the time and space for Persephone herself? It exists only in the interstitial spaces between worlds, the journey from underworld to upperworld and the journey back again. Her self unto self exists only in the most liminal of the already liminal.

JOURNAL: How will things shift as young women the world over gain more education, empowerment, and independence?

ACTION: Do something to support independence in young women, whether that is your independence, or for the independence of young women in other parts of the world. Or both!

Revisioning the Youth

In moving away from the designation of *maiden*, we move away from the sense of owner-ship so prevalent in the mythology and archetypal reality of that concept. For many of us, the term *youth* may call up an image of a strapping young man. That's okay, we'll take it! Again, moving beyond the rote genderization that pervades dominant culture is part of the work we are doing here.

Claiming youth as part of our female experience and part of our divine feminine is part of us healing into the whole people we are as girls and women. Like child, youth is a station unto itself. It is devoid of sexualization or biological designation, has no con-notation of ownership, and is free of the strictures that many of us think of when we say even "young woman."

The youth stands on her own, facing her own future.

> JOURNAL: What thoughts does the term youth bring up for you?
>
> ACTION: Again, building on the previous chapter, notice when you think of something as "girly" or "that's a boy for you!" or even have thoughts of what men or women are like or "should be" like. This time instead of just noticing it, do something about it. Confront genderized thinking in yourself, in your fam-ily, in your circle of friends, in your place of work. When some-one says something that is reactionarily gender-based, say something. When you find yourself judging someone's gender presentation, rethink your judgment.

The Virgin

There is another set of goddesses at least partially within the purview of Potens, the arena of the virgin goddess. (The virgin will be revisited in upcoming chapters as well, because it is an archetype spanning the whole of women's lives.)

The term *virgin* is confusing when it comes to goddesses and also in contemporary versus archaic use. The word may mean a woman who is unto herself, or it may mean chaste, untouched, celibate. It may also mean naïve, inexperienced, or new.

Some virgin goddesses easily align with the archetype of Potens, as with Diana, Artemis, and Anat. This version of the virgin is youthful and remains ever under her own power. In some versions of her story, she is granted permission by a "greater" god, as in the case of the Hellenic story of Artemis, who was given her independence by Zeus.

There are other stories that place Artemis as a pre-Hellenic goddess who had no relationship with Zeus whatsoever and came by her own self-definition as a virgin. In some ancient stories, Artemis remained a virgin even though she took lovers.

Virgin goddesses may also be mothers, like the Norse Gefjon, falling into Creatrix, or Sapientia like the Greek Athena, the Roman Minerva, or the multivalent Sophia.

Some virgin goddesses may be equally at home in many of the five faces like the Hellenic Hebe, daughter of Zeus and Hera, wife or consort of Heracles, and mother to Alexiares and Anicetus. She is all of these things and still considered a virgin.

JOURNAL: *What are terms that you would use to describe the freedom that some Goddesses (and women) designated as virgins may have felt? What about some areas of restriction?*

ACTION: *Examine your language regarding women's lifestyle choices. Remember that a woman's right to self-identity is part of gender equality. As we examine and dismantle our hidden assumptions regarding how other women "should" or "should not" behave, we give all women more freedom to be who they truly are.*

Deities Who May Embody Potens Energy

Artemis is goddess of the hunt. She is personified as the archer. She is associated with both animals that are hunted and those that hunt. Stags and hounds are both sacred to her. She is envisioned as a young woman, often mid-run surrounded by stags or hounds. She holds a bow or wears one slung across her chest. Sometimes she is pictured wearing a crescent moon on her brow. She was known as Diana to the Romans.

Her attributes are courage, independence, action, wildness.

Aurora is the Roman goddess of dawn. She is often personified as a young woman, fresh-faced and radiant. Saffron robed and rosy fingered, she opens the gateway for the sun. Aurora is a goddess who was beloved by Roman and later, English poets. She was and is often written about as a symbol of erotic love.

Her attributes are light-giving, glory, gentle passion, inspiration.

Babalon is the Thelemic goddess of the new aeon. She is the sacred whore written of in the book of Revelations. She rides astride a beast (or *the* Beast), which some say symbolizes the unconscious forces of nature within each of us. She is also known as the Scarlet Woman.

In the writings of Aleister Crowley and others after him, she is seen as the salvation of women and the divine feminine. She is the woman girt with a sword. That sword, according to some, represents Will, something the feminine archetypes of the Bible lack. Babalon is a new aeon interpretation of the syncretic Ishtar, Astarte, Ashtoreth goddesses.

Her attributes are passion, vengeance, connection with the subconscious, raw sexuality, breaking of taboos, empowerment.

Erzulie-Freda is a Vodoun lwa (spirit) of love. She is by turns coquettish and despondent, as she knows well the joy of sensuality and pain of love as separation. She has three husbands—Damballa, Agwe, and Ogoun—and thus wears three wedding bands. She loves jewelry, dancing, sweet foods, fine champagne, and sweet liqueurs. She is known to dance and love with fervor and to weep just as passionately.

Her attributes are wealth, fine tastes, romantic love, luxury, and beauty.

Ishtar is the Babylonian queen of heaven. She is Venus in the evening sky. She is a goddess of love and fertility but also war. Ishtar was later known as Astarte to the ancient Greeks. She is also closely related to—and perhaps syncretic with—the Canaanite goddess Ashtoreth. However, Ishtar, Ashtoreth, and Astarte each have their own stories, so while we can see them as a grouping of goddesses with similar attributes and meanings, they also are their own beings.

Ishtar is likely to have been the "Whore of Babylon" referenced in the Bible. She is known as the queen of heaven in the book of Jeremiah. Some scholars say that in ancient times, worshipers of Ishtar may have practiced sacred prostitution.

Her attributes are magnificence, sexual desire, martial thinking, and action.

Tamar is a Georgian sky goddess. She is an eternal virgin who rides a serpent bridled and saddled with golden raiment. She controls the weather.

Her attributes are strength, power, courage, valor.

Additional Goddesses

- *Anat*: Canaananite
- *Ayao*: Santerían
- *Cessair*: Irish
- *Gersemi*: Norse
- *Hebe*: Greek
- *Hlín*: Norse
- *Hnoss*: Norse
- *Iris*: Greek
- *Juventus*: Roman
- *Kurukulla*: Tibetan
- *Melissa*: Greek
- *Ochun*: Yorúbá
- *Ostara*: Germanic
- *Oya*: Yorúbá
- *Pele*: Hawaiian
- *Persephone*: Hellenic

- *Sibyl*: Greek

- *Skadi*: Norse

- *Xochiquetzal*: Aztec

JOURNAL: What deities feel the most like Potens to you?

ACTION: Find a story about a goddess you don't yet know from the list above or from your own lineage, and read it.

Rites of Passage Related to Potens

Some of the rites of passage that belong to Potens are obvious: leaving home is a central one, the first big solo journey, being seen as an individual in one's community in some way instead of "the child of so-and-so."

The taking of one's first lover might be dedicated to Potens as might falling in love, exploring sensual and sexual identity, and all pleasures of the field and bed.

Situations that call on exploring one's power are perfect rites for Potens to preside over. Starting the path of the Warrior through martial arts or military training. The pleasure of the hunt, and of power. She is stepping into activism, which one may see as the path of the peaceful warrior. Moving into the willingness to confront injustice. Standing on the front lines as a guardian of Earth or community.

Did you know that many of the old goddesses of love are also goddesses of war?

Also under the purview of Potens: starting a business, a venture, or a new project; diving into a new area of study.

The nonlinear aspects of this model allow us to honor the new awakenings that happen again and again in the range of possibly ninety years that we potentially get to inhabit our bodies.

We feel again and again into the promise and potential of Potens.

> *JOURNAL: What rites of passage can you think of that belong to Potens?*
>
> *ACTION: Create a rite of passage for Potens.*

Offerings to Potens

Potens wants offerings of experience more than items. She is very much about *experiencing!* If you want items for her altar, trust your gut. And you can always look to the goddesses you may already worship as Potens for hints.

Consider a statue of Artemis, or an arrow.

She may love a mirror or a picture of yourself that makes you feel strong, sexy, or powerful or all three!

You could offer perfume or essential oils, jewelry, or makeup. Or you could place a knife, shield, and war paint on your altar. Or you could use all of these.

What about an anarchist patch? A military sticker? A rainbow flag? A bumper sticker that sums it all up for you?

She'll love tickets to a show or to a distant continent. (They can live there on your altar until you use them! When you go, be sure to take her with you.) You could offer your passport or money from the countries you have visited or will visit in the future.

> *JOURNAL: What offerings does Potens want from you right now?*
>
> *ACTION: Make an offering to Potens.*

When to Call on Potens

The times to call on Potens are when you need guidance or courage in the beginning of something. Potens will bring the spark that will kindle your dream into action. Call on her when you are looking for adventure.

You may call on Potens when you are traveling on your own, or going into battle—literally or figuratively. You may invite Potens in as the lover, or the beloved. Call on her when you are:

- Planning a journey.

- Leaving home.

- Starting a new project.

- Starting out in a new line of education.

- Looking for a fun, joyful romance.

- Looking for sexual engagement, whether for fun or spiritual fulfillment—or both!

- Wishing to renew an existing sexual relationship.

- Going into battle—warlike or peaceful.

- Going into humanitarian service.

- Consecrating a new pair of shoes or glasses.

- Buying a car.

Some Days Sacred to Potens

Feast Days of Artemis—Sixth day of new moon

Artemis has many feast days, but the easiest to remember and to build regular ritual around is the sixth day of the new moon. Mark it on your calendar and make it a monthly devotional!

Feast Days of Artemis—Great Feasts

Full moons throughout the year are dedicated to different aspects of Artemis. Also, November 22 (approximate) when the Sun goes into Sagittarius, the sign of the archer.

The Feast of Babalon

The feast of Babalon can be performed at any time that seems relevant to you, although the dates of May 23 or June 17 are both relevant to the unveiling of the goddess Babalon. The Feast of Babalon is honored with a ritual and feasting and pleasure in her honor.

Armed Forces Day

Many countries observe Armed Forces Day as a national holiday. The date of the celebration differs nation to nation. In the United States, it's observed on the third Sunday in May.

Peace Corps Week

Peace Corps Week is a floating-date observation. It's a celebration that recognizes the ways in which the Peace Corps organization and its community contribute to positive change.

Amelia Earhart's Birthday—June 24

Amelia Earhart was the first woman to fly an airplane solo across the Atlantic Ocean. The aviator, or *aviatrix* if you prefer, was dedicated to her love of flying and broke many records for solo flights. In her life and work, she championed women's rights and took as a challenge the attitudes against women and girls in her era.

Amelia married, but on her wedding day sent her husband-to-be a letter reminding him of the primacy of her commitment to her work and stating that she did not expect him to hold to "a medieval code of faithfulness," nor would she be held to one.

Amelia is eminently quotable in her written and spoken unwillingness to be constricted by the norms of her time, and her pride and courage in the accomplishments of herself and other women. One of her quotes that exemplifies Potens is: "Adventure is worthwhile in itself."

She, her aircraft, and her crew disappeared while undertaking an attempt to fly around the world. No trace of her remains nor the wreckage of her Electra 10E has yet been found.

Summer Solstice

Summer Solstice is the height of the summer. The sun is a very directed force; powerful, bold, strong, hot.

High School Graduation Ceremonies

This is a good time to celebrate the end of one educational chapter and life phase.

College Orientations

This is a good time to celebrate the beginning of a new educational chapter.

Seasons Sacred to Potens

Once again recognizing that there may be overlap in the year-wheel, Potens easily arcs from perhaps Ostara/spring equinox, to Litha/summer solstice. She is the sap rising, the Beltane fire, the bursting forth of spring into high summer.

Weather Patterns Associated with Potens

Late spring and early summer heat. Flash floods. Thunderstorms.

Her Time of Day

Potens is the rosy blush of first light, and she is midmorning. She is dappled ground under tall trees as heat descends.

As Moon Goddess, nighttime is also a place you will find her.

Her Colors

Pink, orange, yellow, red.

Animals Sacred to Potens

Dogs and hounds, stags, all game animals; in her more gentle aspects all creatures of the waterways; morning birds; horses, the phoenix.

Plants Sacred to Potens

Trees, wild foliage, late spring and summer flowers, kudzu, ginger, bird of paradise.

Suggested Elemental Correspondence for Potens

The suggested elemental correspondence for Potens is fire. Some possible elemental attributes; passion, desire, forceful transformation (from wood to ash), sexuality, innocence, youth, play, warmth, divine will.

JOURNAL: How does this elemental correspondence fit with your existing magickal practices?

ACTION: Work on your magickal wheel, starting with placing Potens in the south. Or elsewhere if you get different information from Potens herself.

An Invocation to Potens

Have you seen the youth, strong and wild
Leader of Hunts
Breaker and Healer of Hearts
Warrior and Lover

Potens, Powerful One
Dawn glowing, sister to moon and sun
I stand with you

Potens, Mistress of the Hunt
Arrow strikes its mark, prey falls
I hunt with you

Potens, She Who Goes
Sack on your back and bells on your ankles
I roam with you

Potens, Warrior Woman
Sword in hand and shield aloft
I battle at your side

Potens, Lover in the field
Flowers in your hair and grass-stained skin
I love with you

Potens, Sacred Whore
Healing arts reclaimed, bed as altar
I heal with you

Potens, Fool and Hero
I walk the tree with you
Arriving at the crown together, we merge

JOURNAL: How does this invocation affect you?

ACTION: Write your own invocation to Potens.

5
Creatrix

Creatrix's sigil

Creatrix—She Who Creates

Creatrix means *female creator.*

She creates worlds, beasts, babes, books, artworks, armies, stories, songs, languages, life, evolutions, and revolutions of thought. She creates culture and she creates the wild.

Creatrix sits at the head of the table. She is holding all that she has brought forth, even as more rushes in through her. She offers her creations forth, sometimes with grace, sometimes with fury. She breathes in, and gives breath to the creations that come through and from her.

In the languorous heat of mid-afternoon, she tends to the gardens and fields, nurturing and harvesting as she goes. Both are her work. She sows and she reaps.

She weaves, she sews, she writes, she sings. She spits, and worlds are born. She is |the clay, and she is the hand that works it. She is the kiln, and the fire that burns therein.

She is the mother at labor, and at rest. Her vulva swells with life. From her breast ambrosia issues forth. Her very flesh is manna.

She holds long enough to give her creations form, then releases them. She tends them until they are able to break free of her protective cradling. They emerge from her and find their way into the world, propagating her powerful seed across the plains, mountains, valleys; telling her stories, singing her songs, tending the fields that are the gift of her body.

She is the pit of death and regeneration; her womb is the resting place of winter's long night. She is flesh on charnel grounds, bone meal ash on freshly furrowed soil. And her hair, the trees of eternity.

Gathering some of this and some of that, she creates whole new ways of being. Her creations are of beautiful form and grotesque, each serving its own purpose.

Creations of mind, heart, spirit, body. Tapestries of sound, and tapestries of art. Civilizations and the wildness that changes them. Ghost children, and living gods.

All things come from her; her mind, her fingers, her feet, her heart, her womb, her vulva, her mouth, all gateways of creation.

We're used to this face of the goddess being called "the mother." Mother is one of her expressions, and there are so many more. The word *creatrix* is much more layered than the Latin *matrix*, which means mother, womb, and the place from which we come forth. Matrix is beautiful but is solidly womb-defined.

> A **rhizome** is a creeping rootstock; a plant that sends out roots and shoots as it grows. A rhizomatic plant has no center and no defined boundary. The rhizome model is a philosophical concept developed by **Giles Deleuze** and **Felix Guattari** that is applied to communication, education, community building, and more.

When we deify Creatrix and allow ourselves to align with the archetype of she who creates, we acknowledge that feminal creative power is rhizomatic, multiplicit, multivalent, multitudinous, infinite.

In this way it becomes possible for us to step away from biological languaging and ultimately from biologically constrained thinking in regards to feminal creative power.

With her liberation from biological predesignation, we claim a bold new freedom in our creative and generative power.

Creatrix builds in addition to birthing. She names. She shapes. She paints and draws. She crafts. She is the architect, the programmer, the author; she designs works of function and form, creates whole universes in code, pulls mythologies and cultures into being from the void.

She is the founder bringing things to ground, laying foundations. Building from the base up, she raises the roof and walls, her hands coax mysteries out of wood and stone.

She is the maker. She casts metal and forges blade, coin, and trowel. She tills and feeds and seeds the soil. She waters and weeds the rows, carries and swings the scythe, threshes the wheat. She grinds the flour, and bakes the bread.

She is the word, and what was before the word. She sings the wilds into synergy, sings the ancient songs that cause roots to reach toward water and branches to strive toward the sun. Her voice is the miracle of a new galaxy being born; she sings the stars awake.

It is a worthy challenge to confront the preeminence of pregnancy and birthing language and metaphors in speaking of the power of Creatrix. This conscious shifting is a turning point where we may claim liberation and sovereignty.

Building more versatility into our language we become able to recognize the capacity for feminal creation as a fully developed, diversely manifesting process of myriad form. These forms include but are not limited to the procreative process.

We embrace the full potential of our creative impulses as we move away from the idea that all acts of female creation are an outcropping of, or stand-in for, the processes of fertility, pregnancy, and birth. There is only one form of creation that has to do with the uterus, yet that act has claimed much of the conversation in speaking of the feminine divine.

In reality, Creatrix may create physical progeny or she may not. She can create anything. She creates alphabets, pantheons, landmasses, gods and goddesses, angels and demons, crops, new ways of being, new places of being.

Creatrix brings forth form from the formless. She crafts continents from whispers, gives life by sharing her own breath. She dances, tearing her clothes and tossing them to the wind, tearing her flesh and offering it up, singing, wailing, laughing, talking with spirits and animals and stones.

There are uncounted ways in which goddesses have created and in which women have created, too. Creatrix is all of this. She is the act of creation, and she is creation itself.

> *JOURNAL: What aspects of Creatrix speak most strongly to you so far?*
>
> *ACTION: Notice how Creatrix shows up for you over the coming days as you read this chapter.*

Her Occult Expression

An aspect of Creatrix's occult expression is a rageful, wrathful one. She births demons and monsters. She is the creation of rage and the rage of creation. She generates a space between worlds where those who live in the pause between doorways come into their fullness in the presence of her grace. Some goddesses fall solidly into this category while others have facets of themselves that show up as this aspect.

Lilith is a Hebrew goddess whose old stories say she was created alongside Adam. She refused to subjugate herself to Adam or God and was cast out of the garden. She screamed out the ineffable name of god and transformed herself. She became the Hidden One. She is the Mother of Demons. She steals men's secretions at night and births their fears.

Kali-Ma, Kalika, or Kali, is an aspect of the Indian goddess Durga. Kali is related to creation, destruction, time, and annihilation. Her name means "black," and she is known by some as the Dark Mother. She wears a necklace of severed heads or skulls, and dances on the belly of a dead Shiva. Her four hands are often imaged as holding a sword, a severed head, a trident, and a skull-bowl.

Coatlicue is an Aztec goddess of birth and destruction. She represents the destructive side of nature where the womb and the tomb both exist. Coatlicue was also sacrificed by her own children in the continuance of creation. Her head was severed, and now she has two serpents growing from her neck, which were formed of the two streams of blood that burst forth when she was decapitated.

This often-obscured face of Creatrix brings forth new forms from the anger of what has gone before. She takes the broken hearts, broken parts, and makes them whole again in the cleansing fire of her wrath.

Sometimes she burns it all down and starts over.

In another occult expression she is the Vengeful One. Sometimes she is justified in exacting her price, and sometimes her actions come from hurt pride. She is the grief-stricken and righteously angry Grain Mother, Demeter, who refuses to let the spring come until her daughter is returned, but she is also the jealous face of Aphrodite setting out impossible tasks to those willing to challenge her claim on her offspring, as in the story of Eros and Psyche.

The voice that tells you that you cannot or should not try to create a thing is an occult manifestation of Creatrix's power. Sometimes this is good advice. And sometimes it is the repressed part of us that believes that we are better off if we do not try.

Her most secret name is *She Who Creates Endings*. She is the storm that washes out newly planted fields. She is the one who calls forth legions of warriors and brings destruction to those who oppose her. She is the fire that cleanses the old away, in order to make space for the new.

This expression of Creatrix may burn out of control and destroy relationships, communities, worlds. Drought, famine, flood, fire; in her pain she scorches the Earth, leaving bare ground in her path.

In time this soil will spring forth with new life; seeds under the surface tempered by heat will burst, sprout, grow.

*In 1994, **Rwanda**, a country in the African Great Lakes Region, was nearly decimated by a 100-day, ongoing genocidal conflict between two warring groups; the **Hutu** and the **Tutsi**. Over a period spanning months, a nation of women saw their husbands, children, and loved ones mutilated and brutally murdered. They withstood rape and torture. And after months of bloodshed, terror, and grievous loss, the country was left with a genocide-scarred population that was 70% women.*

These women have rebuilt Rwanda.

With husbands, brothers, and fathers dead, women formed widows' associations, and claimed their power as survivors. They fought to have rape recognized as an instrument of genocide on an international level. Some of them raised the children conceived through that same rape. They adopted orphaned children from both sides of the war and raised them as their own.

Before the genocide, Rwanda was solidly under patri-archal rule. It now holds among the highest percentage of women in governmental positions in the world, with mandatory minimums of female representation built onto the governance of the nation. Women who had no experience with ownership became home- and business-owners over-night. They became the heads of their households.

Shoulder to shoulder, women became the force for accountability and reconciliation. Women fed one another's children, made sure people were housed. They ran local councils, participated in a generation of solutions, and ran for office. And they won.

There were no feminist marches that shifted the axis of power in Rwanda; just a group of women stepping in to pull together a ravaged country. The effects are seen in the large strokes and the fine details of Rwandan society; 98 percent of girls are educated at the primary school level. In 2014 women held 64 percent of the seats in parliament.

In the aftermath of unthinkable devastation, Rwandan women learned to mother a country and became Creatrixes of a new aeon.

JOURNAL: How do you see these occult areas playing out for you?

ACTION: Notice when your unexamined patterns or behaviors mirror Creatrix, and address the parts of you that are not yet fully known. If you feel the wrathful Creatrix coming up in you, it will benefit you to check in and see what it is that needs to be offered up, so that you do not burn away things that may still be serving you.

Her Empowered Expression

In her empowered aspect, Creatrix is blissfully and powerfully engrossed in her process of creation. She is the center of the universe, expanding. She is the process as it becomes itself. She is the kitchen witch bustling at her hearth. She is the CCO (chief creative officer) bringing new marks and symbols. And she is birth and growth. Her gifts are nurturance of the body, but also of the mind, heart, and spirit.

In her empowered aspect, Creatrix is in communication with her process, and with creation itself, and with those creating with her. In this relationship She is a powerful co-creatrix reveling in the synergy of comingled skill-sets, influences, and mediums.

The empowered aspect of Creatrix takes something old and crafts a new thing of it. She recycles, reuses, upcycles. Hers is the cauldron of changes.

Creatrix is the grounding of things, and the genesis of them. She is the foundation, the bedrock, the altar. She is the rootstock, and she is the new growth. Centered in her gifts She is writing, singing, painting, making children, feeding the people, designing eco-villages, writing symphonies, reciting the magick words. She creates the present moment that grounds us all in our purpose, too.

> JOURNAL: *What does the empowerment of Creatrix feel like in you?*
>
> ACTION: *Take action on some part of what you notice in feeling the power of Creatrix.*

Her Sexual Expression

Creatrix's sexual expression is part of her dance of creation. Her sexual expression may be shared or held unto herself. Either way it is fuel that fires her process of creation. Her sexuality is about desire and culmination.

Her sensual, sacred, sexual dance is a dance of creation; the dance of building and growing, and grounding. Desire and consummation. Sometimes it is a dance of consumption, as she gives herself fully over to the process of creation, becoming both that which she creates and that which the creation is creating of her.

Creatrix's sexual experience and expression is an intentional and directed dance. Its most joyful articulation comes in the form of a devotional as she loves her creations into being.

Sometimes her sexuality is also about securing the bonds of companionship, love, and partnership. It is the secret dance of communication: bodies humming together, nurturing desire and comfort where these have flagged. Hers is the oxytocin release that forms bonds of love through the alchemy of sex.

JOURNAL: In what ways does Creatrix's sensual and sexual expression speak to you?

ACTION: Allow yourself to feel into the power of your sexuality as a force for creation, whether procreative or generative purely on the energetic level.

Creatrix in the Linear and Nonlinear Trajectories of Womanhood

In the linear sense, Creatrix is the middle stage of life. She holds the position of grounding the energy of Potens and laying the groundwork for the coming time of wisdom.

She is no space-holder though; except in that she contains *all* space. Creatrix is the finding of her place in the world, finding her purpose. Her time in the linear model is the point where questing finds its way to homing in. She stands at her hearth, in her studio, at her books, in front of her empty page awaiting the creation coming from absolute potential.

She stands in relationship to a family or community context. She may spend times of creation alone, but her acts of creating tie her to her community, world, family of choice, blood, kin.

She creates because she creates. It is what she does. And her acts of creation tie her to those who are created from it, inspired by it, or changed by it.

Sojourner Truth, born Isabella Baumfree, c. 1797–1883, was an African-American abolitionist, feminist, writer. She was mother to five children. In 1826 Sojourner escaped slavery with her infant daughter, Sophia. She was forced to leave her other children behind. Soon after, she sued a slave-master for custody of her youngest son. She won, becoming the first Black woman to prevail against a white man in such a case.

*Sojourner is most well-known for a speech known as
"Ain't I a Woman?" which was delivered extemporane-
ously at the Ohio Women's Rights Convention in Akron.
While that speech was later shaped to include elements
not spoken by Truth, and to infer a Southern dialect
(which Truth would not have had, since she was born
and raised in the North), it became a rallying cry that
still holds unfortunate relevance for the rights of
Women of Color.*

*A woman well ahead of her time, Sojourner owned
not one but two homes in her lifetime. She traveled,
preaching the word of abolition. She rallied Black troops
to fight in the Union Army. She fought against slavery, for
prison reform, against capital punishment, and for the
rights of women until the day she died at 86.*

In the nonlinear sense, Creatrix is an archetype most girls and women step into again and again. One may be solidly in one or more of the other phases, and still be in Creatrix. And a teacher who moves into Sapientia and still continues growing her offerings is standing in both aspects potentially for the greatest balance of her life.

One may also be in Potens at the same time, finding the exciting edges to her field and exploring them as she simultaneously creates from the center of her full potential. She teaches from the wealth of wisdom that as Sapientia she has already rooted herself in.

If one becomes or has already become mother to physical children—by birth, adoption, or marriage—Creatrix may be a role central in her life for the duration of early childrearing or even extended childrearing.

Again, this woman who is experiencing Creatrix as a mother of flesh and blood children may also be a scientist or teacher (Sapientia) in her career. She may even be Antiqua, an old woman, raising her grandchildren as her own children.

> *JOURNAL: What are some of the ways in which the archetype of Creatrix shifts your relationship with your idea of the divine feminine?*
>
> *ACTION: Create an image of Creatrix.*

From Matrix to Creatrix

In Paganism and goddess spirituality, the mother goddess archetype is one of the most revered, most commonly invoked, and most loved of the goddess archetypes. As an archetype, the mother is—understandably—nearly universally adored. And deservedly so; without mothers, where would we be? Without the Mother, where would we be? The mother (our mother) is the place we all and each come forth from. She literally forms us, and informs us. We exist because she made us. And we exist as we are because our mothers informed our development. As William Makepeace Thackeray said, "Mother is the name for God in the lips and hearts of little children."

A mother goddess makes sense. Mother goddesses exists all over the world, and have almost certainly existed for as long as we have had consciousness as a species. And even still, as we all know, mothers are not valued under patriarchy. Things would shift for the better if the world were to recognize the mother as worthy of worship, to recognize mothers as worthy on the mundane level. They are worthy of consideration, support, commensuration; paid maternity leave, equal opportunities for work and housing, and compensation for their work.

Mothers will not be valued until women are valued. Beyond valued, until they are liberated; until the people are liberated. Until we have broken free of concepts like *utility* and *value*. This is a long-haul struggle. We are still working for this, still fighting for this. Still dancing for it. Still doing magick for it.

> *Mother of the New Time, a project of **CAYA Coven**, is an ongoing, global magickal happening. As part of the full moon observation offered on the Mothers of the New Time website and Facebook group, women are encouraged to participate in a ritual that includes a directive to burn the patriarchy and create the New Time together. Every*

full moon, countless women around the world write the word "patriar-
chy" on pieces of paper, and then, under the moon, they burn them.

> *JOURNAL: What are some things you believe about mother-*
> *ing or about being a mother?*
>
> *ACTION: Support a mama. If you are a mama and you need*
> *support, ask for something you need.*

All Forms of Creation are Her Creation

We are shifting, and so our spiritual archetypes must shift with us. As undervalued as the work of mothering is, it is still seen as the quintessential achievement—and essential purpose—of womanhood.

In consigning the mother as the exclusive face of the creative aspect of goddess expression, we ignore numerous limiting elements; because we create in myriad ways, so must she. It's no longer viable, if it ever was, to conflate *woman* with *mother*. Not every woman is born with the ability to bear children; not every woman is born with a uterus. Not every woman is born with ova. Not every woman is born with hormonal balances allowing for a regular menstrual cycle. Some women are unable to become mothers by womb.

As importantly, some women are born without the *desire* to breed. Other may have the desire but choose for reasons relevant to them not to procreate. Not every woman wants or needs to be a mother, by blood or by vocation.

According to the Pew Research Center, the US childbirth rate dropped by 9 percent between 2007 and 2011. The study showed that the number of those choosing to be childfree was rising across all races and ethnicities. In 2003, the US Census found that 19 percent of women in the US between the ages of forty and forty-four didn't have children, as opposed to 10 percent in 1976. A 2004 US Census study stated that 18.4 percent of women between thirty-five and forty-four were childfree.

Those who have chosen to be childfree cite many reasons for their choice, from quality of life (their own, and that the children might have had), to financial concerns, marriage status, environmental concerns such as resource scarcity, over-population, and pollution, religious adherence, lack of interest in pregnancy, childbirth, and child rearing, and career orientation, to name a few.

Many women who choose to remain childfree face pressure within the dominant culture to produce children. Many face judgment from their mothers, their sisters, their grandmothers, their childbearing friends. Somehow, everyone thinks it is their right to say when, how, and with whom women should breed.

When the mother stands as the pinnacle of feminal creativity, we enter into a realm of near biological predestination. It is seen as our fate, as women, to procreate. It is implied—if not directly stated—by media, friends, parents, loved ones that we are seen as "not fully women" if we don't. Again and again we unthinkingly reinforce the idea that a woman's body is not for herself. Her body is, in short, an incubator *in potentia*.

The weight of the "miracle of life" is a heavy one. Not every woman wants to transform her body into a living ark for nine months. And the nine months of pregnancy is a fraction of the trajectory that motherhood requires.

In a culture that sees women as potential mothers, women are considered producers. The product is the body that issues forth from their own. This is, in the eyes of the patriarchy, the least—and the most—we can offer. It is our womanly duty. Our obligation to family, God, and country. Heirs. Offspring.

It is no mean feat to be relied upon to birth the future.

Does this make the women who choose a different path less like the goddess? Because around the edges of the circle, in the hallways, in the kitchens, in the classrooms, women are talking about not feeling like they are recognized in the guise of the mother goddess.

Even in the circles of goddess spirituality, many of the women who create via different means have felt unrecognized. Until now, they have been given no way to wear her face, because her face is not theirs.

In this new time we are creating new stories. We are giving the goddess our own face. We are singing new songs about creation. We are talking about how we're building, how we are shaping, how we are cooking, how we are breathing our breath into new beings and worlds.

Creatrix, *She Who Creates*, liberates us from our ages-old shackles, and allows us—if it is what our souls want—to choose not to give birth and instead to create in the ways that make our souls sing and our hearts beat to the rhythm they were born to.

And in this way, if we do give birth or raise flesh-and-blood children of spirit, we do it because it is the option we have chosen for ourselves—not out of fealty nor duty nor guilt, but out of pure desire. Matrix by choice; Creatrix by design.

> *JOURNAL: What is your natural mode of creation? How do you feel when you are in your creative process? What have you felt pressure—internally or externally originating— to create? How did you respond to those pressures?*
>
> *ACTION: Allow yourself to create from pure desire. Give yourself the time and space to give yourself over entirely to your creative process.*

The Virgin, Revisited

Here we examine the Virgin in the context of Creatrix, who may or may not be a physical mother of gods—the Virgin Mary comes to mind as does Hebe, as discussed in the previous chapter.

Again we decipher deeply into what terms meant, and what they mean. Some of these virgin mothers were mother via divine intervention, or parthenogenesis. Some were just wildly independent, who took lovers or did not, had children or did not, and still remained their own ultimate authority.

> *JOURNAL: What thoughts does the term* virgin *in the context of Creatrix bring up for you? How do your ideas of sexuality, coupling, and independence, all shift when you think of Creatrix as a Virgin—either as sexually chaste or in the older meaning of "Unto Herself."*
>
> *ACTION: Be a force unto yourself! What would it be like for you to be held only to your own creative desires and drives? Allow yourself some time and space to experience it.*

Deities Who May Embody Creatrix Energy

A'akuluujjusi is the Mother Creator of the Inuit people. She also created the animals her people eat to survive. She created the caribou from her pants and the walrus from her jacket. She gave the caribou tusks, and the walrus antlers. Then she switched them because they were too hard for her people to hunt the first way.

Her attributes and powers are creation, power, caring, creativity, problem solving, mothering.

Ak Ana is also known as the White Mother. She is the Mother Creator of the Turkik and Indigenous peoples of Siberia. She is the Water, from which everything came forth: the land, and all the creatures on it, including humans. Even the foreign and hostile elements are from her.

Her attributes and powers are life, fertility, productivity, spirits, entrance to the other realm.

Coatlicue is an Aztec goddess who birthed gods and goddesses and the moon and stars. She possesses attributes of both life-giving and life-taking. She wears a skirt of snakes and a necklace of human heads. In her the womb and the grave both exist.

Her attributes and powers are birth, death, power, will, terror, creativity, regeneration.

Demeter is the Hellenic grain goddess. She is the fields, the soil, and the stalks that grow. In Hellenic myth, Demeter is the one who rules the surface of the planet. The Eleusinian Mysteries are her rites.

While Demeter is often thought of as the fertile queen of the harvest, she is also the barren ground of winter. When Kore was stolen from her, she let her fields lie fallow. In hurting her daughter the gods of Olympus almost lost all of humanity to starvation.

Her attributes are generosity, love, compassion, and also righteous anger.

Lalita Devi is a Hindu goddess. Her name means "playful one," and she is life and creation as play. Her play is the creation of all things. Lalita is also called the beautiful one, the beloved, and the divine mother. According to those who worship her, all existence is the Divine Play (the Lila) of the Mother. Consciousness and manifestation emanate from her.

Her attributes and powers are creation, organization, love, life, play, joy, karma.

Persephone is the Greek queen of the Underworld. Her name may mean Thresher of Grain, Speaker (or Bringer) of Death, or Bringer of Light. Those who know her know that all three are fitting names. Persephone presides over the souls of those who have died, and she allows them the hope of rebirth. As she herself is born again each spring as the innocence of Kore, so are we all. Persephone holds the mysteries of life and death.

Her attributes and powers are devotion, sacrifice, compassion, power, light in the darkness, grace, transformation, choice.

Additional Goddesses

- *Amaterasu:* Shinto
- *Aphrodite:* Greek
- *Beaivi:* Sami
- *Bhuvaneshwari:* Hindu
- *Bi-tsin' ma-ca (Frogwoman):* Indigenous Californian including Pomo
- *Brigid:* Celtic
- *Cerridwen:* Welsh
- *Cura:* Roman
- *Demeter:* Greek
- *Devi Ma:* Hindu
- *Eingana:* Australian Aboriginal
- *Eithinoha:* Iroquois
- *Erzulie Dantor:* Vodoun
- *Estsanatlehi:* Diné
- *Freyja:* Norse
- *Gaia:* Greek
- *Guadalupe:* Mexican, Pre-Christian and Spanish Catholic

- *Hathor:* Ancient Egyptian
- *Hera:* Greek
- *Inari Okami:* Shinto
- *Isis:* Ancient Egyptian
- *Ixchel:* Mayan
- *Kali:* Hindu
- *Lakshmi:* Hindu
- *Lilith:* Hebrew
- *Maderakka:* Sami
- *Mami:* Sumerian
- *Ninhursag:* Sumerian
- *Nuit:* Thelemic
- *Nyx:* Greek
- *Ochun:* Yoruba
- *Oya:* Yoruba
- *Quan Yin:* East Asian
- *Radha:* Hindu
- *Sara-la-Kali:* Romani
- *Tiamat:* Mesopotamian
- *Tripura Sundari:* Hindu
- *Yemaya:* Yoruba
- *Yeshe Tsogyal:* Tibetan
- *Yolkai-Estsan:* Diné

JOURNAL: What deities feel the most like Creatrix to you?

ACTION: Find a story about a goddess you don't yet know from the list above or from your own lineage and read it.

Rites of Passage Related to Creatrix

Rites of passage related to Creatrix are the times of taking on the creation of anything. Writing a book, becoming pregnant and carrying a child, becoming a parent (through birth or otherwise), creating a music album, starting a business, creating a community, starting a home, creating a spiritual path, or creating a spiritual community.

Stepping into one's self-definition as an artist, having one's first showing, committing to creating a body of work, are related to her also.

Transitioning from one sex to another, coming into profound alignment with one's core, and taking a true name are under her protection as well.

Her Rites are active rites of making. Creating from nothing. Bringing forth from the void.

JOURNAL: What rites of passage can you think of that belong to Creatrix?

ACTION: Create a rite of passage for Creatrix.

Offerings to Creatrix

Creatrix wants your *creations*. The items you put on her altar may be representations of the thing or things that you're pulling or breathing into being: spell workings, prayer candles, or any and all of the tools of your craft can be placed there as an offering. You can also do so to charge them with her power.

You can put any items on her altar that have to do with stories of creation, or that represent creation to you. You may put images of her there as a way of honoring her.

She loves flowers, water, grain, fruit, bread, offerings of meat—especially pork and lamb—honey, and wine.

When to Call on Creatrix

Calling on Creatrix is a helpful way to dedicate you to your work, and it is also a way to enroll her in your project. You are creating in her name, she is creating through you.

Call upon her when you are:

- Working on your craft.

- Creating a garden, planting seeds, harvesting food.

- Slaughtering or butchering an animal.

- Cooking, canning, baking, pickling.

- Crafting.

- Building.

- Trying to get pregnant, are pregnant, are ready to give birth.

- When you are ready to find a home space and ground your life.

- Looking for partnership, be it sexual, business, or loving.

- Looking to build community or family ties.

- Practicing gratitude for your abundance.

Some Days Sacred to Creatrix
Feast Day of Sojourner Truth and Harriet Tubman—March 10

These two women, mothers of abolition and the women's rights movement, are honored by the Lutheran Church because they were both very spiritually driven women who received the directive to undertake their dangerous and brave work as an edict from God.

Araminta Harriet Tubman, also known as Mother Moses, may not have mothered any children, but she birthed uncounted souls from a life of slavery into one of freedom.

Workers' Day—May 1

International Workers' Day is celebrated on May 1 by the International Workers of the World (IWW) Unionists. May 1 is also observed as a day to honor workers by many governments.

Mother's Day

The observation of Mother's Day in the United States emerged during a potent period in American history—the Civil War. The only war to have been declared and fought on American soil, the American Civil War destroyed lives, tore families and communities apart, and divided a country.

The response to the bloodshed on the part of many American women of the time was to call for an end to war.

No solitary woman can be credited with the beginning of a movement toward the Mother's Day holiday, but every thread that ties into the entangled roots of the emergence of Mother's Day is cut from the same skein; the day was a celebration by mothers, about motherhood, and about the largest gift a mother ever gives her child, the gift of life.

The Mothers' Day Proclamation, written in 1870 by Julia Ward Howe, a feminist and abolitionist, states it plainly:

> Our sons shall not be taken from us to unlearn all that we have been able to teach them of charity, mercy and patience. We, the women of one country, will be too tender of those of another country to allow our sons to be trained to injure theirs. From the bosom of the devastated Earth a voice goes up with our own. It says: "Disarm! Disarm! The sword of murder is not the balance of justice."

The Feast Days of Oshun and Yemaya—September 7–9

Oshun, also spelled Ochun, is the Orisha of love. She rules the rivers. She is joyful, seductive, sensuous, and passionate. In the Yoruba religion, she is the one who ensures through flirtation and seduction that babies get conceived. Her Feast is best celebrated by a natural body of water. She loves offerings of golden things, yellow roses, honey sprinkled with cinnamon.

Yemaya, also spelled many other ways, is the Great Mother Orisha. She rules the life-giving part of all oceans. All creation comes from her. She gave birth to the moon, the stars, and almost all Orishas. She is the Orisha of fertility, motherhood, pregnancy, and fecundity. Her Feast is best celebrated by the ocean or by a lagoon or lake. Her colors are blue and white. She appreciates offerings of fruit, white wine, and fish. Her number is seven.

Labor Day (United States)—First Monday of September

Labor Day is a celebration of the labor movement in the United States, as well as the gains made by unions and workers. It is a day dedicated to recognizing the contributions of American workers as they have contributed to the prosperity and well-being of the nation at large.

The Festival of First Fruits—the First Harvest

This feast or festival is celebrated at the cross-quarter point between summer solstice and autumn equinox. Known as Lughnasadh by the Gaels and Lammas by the Anglo-Saxons, this festival is a time of blessing; it is the beginning point of the harvest season.

Lughnasadh was the funeral feast for Tailtiu, the Celtic Earth goddess who was Lugh's foster-mother. Tailtiu died of overwork from clearing the plains of Ireland for agriculture all on her own. In her honor, Lugh created a festival of harvest.

Lammas comes from the Anglo-Saxon *hlaf-mas* meaning "loaf mass." During Lammas loaves of bread are blessed and then used in protecting the grain harvest.

This festival is celebrated by many modern Pagans as the first of the three harvest festivals; the other two being Autumnal Equinox and Samhain.

Autumnal Equinox, also called Mabon, the Feast of Harvest Home, or the Ingathering

Celebrated on or around autumnal equinox (around September 23 in the Northern Hemisphere and March 20 in the Southern Hemisphere), the second harvest festival is like Thanksgiving. It is a celebration of bounty, beauty, abundance. It is also a time of welcoming the autumn rains. It is a time to celebrate all that has been given of her body.

Harvest's End, the Blood Harvest, Samhain
Cross Quarter between Summer Solstice and Winter Solstice

The third and final harvest celebration falls between autumn equinox and winter solstice. This feast belongs with the Creatrix, and also with Antiqua, the Old Woman, so we will revisit it in her chapter.

Samhain is also known as the red harvest; it was the harvest of flesh. This is the time to cull the herds, harvesting the weak so they won't sicken the healthy livestock in the lean months. The meat is dried, smoked, canned, or frozen in order to feed the tribe through the winter.

This final harvest honors the death-for-life face of Creatrix.

Thanksgiving

In the United Sates, Thanksgiving is a secular national holiday, although it is one with a dirty history. Hidden in plain sight, among the celebration of harvest and bounty is a lot of whitewashing of American history and the genocide of Indigenous peoples across the country.

Some who choose to celebrate Thanksgiving choose also to make offerings and prayers to the souls of those who were violently murdered in the "settling" of the United States.

As this is celebrated as a feast of bounty, it may well be dedicated to the Mother, even if it is one of her more hidden faces.

> JOURNAL: What days would you celebrate as sacred to Creatrix?
>
> ACTION: Create a Feast Day for Creatrix.

Seasons Sacred to Creatrix

Creatrix reigns through the harvest festivals, from First Fruits to Blood Harvest. Your sense may be different; again you are encouraged to feel into your own senses of it.

JOURNAL: What time of year do you associate with the She Who Creates?

ACTION: Continue the process of creating your own year wheel graph that incorporates the five faces.

Weather Patterns Associated with Creatrix

The high heat of summer growth and fruiting, harvest, and the moving into the cooling and crisping of autumn. The harvest, and the putting up. The times of curing and storing foods for winter. The early rain falling on dry soil. The incomparable smell of fall. Did you know there's a word for the smell of rain on dry soil? The word is petrichor. The first cold days, with the wood fires burning in the hearth. The pulling in, and keeping safe against the coming darkness.

Her Time of Day

Creatrix is midday to early evening. She is the afternoon hours of preparation and tending. She is the first blush of sunset, Venus visible on the horizon.

Her Colors

Red, green, brown, blue, yellow.

Animals Sacred to Creatrix

Livestock. All critters that are self-propagating. Creatures that birth and that foster. All female animals. Deer. Buzzards. Beetles. All animals that build, create, tend.

Plants Sacred to Creatrix

Plants that bear food; fruit trees, grains, edible plants propagated and wild; some entheogens like ayahuasca, iboga, and cannabis. Entheogenic means "generative of the divine within." An entheogen is a chemical or medicine that may be used in a spiritual, religious, or shamanic context.

Places Sacred to Creatrix

Gardens, fields, forests, oceans, rivers, mountains. Homes, kitchens, nurseries, offices, workshops, recording, painting, and sculpture studios. Beds and bowers. Caves, tombs, graves.

Suggested Elemental Correspondence for Creatrix

The primary suggested elemental correspondence for Creatrix is Earth. Some attributes: the ground of our being, grounding, earthing, motherhood, nourishment, pregnancy and birth, lineage, protection, stability, strength, sensuality of the dirt and grit, garden, growth; to be silent.

The secondary suggested elemental correspondence is the element of water. Some attributes: transformation, waters of life, birth, nourishment, primordial beginning of life.

> JOURNAL: How does this elemental correspondence fit with your existing magickal practices?
>
> ACTION: Work on your magickal wheel, placing Creatrix with earth or water. Or elsewhere if you get different information from Creatrix herself.

An Invocation to Creatrix

Have you seen Creatrix?
All things arise from her ground of being.

Creatrix, She Who Creates
Show me the way to
Draw form from the formless
Creating newness from nothing

Creatrix, Divine Painter
Show me the way that your brush
Forms meaning
Creating new ways for us to see

Creatrix, She who Writes
Show me our old stories
And our future stories too
Your words are both Vault of Knowledge and Maker of Ways

Creatrix, Mother of All
By will or by womb
Your children come to your life
Bring mine to mine, and let me raise the next generation to love you

Creatrix, Singer of Songs
Your words call worlds into being
Carry us to starry skies and unknown lands
Let me dance to your melodies and find my way home

JOURNAL: How does this invocation affect you?

ACTION: Write your own invocation to Creatrix.

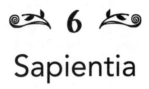

6
Sapientia

Sapientia's sigil

Sapientia—Woman of Art and Wisdom

Sapientia is the *wise woman.*

In Latin, *sapientia* is a more complex word than wisdom alone. It means science, discernment, forethought, perfection of intellect.

Sapientia stands at the lectern, her treatise on the stand before her. She stretches tall, fills the space around her. She makes no excuses for her wisdom; she has earned it. She has walked the miles, spent needed time with her guides and teachers, read the books, tested her theories, and finally built structures of her knowledge.

She stands with both gravity and ease. Her laughter is full-hearted when it comes, and her tears are the power of a late fall storm, unrelenting. She is like the mountains and like the air. She is bright, inquisitive, rooted. She is a force of nature.

In her wisdom she knows that learning is never done; it is a path, not a destination. She holds her hands open to spring rain and autumn rain alike to replenish her well, trusting the process of gathering and letting go.

She tends to the wild herbs and roots, seeks the medicine of dirt, fire, rain, and wind. Holding vigil, she sits in silence while the sun rises after a long night of ritual, ceremony, witnessing. She brings the wisdom into her body, digests it, becomes it; her very being formed and informed by these moments of illumination.

She brings the wisdom forth in words, songs, mathematic proofs, medicine for healing. She sings the chants, tells the stories, instructs the student, heals the one seeking healing. She offers out from her accumulated knowledge. Her acts benefit all beings.

Sapientia is the energy that pulls resources into order, and offers them out again as systems, as teachings. While *sapientia* has the denotation and connotation of wisdom (sapience), the complex meaning of this word also includes science, skilled practice, discernment, and memory.

She is the woman who has mastered her art. She is the wisdom-teacher, the librarian, the storyteller, the spiritual leader. She is the politician, the professor, the chief executive officer. She is the lawmaker, the law keeper, the judge. She is the mediator, and the diplomat. She is the scientist, doctor, mathematician. She is the midwife, the herb woman, the Green Witch. She is the chef, the woodworker, the philosopher.

> Did you know that the word **master** is not a gender-specific term? It means teacher, chief, one who has mastered their area of interest, one with authority. The feminized **mistress** has various, inconsistent meanings; female teacher, female master, and kept woman or illicit lover. Words of power have been perverted in meaning and used against women. We must claim and reclaim words that empower us to stand in our authority.

Sapientia is the wise woman. She is the master of her field. She is the keeper of knowledge. She is the hierophant.

Her Occult Expression

In her occult position her lessons and methods may be harsher than you might have expected. Her hidden face is the strict master offering the arcane arts. You may have to work hard to come into her good graces. With all the time she has spent honing her teachings, she will want to know that you take your studies seriously.

She may be impatient. She may forget how long it takes to attain mastery.

She may cling to her intellectual property, as is her right. She may choose to carry her teachings with her to the grave. She may feel protective of the lessons, or she may fear the power they possess and the outcome that power may unleash upon those who would learn from her.

An obscured expression of Sapientia is that of the teacher or leader who does not help to empower those around her. In this expression, Sapientia may not easily share leadership. She might cling viciously to her power, especially if she feels that her position is all she has built. In her hidden guise, Sapientia may fall into a holier-than-thou mindset or become staid or judgmental about how one might learn, what one might have to offer, or about one's spiritual or educational credentials.

If you take what she has to offer and are not grateful for it, her scorned aspect is very adversarial. She can easily feel martyred in her attempt to make her wisdom accessible. Her pride may be injured, and if it is, she will make it known.

JOURNAL: Have you experienced a teacher or leader falling into these patterns? Have you noticed yourself doing so?

ACTION: In the cases where you see this shadow arise in you, ask it what it might need in order to feel safe or acknowledged.

Her Empowered Expression

In her empowered expression, Sapientia pulls knowledge into systems, and offers those systems out to those around her. She examines, codifies, measures, and distills. She perfects her formulae until she reliably produces outcomes that can be recreated by others.

Her presence may be quiet, but it is subtly commanding. Even when she is not at the front of the room, or holding the still-point in the circle, she is holding, grounding and weaving, cultivating, and maintaining the space she is in.

Her senses are multivalent. She sees, hears, and feels on many levels at once. She has learned how to move between worlds without moving at all.

She is the master teacher. She teaches her subject, and she teaches how to teach.

In her empowered aspect she is the magnanimous professor, the maven, the connector. When fully in her element she has an ease and grace about her because she has nothing left to prove. Her works are her proof. And her offerings are carried out into the world, numerously multiplied.

Marie Sklodowska Curie was a physicist and chemist who performed groundbreaking work on radioactivity. She was the first woman to win a Nobel Prize, and is as of this writing the only woman to win twice. She received the Physics prize in 1903 for her discovery of radioactivity, and then received the Chemistry prize in 1911 for the isolation of pure radium. She is the only person who has won Nobel Prizes in two different sciences.

While her dedication to her art was ultimately fatal—in 1934 she died of aplastic anemia, caused by her ongoing exposure to radiation—she left the world a changed place. Her contributions to the realms of science were immense, and the recognition she received as a woman was unprecedented.

In her later years she headed the **Radium Institute***, a radioactivity laboratory, and she founded the Curie Institutes in Paris and in Warsaw. The institutes remain vital centers of medical research today.*

JOURNAL: How do you express the empowered aspect
of Sapientia?

ACTION: Consider the areas in your life where you are secure
in your mastery. Bring forth some of your unique sapience.

Her Sexual Expression

Sapientia knows what she wants and how she wants it. In most cases, she knows how to get it.

Shared sexual expression and experience may be a central part to Sapientia's practice, teachings, and ways of knowing. The sexual and sensual dance of desire and mergence is one of the areas of mastery available to Sapientia. It is one of the ways she may reach for, touch, and fall into the Divine.

Sapientia may also pull her sexual power into herself, using it as an elemental force that circulates and recirculates within her, replenishing energy for her work and devotion. It is here we revisit the concept of virginity. Sapientia may choose conscious celibacy as her sexual expression, and even as her sexual identity. Sapientia may harness her sexual energy and direct it into her work. She may leave the exploration of interactive sex to the side, temporarily or for a lifetime. She may convert her sexual energy entirely into energy that feeds her learning and teaching.

Her sexuality may be her work. Sapientia is the sacred whore as sexual initiator, teacher, healer, and priestess. She has made a science and an art of her sex. She has studied and practiced and deepened her own experience, and so she shares her sexual illumination.

JOURNAL: In what ways have you explored your sexuality?
Does it play into your spiritual expression and experience?
If so, how?

ACTION: As you move through your day, withhold judgment
on sexual choices or orientations; recognize that sex and sexuality serve different purposes for everyone.

Sapientia in the Linear and Nonlinear Trajectories of Womanhood

In the linear sense of the arc of the fivefold goddess, Sapientia is middle age. It is the point at which one has reached some level of acumen, standing, recognition. Wisdom.

While we often think of this as the silver-haired, newly "croned" or croning woman just past child-bearing age (falling into the biologically ordained, linear model), this stage is one that may be moved through, out of, and back into throughout life as we master new areas of interest.

Additionally, the linear space that Sapientia occupies is different from woman to woman. Some may go more or less directly from Femella to Sapientia. Some may reside in Sapientia for years, decades even, while also calling in the other aspects of the five to enrich and enliven her teachings and practices.

> *Malala Yousafzai is an example of a very young Sapientia. Malala is the youngest ever recipient of the Nobel Peace Prize, and is an activist for educational access for girls and women. After being shot by a Taliban operative for refusing to give up her education, she has become an international icon for the rights of girls to an education. On her eighteenth birthday she opened a school for girls who are Syrian refugees in Lebanon.*

> *JOURNAL: What are some of the ways in which the archetype of Sapientia shifts your relationship with your idea of the divine feminine?*
>
> *ACTION: Create an image of Sapientia.*

Claiming the Wasteland and Rewilding the Ways

Sapientia offers us an opportunity to claim spaces we have previously been discouraged—or expressly forbidden—from entering. As women existing within the patriarchy, whole areas of expression, vocation, avocation, and recognition have been inaccessible to us. Through Sapientia, we claim the keys to the halls of academia, the floors above the glass ceiling, the gateways to the front lines.

We've had to fight long and hard to claim our space in the classroom whether at the front or back of the room, and the fight is far from over. In some sectors, locales, and cultures and subcultures, the progress once made has gone retrograde. Around the world, the long walk toward equality of the sexes has seen uneven results and has been beset at all sides by resistance.

Sapientia is the standard-bearer of the movement. She sings the clarion call to equality, and recognition of equality.

The ways that women walk in the worlds are different ways. The ways women create are different. By birth, by spirit, by body, and mostly by culture and training, we are cast from a different mold.

Sapientia brings the offering of new languages and new systems of language. She carries the languages of women, revealed and hidden. The fluid languages spoken where women gather; languages that start at the edges and move to the center, and then outward again, spiraling languages, the language of pregnant pauses and staccato refrains. It is language that dances, that pauses, that lilts, that lifts, that drops, and climbs.

She crafts languages that are created from, and which then create, the equality we are living into. It is a language of *we-us*, instead of *I-you*. It is a multiplicity of languages, of identity, core, and collaboration; the languages of spheres and of rhizomes.

Hers is the living system of our nonlinear progression. Rejecting the linear model of progress—often conceptualized as a straight line from a "lesser" state to a "greater" one—Sapientia calls us to remember the cycles of seasons, the moon, birth-growth-death-decay-regeneration, seed to shoot to blossom to fruit to seed.

She calls in the patterns that serve as templates for the organic awareness of our place in the larger scheme of things. She calls in new ways of reasoning that are ancient and encoded in our cells. She calls in new conceptualizations of the grid, the matrix, the sphere. New representations for thinking, dreaming, and talking about all things.

She weaves together the ancient forms and new threads, creating the new time. We are invited out of our old, ill-fitting ideas and into the new aeon; one where we are actively writing our own stories, remembering our own stories, and building toward an inclusive and consciously recursive future.

Sylvia Rivera, July 2, 1951–February 19, 2002, was a trans woman of color, a gay liberationist, a self-identified drag queen and transvestite, and a trans rights activist. A New York native of Venezuelan and Puerto Rican descent, Rivera was a lifelong advocate for the rights of trans people. Her approach was radically intersectional and anti-assimilationist.

After an early childhood riddled with loss, Rivera was cast out by her grandmother, who was unwilling to accept or support Rivera's gender identity and expression. Living on the streets and working as a prostitute by age ten, Rivera dedicated her life to the rights of some of the most marginalized members of our community. Rivera stood proudly and said, "Us too. We also deserve recognition of our humanity."

Many consider the Stonewall riots as a turning point for the visibility and rights of queer people and the queer community. While mention of Rivera and the other trans Women of Color who have been central to the movement were conspicuously absent in the mainstream, Sylvia was a highly visible and integral participant in the events leading up to and following the riots.

A woman well ahead of her time, she was a gender non-comformist to the very end. She was known to refer to herself as a gay man, a gay woman, and a drag queen, among other identifiers. In her essay "Queens in Exile: The Forgotten Ones," Rivera wrote, "People now want to call me a lesbian…, and I say, 'No. I'm just me. I'm not a lesbian.' I'm tired of being labeled. I don't even like the label transgender. I'm tired of living with labels. I just want to be who I am. I am Sylvia Rivera. Ray Rivera left home at the age of 10 to become Sylvia. And that's who I am."

Her works and name are carried forward by those who remember and honor her selfless dedication to her communities.

JOURNAL: In what ways has language limited you in the past? What are some ideas that come to you as you think of new ways, old ways, ancient ways, future ways?

ACTION: Notice when old ideas are holding you away from your true intent.

Deities Who May Embody Sapientia Energy

Ame-no-Uzume-no-Mikito is a Shinto kami, or god. At one time the sun goddess, Amaterasu, hid herself away in a cave to avoid trouble with her brother, Susanoo-no-Mikoto, the god of sea and storms. Ame-no-Uzume knew that the Earth and everyone on it needed light of Amaterasu for survival. Ame-no-Uzume tried many things to lure the sun goddess out of her cave. She kindled sacred bonfires and finally ornately decorated herself with moss and leaves and flowers. Then she turned over a washtub, stood on top of it, and danced in front of the cave Amaterasu was sheltering in. Her dance was so beautiful and powerful that all the assembled spirits were overcome with joy. Ame-no-Uzumi showed her breasts in honor of the nourishment the sun brings and her belly to remind Amaterasu that the sun is the ultimate source of life for Earth.

Amaterasu was curious about the laughing, stomping, and music, and she peered out of the cave. Ame-no-Uzemi held up a mirror and Amaterasu was reminded of her own beauty, glory, and power. She left the cave, and all harmony was restored.

Ame-no-Uzemi's attributes and powers are dedication, wisdom, intelligence, humor, ingenuity, creativity, and knowingness.

Athena is the Hellenic goddess of wisdom, courage, inspiration, civilization, law and justice, strategy, mathematics, arts, and crafts. One of her origin stories says that she was born from the head of Zeus, but many scholars believe she was known to have been a daughter of Metis before that—a titan whose name meant "wisdom," "skill," or "craft." It was prophesied that Metis would give birth to a son more powerful than Zeus. When Metis became pregnant, Zeus swallowed her, which is how Athena came to be born from His head. While Athena was in utero, Metis made her child a helmet and armor, and so she sprang forth fully equipped for battle.

Athena is often imaged as wearing her helmet and a full-length chiton. She holds a spear and a shield. She is associated with the owl and the serpent.

Her attributes and powers are intellect, courage, virtue, wisdom, and reason.

Ma'at is an Egyptian Goddess whose name means *truth*. She represents all that is right and good. In ancient Egypt the ways of civilization were considered Ma'at's ways. It was believed that without her influence the world of humans and even the universe would be cast into chaos. Sticking to the upright ways was the worship of her.

Those who meted out justice were Priests of Ma'at.

After death, a person's heart was weighed against the weight of Ma'at's feather before they could enter the afterlife. If the person had erred in life their heart would outweigh the feather. In this case it would be fed to the demon Ammut, the eater of hearts. Being eaten by Ammut meant the final death. However, if one had done service to Ma'at in life, their heart would be light after death. If the heart was equal to Ma'at's feather, the soul of the dead person would go into the afterlife in the Land of Two Fields.

Ma'at's attributes and powers are balance, uprightness, truth, order, and justice.

Saraswati is a Hindu Goddess of knowledge, music, arts, wisdom, and learning. In Sanskrit, *sara* means essence, and *swa* means self, so Saraswati is *essence of self*. Those who worship her believe that she is the one who can deliver *moksha*, the ultimate liberation.

She has four hands, each symbolizing one of the four aspects of human learning; mind, alertness, ego, and intellect. Two of her four hands play a stringed instrument called a *veena*. In her other two hands she holds sacred scriptures and a lotus blossom. She is worshipped by those who prize knowledge: students, teachers, scientists, scholars.

Her attributes and powers are discernment, purity, knowledge, wisdom, consciousness.

Additional Goddesses

- *Airmed:* Celtic
- *Aja:* Yoruba
- *Ariadne:* Greek
- *Bona Dea:* Roman
- *Brigid:* Celtic
- *Cerridwen:* Welsh
- *Cocomama:* Incan
- *Dolma:* Tibetan
- *Dorjne Naljorma:* Vajrayana
- *Eir:* Norse
- *Ekadzati:* Tibetan
- *Frigg:* Norse
- *Fulla:* Norse
- *Ganga:* Hindu
- *Hecate:* Greek
- *Hygeia:* Greek
- *Isis:* Egyptian

- *Ixchel:* Incan
- *Kamrusepa:* Hittite
- *Kitsune:* Shinto
- *Krtya:* Hindu
- *Metis:* Greek
- *Minerva:* Roman
- *The Muses:* Greek
- *Olokun:* Yoruba
- *Oya:* Yoruba
- *Prajnaparamita:* Tibetan
- *Seshat:* Egyptian
- *Sibyls:* Greek
- *Sirona:* Celtic
- *Snotra:* Norse
- *Sophia:* Greek
- *Tara (Black):* Tibetan
- *Waiora:* Pacific Islander/Polynesian
- *Yum-chen-mo:* Tibetan

JOURNAL: What deities feel the most like Sapientia to you?

ACTION: Find a story about one of the goddesses listed above who you do not yet know, and read it.

Rites of Passage Related to Sapientia

Rites of passage under the governance of Sapientia are rites of completion in an educational field, graduations, and auspicious beginnings following completion such as starting a new job in your chosen field, job promotions, graduating from student to teacher.

Other areas of promotion are ordination into a given priesthood, and creating or founding a spiritual community, tradition, or order.

Running for election for a political office, being elected, and serving in the capacity of elected official all fall under her purview, as does becoming an attorney or being elected judge.

She relates to becoming a leader in your community and being called to teach those who need what you have to offer, and when you are given the empowered position of speaker for your people.

When you become a woman of letters or publish your work; when you write down the stories of your people or write your own stories; when you become a storyteller, she may guide you. When you choose an educational path or profession in the sciences or healing arts such as becoming a doctor, midwife, herbalist, scientist, theorist, or mathematician, or opening your own practice, Sapientia's energy is there.

She stands for choosing to serve your purpose, your path, your people.

> JOURNAL: What rites of passage can you think of that belong to Sapientia?
>
> ACTION: Create a rite of passage for Sapientia. (Not ready to build a rite on your own? See the appendix for ritual templates to work from.)

Offerings to Sapientia

Sapientia will best be served by your works, and in the process of working with her, the tools of your trade (in my case, pens and paper, my computer) can be both offered to her and consecrated in her name.

She also takes your mistakes, missteps, and trials as offerings, as she knows that these are where learning comes from. You honor her with your failed experiments and botched attempts.

She will appreciate artifacts from your traditions, your times of learning, your travels that have brought you to her (and home to yourself); your diplomas, your published works, your proofs and spells are all righteous offerings.

Keys are sacred to her, as are feathers, skeletons, and bones used for learning. Also sacred are healing gemstones and crystals; templates, systems, and tables.

She may appreciate candles, resinous incenses, rare flowers, and images or representations of the galaxy, distant star systems, and the Earth.

> JOURNAL: What offerings does Sapientia want from you right now?
>
> ACTION: Make an offering to Sapientia.

When to Call on Sapientia

Calling on Sapientia will bring wisdom, problem-solving skills, innovative thinking, authority, and calm. She can help you to find your center and look at things with reason.

Times you may want to call upon her for assistance could include:

- Readying yourself to take an exam

- Interviewing for a job in your chosen field

- Getting ready to teach

- Getting ready to study

- Before you begin your work

- When you are looking for a solution to a problem

- Blessing or consecrating your tools

Some Days Sacred to Sapientia

Athena's Feast Days

Athena's feast days were celebrations of her birth and her continued influence on her culture, on December 2, March 19, May 20, the month of July, and September 21. The Lesser and Greater Panathenaia were approximately June 8 and August 13. Historically, the lesser Panathenaia happened yearly, and the greater every four years. On the year of the greater, the lesser and the greater were observed together. There were games and contests devoted to different aspects of her expression; music, gymnastics, arts of war. There were dances and choruses and processions and sacrifices.

World Day of Social Justice—February 20
World Day of Social Justice was proclaimed by the general assembly of the United Nations in 2007. There are annual themes designed to bring awareness to global issues and to encourage and promote positive change in law, education, and culture.

World Thinking Day—February 22
World Thinking Day was founded by the World Association of Girl Guides and Girl Scouts.

World Contraception Day—September 26
While originally founded by a global pharmaceutical company, the goal of World Contraception Day is laudable; that every pregnancy everywhere be a wanted one. World Contraception Day is supported by twelve international Non-Governmental Organizations (NGOs), including Women Deliver, an advocacy group focused on improving health and well-being for girls and women.

World Teachers' Day—October 5
Founded by UNESCO, World Teachers' Day is an effort to outreach to teachers to offer them resources, training, and services that will allow them to do the world-changing work before them.

World Science Day for Peace and Development—November 10
Created by UNESCO as a way to engage people in an awareness of the value of application-based science, World Science Day is an opportunity for the science communities, governments and general populations to work together to create positive outcomes through science.

World Philosophy Day—Third Thursday in November

Another day of observation brought by UNESCO, World Philosophy Day was founded as an opportunity to recognize the power of philosophy as a discipline that encourages "critical and independent thought," self-examination, understanding and tolerance.

Here are some bonus days, because Sapientia has so many good ones:

- *International Science Day:* February 22
- *International Women's Day:* March 8
- *International Day for the Elimination of Racial Discrimination:* March 21
- *World Poetry Day:* March 21
- *World Health Day:* April 7
- *International Day of Human Space Flight:* April 12
- *World Book Day:* April 23
- *World Intellectual Property Day:* April 26
- *World Press Freedom Day:* May 3
- *International Midwives Day:* May 5
- *Festival of Minerva:* June 13
- *World Goddess Day:* September 7
- *International Literacy Day:* September 8
- *World Mental Health Day:* October 10
- *United Nations Day:* October 24
- *Veterans Day: United States:* November 11
- *Human Rights Day:* December 10

> JOURNAL: What days would you celebrate as sacred to
> Sapientia?
>
> ACTION: Create a Feast Day for Sapientia. It may be a com-
> memoration of your own day of stepping into the power of
> Sapientia; a graduation or other turning point.

Seasons Sacred to Sapientia

Sapientia reigns in the newly darkening time, when the veils are growing thin. Her time of year is what could be conceptualized as the twilight of the year just moving into the full night; from fall equinox to winter solstice. It is the nurturing lull of the time after the harvest and before the coldest months.

Your sense may be different, and again I encourage you to go with your intuition—it will always work best for you.

> JOURNAL: What time of year do you associate with the
> Woman of Wisdom, Science, and Art?
>
> ACTION: Continue the process of creating your own year
> wheel graph that incorporates the five faces.

Weather Patterns Associated with Sapientia

She is autumn rains, the first frost, days cold enough to light a hearth fire. She brings cleansing and nourishment through the alchemy of the shifting seasons.

Her Time of Day

Sapientia is the gloaming, the time between true day and true night. Past evening, the times when you see with more of your senses than just your eyesight. She is the darkness setting in, stars shining forth in the firmament. She is also the morning gloaming, the ancient, waning moon setting on the western horizon.

Her Colors
Yellow, gold, black, purple.

Animals Sacred to Sapientia
Owls, the white stag and white doe, foxes, whales, cows, ravens, salmon.

Plants Sacred to Sapientia
Rare flowers and plants; cacao; medicinal herbs; some entheogens: coca leaves, morning glory seeds, salvia divinorum, perhaps peyote. LSD, MDMA, and other synthesized entheogens when used in an intentional setting for healing or mind expansion are also sacred to her.

Suggested Elemental Correspondence for Sapientia
The primary suggested elemental correspondence for Sapientia is air. Some attributes: intellect, innovation, logic, new ways of thinking, language, communication, breath.

The secondary elemental correspondence is earth. Some attributes: wisdom, strength, history, lineages, ancestry, duration, stability.

> JOURNAL: How do these elemental correspondences fit with your existing magickal practice?
>
> ACTION: Work on your magickal wheel, placing Sapientia with air, or with earth. Or elsewhere if you get different information from Sapientia herself.

An Invocation to Sapientia
Have you seen the Woman of Wisdom?
Her voice is strong,
And she stands like a mountain.

Sapientia, Woman of Science
You are the art of numbers

Your grace exists in vaulted skies
And crystalline formations of mineral
Resting in the heart of Earth

Sapientia, Woman of Knowledge
You are the echo of things recursive
Vibrational bonds
Tying all things to nothing
In the timeless spaceless place of all that has ever been

Sapientia, Woman of Letters
You tell the ancient stories
That let us remember who we are
And the new stories
That allow us to create that which we will be

Sapientia, Woman of Art
You hold the mysteries
At the heart of things
The cycles of birth, growth, death, regeneration
All sacred in your eyes

Sapientia, Woman of Wisdom
Bring your powers that I may know healing
Bring your arts that I may know magick
Bring your laws that I may know order
Bring your words that I may create new worlds with them

JOURNAL: How does this invocation affect you?

ACTION: Write your own invocation to Sapientia.

Antiqua

Antiqua's sigil

Antiqua—The Ancient One

Antiqua means *ancient woman.*

Antiqua stands, body bent, fingers twisted like bare branches. Her face is a map of the million times and places she has been. Weathered mask crowned by silver hair, she is as old as Night itself.

Her faded eyes graying with the slow loss of sight, she looks at the world from the distance the aged see from. She sees shadows come to life, replaying long-forgotten sequences of her own story.

Antiqua's steps are little earthquakes, each one a movement closer to the grave. She dances in slow and halting arcs under starry skies. Body bending toward the soil, she moves from a different strength; Will alone is her helpmate. When that wilts, she wanders among timelines, one foot in this world and one in the next. She moves in all directions at once. Time and the counting of it ceases in her moments of forgetting.

Antiqua is by turns terrifying, infuriating, and dear. Vibrant and fading. In all of these she is vulnerable, and venerable. Her basic being, inconstant as it may be, commands respect. She has been on this long and varied road for a time outside of time.

Sometimes she forgets herself. She becomes one with everything, nothing left as she drifts between worlds. Half sleeping she talks to the spirits of those who have gone before, making her way toward the western gate.

Antiqua is the old woman seated near the ritual fire. She is the priestess who has served her community and is now ready to rest and be taken care of by it. She is the aged one in need of an arm to rest on for stability during the walk up the hill to circle. Later, in her final rest, she will need to be carried there.

She is the ancient and weathered professor emeritus, sitting rapt and attentive in her academic regalia, and she is the lifelong teacher becoming foggy on her subject deciding to surrender her position.

Antiqua is the supreme court justice tearing holes in bad judgments—and sometimes nodding off in session. She is the actor getting fewer roles because women are not shown in our process of aging. And she is the new face of the old woman; she who is shining a light on the ways her years wear on her.

> *Supreme Court Justice Sandra Day O'Connor* was the first woman appointed to serve on the Supreme Court. She was appointed in 1981. Though she served for only 11 years—stepping down because of health issues—at 85 (as of 2014) she now spends much of her time and energy teaching younger Americans about how the courts work. She shines a light on the elements of big money influence, and arms Americans in the struggle to maintain meaningful civic involvement.
>
> *Justice Ruth Bader Ginsburg* was the second woman to be appointed to serve. She assumed office in 1993. In 1999 Justice Ginsburg was diagnosed with colon cancer. In the process of her treatment—surgery, chemotherapy, and radiation therapy—she never missed a day on the bench. As of this writing, she is 82 and still serving.

Justice Ginsburg has been, and continues to be, a tireless feminist activist. She stopped observing her familial faith, a conservative line of Judaism, because of gender inequalities. She refused to attend a prominent mass other justices attended due to anti-abortion rhetoric.

In an interview on National Public Radio in October 2014, Justice Ginsburg was asked how many female justices she thinks would be enough. Justice Ginsburg is quoted as saying, "When there are nine." She added, "For most of our country's history there were nine, and they were all men. Nobody thought that was strange."

She is the stately and powerful maven, and she is also the moment the maven begins to crumble back into the Earth.

She is the body giving way to gravity, mind slipping—perhaps slowly, perhaps more rapidly—into the quicksilver glisten of forgetfulness.

She is the ancient woman sitting in the rocking chair or lying in bed, no longer able to read, write, knit. Perhaps too old to walk. She is the elder ready to be taken by death, or fighting death tooth and nail. She is the one aware that death is near.

She is the one who shows us the ways to care for those in need. She is the one who teaches us about dying. Antiqua is the beloved one who is cared for in her final days.

In her slow-moving decrepitude, Antiqua's memory is less linear, part dream and part time-travel. Antiqua is wise beyond knowing; her years have left marks on her.

She may have already passed into the reborn innocence that lies beyond memory and forgetting. Yet even in her forgetting she holds wisdom.

Antiqua is the senile woman. The crazy old lady. The mad woman. Sometimes furious in her lapses she lashes out, flailing for a ledge to catch her fall.

She is the wild one retreating into her cave. The hag in her thatched hut. The witch in the woods, wandering, seeking what is lost. She is the old ways, in danger of falling away. She is the guardian at the edge of the circle. She is the one with the crescent-shaped blade.

Antiqua is the ancient one, wending her way toward the summerland, the world beyond this one. She is the cutter of threads. She stands between worlds.

> JOURNAL: *How does Antiqua live in you?*
>
> ACTION: *Safeguard some of the teachings of Antiqua. This may mean writing down one of the stories from your lineage, or your life experience, or it may mean finding an elder and asking her to share a story with you.*

Her Occult Expression

In her obscured expression, Antiqua is sometimes wrathful, sometimes confused, sometimes stubborn, sometimes terrifying. She holds up for us the obsidian-mirror face of death. She carries all the weight we place on the process of aging.

In the most complete aspect of her occlusion, she is the personification of old age, decrepitude, and death. Even before that, however, her energy grows more and more finite in her waning days. She must hand over power and delegate it in her areas of authority. And as she passes on her duties to those coming up behind her, her desire for perfection may be exacting.

Antiqua is attached to tradition and fears the loss of her heritage and teachings. Because she sees the value in the old ways, she may overlook—or even try to override—new ways of thinking or doing things. Her stubbornness in clinging to tradition over innovation may isolate her, which in turn may leave her feeling abandoned.

A hidden aspect of Antiqua is the fear of being forgotten—she is the specter of the old woman in her cave or hovel. In this aspect she is often unwilling to participate in things that don't work out the way she would prefer.

Sometimes she acts from a sense of unexamined privilege. She wants things her way. She believes she deserves it, and so she may. Antiqua may have a challenging time transitioning to the expectations others have for her. She has passed through all the other stages of life, and now she is at risk of being told what to do, how to do it, why, when, where, and with whom. Antiqua is used to having some say in her life circumstances, as all of us are. The harsh shift toward elements of powerlessness leaves her shocked, angry, and confused. Even her body is betraying her. As an independent woman, the process of losing power is infuriating.

Her anger flares up when she feels the sting of objectification or perceives paternalism toward her. Don't "help" her against her will; if you do you will surely be on the receiving end of Antiqua's fury. At the same time, she may forget (or be unwilling to) ask for help, so taking care of her may feel like a fool's errand, a job never done that you can never get right.

She is the nightmare hag; the thing that goes bump in the night, the heart-chilling cry of the bansidhe. She is the thinnest crescent of the waning moon, no light cast upon the ground. She is the rotting stench of death. She is the toothless, bruised, tattered, angry, senile old lady, cursing and pissing in the street.

In her most hidden aspect—the one we are most deeply afraid of—she is the Forgotten.

> In **France** in 2003, a **heat wave** resulted in the deaths of close to 15,000 people. Most of these people were 75 or older or in frail health. Many of the old people who died were living in isolation; they died without anyone noticing.
>
> Morgues overflowing, refrigerated trucks and warehouses were turned into temporary storage for the bodies. When the crisis was over, hundreds of bodies were left unclaimed.

> JOURNAL: What is it like to have your will and power gradually taken away by age or other circumstance?
>
> ACTION: How would you most like to be helped in achieving your needs and desires, even as the amount and type of power and energy you have available to you shifts?

Her Empowered Expression

In Antiqua's empowered alignment, she is the ancient storyteller, keeper of the old ways, spinner of tales. She is the living cauldron of our collective knowledge. She reminds us of the things that make us who we are—of where and what we are from.

> In traditional **Wyandotte** (also known as Huron) culture, each clan's senior women chose those who would step into positions of leadership.

She is the soothsayer, the fortuneteller. She can see the future and the past. Her raspy, breathy, haunting tenor is the voice of fate itself.

In her empowered position her fierce and furious fire is expressed as passion, will, and mirth. She laughs at the comedy of it all; of how short life is when all is said and done, at impermanence, at our fear of death and transitions, at the grasping we are prone to throughout the years.

She tosses her wild head back and howls at the moon. She is a lunatic. She wears night like a cloak. She does not fear the dark.

She is the one who teaches us how to midwife death, teaches us how to mourn the passing of loved ones. She teaches us how to live with death as a constant companion.

> While the **Greek goddess Hecate** may not have always been seen as an old woman, most who worship her now know her as an ancient woman standing at the crossroads, carrying a torch to show the path through the darkest nights. She helps us choose the way. She is a midwife in birth and in death.

In her empowered aspect, Antiqua teaches us to let go, allows us to rage and cry, and sits with us at all endings, large and small. At the breaking of ways, at the sickbed and the graveside.

She shows us the new tendril sprouting from the rotting fruit. She sings the death-chants; hers is the chest-heaving dance of the final release.

> JOURNAL: How does the empowered aspect of Antiqua express itself in you?
>
> ACTION: Take that empowerment and do something to safeguard the empowerment of elderwomen, yourself or others.

Her Sexual Expression

Antiqua's sexual expression is a hidden mystery. A last taboo, like Baubo she reveals her desire. Her pleasure is for pleasure's sake. She reaches out to her lover and holds to this world and time through the passionate fire of love and sacred sexual desire.

*Baubo is the **Greek goddess** who made **Demeter**, the **Grain Mother**, laugh by dancing a flirtatious dance and revealing her vulva to her. This broke Demeter's rage and grief over the loss of her daughter, Kore. In a flash, Baubo's bawdy reminder allowed Demeter to see humor in the processes of death and life.*

In her long years she has tasted many forms of sexual expression. This does not inure her to seeking the edge of her own sexual experience; she has little to risk now. She welcomes her final throes of ecstasy as part of her journey to the next world, her pleasure birthing her to new expansions.

> JOURNAL: Sexuality belongs to all. How does age affect your relationship with your sexuality?
>
> ACTION: Imagine yourself moving toward death and still reaching out to lovers for sexual pleasure.

Antiqua in the Linear and Nonlinear Trajectories of Womanhood

In the linear sense, Antiqua is the oldest of old women. In the nonlinear, you may experience Antiqua when you're moving through rites of passage such as retiring, losing loved ones to illness or death, spending more time on your own. You may come to know her while living with an illness that leaves you incapacitated.

You may feel her in a divorce or ending a long-term companionship, or when children move out of the home.

You may feel Antiqua's power when you are looking at your own mortality, or experiencing the death or illness of someone close to you.

You may feel her as you gather your family's stories, study your traditions, research your genealogy.

> JOURNAL: What are some of the ways in which the archetype of Antiqua shifts your relationship with your idea of the divine feminine?
>
> ACTION: Create an image of Antiqua.

Reclaiming the Hag

The folk and faerie tales that survive in the dominant narrative have roots that reach far back into the culture of colonization. In those stories, the hag is one of the most fearful of creatures. Stories about wild hags lurking in the night have been used to make children behave for even longer than stories have been written.

If you go out in the dark, Black Annis will get you! Stay nearby, or the Cailleach will take you. Don't go near the water or Jenny Greenteeth will make short work of you. Be careful in the night, or Bakhtak, Mara, the nightmare will crush your chest.

We have been taught that the dark is to be feared. We have been taught that the darkness is an old woman. We have been taught that old women are to be feared.

But we know who wrote the stories down. Remember this; the greater weight of the stories that have been committed to ink serve to secure the power structures of dominant culture. History is written by the victors.

And we know whose stories were given to the winds. Our living stories shifted off the page and ran to the hills; they grow there still, craggy roots deep in the soil. They embedded themselves in herb pots and patch gardens and told themselves to us as we touched the dirt and smelled the sacred scent of decay. Secrets slid gently into sewing threads and twine and gave themselves to the cross-stitch.

We know in our bones that the Witch in the Woods was not always evil. Some stories predating or existing outside of the patriarchy tell a different story of the Old Woman. In these stories she is powerful, wise, and independent. Perhaps she uses some trickery to get done what needs to be done, but this is not out of evil intent. The Suppressed Histories Archives, founded and directed by Goddess Historian Max Dashu, is a storehouse of these stories. She has compiled folk stories and faerie tales that show the old woman in a different light.

You can also find these stories in living oral traditions within Indigenous cultures that have been able to keep their languages alive. Many Indigenous cultures in the occupied territories known as the United States have stories of Grandmother Spider, and some have stories of First Mother, also known as Ancient Bodied Woman.

The dark of night cannot be colonized: it is a wild land, still living free. It is the leftover part, considered inhospitable. Hidden territories left to their own devices.

Attempts at colonization continue, and each of us are colonized and colonizer. We tell the stories of Hansel and Gretel, Snow White, and Sleeping Beauty, introducing our young charges to the same fear, commingling ideas of advancing age, struggles for power, and fading beauty as an impetus for wrong-action, and the overall evilness of women.

> *Lateral aggression, or lateral violence, is directed at one's peers instead of one's adversaries.*

In our fear, or foolishness—or both—we reinforce the normalization of lateral aggression; women fight against women for the scraps, the meager spoils available. We have been taught this as the way of women; the evil stepmother, the wicked witch, the old hag.

Of course there *is* a place for folk and faerie tale; folk tales are our living stories. We will take the stories back and eat them, hags that we are. We will let them digest. And after a time, we will cough them up, spit them out, and tell new stories about the magick that lives in dark and wild places. About the glory of stars and the comfort of darkness.

About age rolling over us like a blanket. About death coming to us as an old, haggard, beautiful, beloved friend.

> JOURNAL: What stories would you rewrite to reclaim the power of the hag?
>
> ACTION: Write, or tell, that story. Or write or tell a brand-new story with a hag as the hero.

Old Age

In dominant Western culture, we don't have a place for our very oldest elders. An unforeseen product of longer life spans, industrialization, economics, and shifting cultural values and expectations, the oldest among us are most often left alone.

There are also gender-based implications of course, because while this is true for old men, it is especially so for old women. While somewhat old men are still seated at the figurative head of the table, somewhat old women still have to fight for every inch of political and economic power.

Once women get very old in Western culture—and women *do* get older on average than men—they're often seen as a burden. And as often, they're not actually *seen* at all. Often they are put in nursing homes or assisted living centers by families who do not have the capacity to offer full-time care to parents and grandparents. In the dominant, industrialized culture, the idea of the grandmother, great-grandmother, or the elderly aunt or family friend caring for the young children is not a realistic one. The requirements of the two-income nuclear family model have trumped the comparably more tried-and-true format of extended family structures. In a (more and more global) culture built on rugged individualism and an acquisitive drive, economy of scale has not been highly prized.

On our own, the likelihood of isolation and loneliness increases the older we get and with it, more and more severe repercussions. A meta-analysis of studies on loneliness and isolation compiled at Brigham Young University found a 30 percent increase in mortality in cases of extreme loneliness. One of the review's authors, Dr. Julianne Holt-Lunstad, said about the analysis that the data shows "greater longevity if you're well connected."

Studies are showing that loneliness is more of a health risk for older people than is obesity. Yet in the dominant culture, there is no integration of the truly aged.

> *JOURNAL: How vibrant are your social networks? How many close friends do you share intimate details of your life with? How often do you see people you love in person?*
>
> *ACTION: Make plans with a friend or friends. Or, do something you enjoy and find ways to meet others who enjoy that thing too.*

Creating Solutions to the Isolation Epidemic

It begins with the rhizome. We take root, and send out shoots, runners, fibers, fingers. We reach through the soil—fertile, dry, and waterlogged. We thread ourselves to one another. We weave a new world together.

We need one another. We are beginning to comprehend how our relatively short (in the scheme of things) experiment in isolation is harming us. Yet globally our social habits and lifestyles are leading us farther from the community fire circle and closer to desolation.

At the edges, we are seeking ways to come back into a collectivist experience. And from the edges, the methods are filtering slowly into the mainstream.

Cohousing is a communitarian model of intentional, collaborative living. Combining elements of close community and privacy, cohousing villages or neighborhoods often include a shared common house as the community center and single-family homes for all residents. Communities are often designed by members from the ground up. Membership in established cohousing communities can also be bought into and in some cases residences may be rented or leased.

Most cohousing communities have regular membership meetings and ongoing, shared social events such as community meals, dances, game nights, movie nights, and group outings.

While the cohousing movement started in Denmark in the 1960s, cohousing communities started popping up across the United States in the early 2000s. The model is taking off in other countries as well. In Denmark, elder cohousing communities are being built in proximity to multigenerational cohousing communities to ensure a sustainable model.

In the Netherlands, university students are being offered housing in retirement communities as a way to increase intergenerational friendships and community building. The students pay no rent but offer thirty hours a month of support to the elders living in the communities. They may teach a class—like computer skills or graffiti art—or take an elder shopping, prepare meals, or simply hang out. The elders are not required to spend time with the younger community members, but so far, most choose to.

In 2013, the Babayagas' House opened in France. This feminist-focused old age home was brought into being by Thérèse Clerc and a collective of other dedicated women. Clerc was in her sixties when she conceptualized the home. The doors opened and she moved in at eighty-five.

The project won attention, support, and financing in the wake of the disastrous effects of the 2003 heat wave. The support was bolstered by the daunting fact that more than a quarter of the population of France is older than sixty years old. The French government and people recognized that it was time for real solutions.

The Babayagas' House is a built-to-purpose, four-story building in an active, suburban neighborhood. In addition to the twenty-four self-contained units, there is a shared common space designed to house a spa and a university that will serve the Babayagas and other senior citizens.

To become a Babayaga, an applicant must have an active track record in civil involvement and activism. The central values held in common by the Babayagas are civic sense, solidarity, self-management (independence), and ecology.

As of 2015, numerous projects inspired by the Babayagas' House are underway.

JOURNAL: What do you envision for your final years?

ACTION: Research options or have a conversation with loved ones about what your old age may look like. Begin discussions about aging in your intimate circle.

Death and Dying

As a culture, we have a generally negative and fearful relationship with aging and dying. It is easy in a sense to conceptualize this aspect as the old crone—root word *caro*, shared with "carrion." She is death incarnate.

Death is seen by many as the enemy. We are taught to fight against her tooth and nail. In Western culture we spend exorbitant amounts of money warding off the inevitable. We throw good money after bad in an effort to prolong life when it may truly be time to surrender into the arms of Old Mother Death.

> *While ancient cultures may well have had death a little bit more normalized than "modern" culture does, different spiritual paths in industrialized nations are currently introducing, or reintroducing, healthier views of death and dying. Drawing on Tibetan practices, depth psychology, Paganism, and other sources, people are finding ways to move toward more* **conscious ways of dying***.*

Instead of facing death with fear, what if we could face her with acceptance or even curiosity?

A subtle shift has begun. In the United States and Europe, conscious death has recently become somewhat of a growth industry. Innovation and spiritual exploration are hallmarks of the baby boomer generation, and as boomers begin facing the prospect of their own death, these inclinations appear to be affecting choices in end-of-life experiences.

In 2004 Swiss sociologist Bernard Crettaz hosted the first *café morte*, or "death café." Over the next ten years, Crettaz hosted numerous death cafes in Switzerland, and then in France, and then in the United Kingdom. In 2011 Jon Underwood, a government employee living in East London, heard about Crettaz and his work. Underwood was an immediate convert and is now in his own words, a "committed death-activist." He runs a not-for-profit social franchise called Death Café, which facilitates people in gathering to "eat cake, drink tea, and discuss death."

Also in 2011 (which was apparently a good year for death), the Order of the Good Death was founded by Caitlin Doughty, a mortician and writer living in Los Angeles. According to their mission statement, the Order is, "a group of funeral industry professionals, academics, and artists exploring ways to prepare a death phobic culture for their inevitable mortality."

Generation Xers are facing the questions of death with perhaps a more jaded tone but with the same desire for different end-of-life outcomes. Increasing awareness of the wastefulness of the death industry as it stands—the ill-effects on the environment of options such as cremation, embalming, and space considerations with funeral burials—have led to solution-seeking on the basic levels of consideration regarding death.

It is clear that our values about death and dying are being examined. Laws that restrict choice in the hows and whens of death are being evaluated and changed around the world. Known most commonly in the United States as Death with Dignity laws, conscious end-of-life choice is the cause of our time. As of this writing conscious, consensual euthanasia has been legalized in Luxembourg, the Netherlands, Belgium, Colombia, Switzerland, Germany, Japan, Albania, and in the US, in California, Washington, Oregon, Vermont, New Mexico, and Montana. Sixteen other states have Death with Dignity laws in process.

The true force of this change in attitude is only now beginning to hit the mainstream. Training and certification programs for death doulas and midwives are beginning to appear. Perhaps another outcome of boomers facing death, more people are choosing not only how they die, but also how their bodies will be laid to rest and how they will be commemorated. Green burials are available if you look for them. There are death professionals, planners, and funeral celebrants to help with the process. Celebration of Life ceremonies are becoming more common and are often planned out by the commemorated themselves.

While some of this is undoubtedly pure in its impulse, some of it is surely a further grasping at control over the inevitable. But we have no way to control the inevitable, ultimately.

There is no way to truly know what lies on the other side of the body's last breath, but some among us have traveled there and returned. They have told us not to fear her. And even if we do fear her, she wins out in the end.

Knowing this is so, what can we do in our lives to create a better relationship with her? What can we do to become more familiar?

> JOURNAL: Begin planning your death. Do you want to die at home? Who do you want to make your end-of-life decisions once you are no longer capable? Do you want certain readings done to help you through the process of dying? What about your funeral or memorial? Burial or cremation? Green burial? Where?
>
> ACTION: Start writing out your end-of-life wishes, and share them with someone who needs to know.

Embracing Antiqua

The process of coming into a graceful relationship with this face of the fivefold goddess is sure to challenge some of us. In coming face to face with Antiqua, we confront our fears of aging and of our eventual death.

Making peace with Antiqua means coming into a harmonious relationship with our very old elders and with Death herself in the cultural and communal sense. It means learning how to care for Antiqua and our elders in a collaborative way. We strive for solutions that make her feel cared for, welcomed, at home. We want her to be safe, cherished, honored even. Because Antiqua deserves honoring.

Perhaps if we have a name for her, a divine face of the goddess that represents this old, old woman, we will be able to look at her more fully and with more care and compassion.

We will welcome her at our table. We will offer her rides to gatherings and invitations to dinner with the family. She has a place by the fire, and a voice in council circles; even when she stops making perfect sense to us. (After all, we never know when the voice of the divine might find its way to her lips.)

Perhaps we can learn to honor her, by honoring Her.

> JOURNAL: What do you hope to see, do, experience in your final years?
>
> ACTION: Do one of those things now. Bonus points: invite an elderly loved one along and trade stories.

Deities Who May Embody Antiqua Energy

Ayizan, also known as Grande Ai-Zan, and Ayizan Velekete, is known in Voodoo traditions as the primal Mambo; the first priestess. She and her husband, Loko, is the first Houngan, or priest. Together they guard the secrets of healing and initiation. Grande Ayizan is an ancient woman who wears an apron with deep pockets. She brings birth and death.

Her symbol is a palm frond. It is used for clearing magickal space for rituals. Ayizan holds the space for her children—and all children of the Lwa are her children—to be reborn through initiation.

Her attributes and powers are transformation, initiation, healing, rebirth.

Baba Yaga is a Slavic Witch who lives deep in the forest in a hut that stands on giant chicken legs. The fence around her hut is made of human bones and skulls. Baba Yaga flies about in a mortar, using the pestle as a rudder. She uses a broom to erase her tracks.

If you seek Baba Yaga for help—or if she happens across your path by accident—she may aid you in your plight, or she may make it worse. You must take care with the way in which you approach her and in the ways you ask her for assistance.

Her attributes and powers are enchantment, power, will, movement, stealth, transformation. She has control of the elements, the sun, and the moon.

Grandmother Spider, or Spider Grandmother, has many stories. She is honored by many Indigenous tribes in the lands now called the United States. In one story, Grandmother Spider is the earth herself. In another, she stole fire for the people. In yet another, she stole the sun to bring light. Another tale says that it was Grandmother Spider's dreamsong that created everything that exists.

Her attributes and powers are creation, bravery, selflessness.

Hukluban is an ancient Philippine goddess of death. Her name means hag. She is one of the goddesses of the Kasamaan—the Tagalog equivalent of hell. She is a shapeshifter, and is known to sometimes trick humans off of their paths to take them off to the land of the dead. But she can also heal as easily as she can slay.

Her attributes and powers are transformation, temptation, healing, and death.

Jabmiakka, also spelled Jabme-Akka, or even Yambe-Akka, is the Samí Goddess of death and the underworld. Her name means "Old Woman of the Dead." The trembling of her hands is the cause of earthquakes. *Samí* shaman healers, the *noaidi*, use the beat of the ceremonial drum and chants to find their way to Jabme-Akka so they can ask her to release the souls of those in need of healing. While she is not known to be the most gentle of souls, she is reputed to offer a special kindness to the souls of babies lost in childbirth.

Her attributes and powers are the decision point between death and life, intercession, and healing.

Manåt is a pre-Islamic Arabic goddess whose name means *fate*. Ancient as the soil in the fertile crescent, she was worshipped by her people along with her sisters, Al-Uzza and Al-Lat, until their worship was pushed under the surface with the coming of Islam. But fate outlasts us all; perhaps she is waiting for us even now.

Her attributes and powers are gravity, duration, sacrifice.

Additional Goddesses

- *Annis:* Celtic
- *Batibat:* Ilocano
- *Baubo:* Ancient Greek

- *Boo Hag:* Gullah
- *Cailleach:* Gaelic
- *Eagentci:* Seneca
- *Escheman:* Arapaho
- *The Fates:* Ancient Greek
- *Granne Erzulie:* Vodou
- *Ketq Skwaye:* Huron
- *Keyuri:* Tibetan
- *Kikimora:* Slavic
- *Muma Padurii:* Romanian
- *Nana Buruku:* Candomble
- *Nokomis:* Ojibwe
- *The Norns:* Norse
- *Sedna:* Inuit
- *White Tara:* Tibetan

> JOURNAL: *From your own lineage, what deities who you work with feel the most like Antiqua to you?*
>
> ACTION: *Learn about one—or more—of these goddesses.*

Rites of Passage Related to Antiqua

Her rites of passage have to do with age, growing older, and death. As a woman ages, it may benefit her to put an offering for Antiqua out on her birthdays. However, her rites of passage don't have only to do with your aging; they also recognize the rites of passage of the elder women in your life, and how those passages affect the arc of your life.

Transitions are sacred to her—becoming a grandmother by blood or spirit, or great-grandmother; retiring from your job. If you were a mother, moving out of the home you raised your children in and into a home of your own is an opportunity to honor her.

Death and dying are under her purview. If you become a hospice worker, your work may be dedicated to her. Your licensure and promotions will be opportunities to recognize and honor Antiqua.

Becoming a keeper of your lineage or family stories is also a rite of passage that may be dedicated to Antiqua.

JOURNAL: What rites of passage can you think of that belong to Antiqua?

ACTION: Create a rite of passage for Antiqua.

Offerings to Antiqua

Antiqua will appreciate things that belonged to your ancestors; old letters, old pictures, family heirlooms. She wants the recipes passed down from your grandmother's grandmother. She wants the rolling pin and kneading bowl, mortar and pestle, grinding rock. She wants the knitting needles and the quilt needle, commemorations of the secret textile languages passed from woman to woman. She wants reminders of the quilt code that delivered slaves to freedom. She wants the pauses that are words, brief punctuation revealing through hiding. She wants sweets, tea, cakes; scissors, yarn, thread, or twine; a crescent blade.

Antiqua wants your stories, poems, songs, written and spoken in your mother tongue, or the mother tongue of your mother's mother, brought back from the dead. She wants starry night skies, wood smoke, a sip of spirits, and a bowl of sweet hashish. She wants poppy pods and valerian rhizomes.

She wants pure essential oils, overwhelming and wild. She wants wild sage, a rocking chair, a luxurious shawl, rose water, jasmine flowers, and violets.

JOURNAL: What offerings does Antiqua want from you right now?

ACTION: Make an offering to Antiqua.

When to Call on Antiqua

Antiqua will manifest on different fronts at different times in your life. She will sit with you when you are on deathwatch for a loved one, when you are grieving, when you yourself are facing mortality.

If you suffer a debilitating illness that causes the necessity of extra care being offered from the community, Antiqua can be your ally. Call on her when:

- You pass on the mantle of leadership.

- A thing ends.

- You need to find the internal courage to let go of external requirements that are not aligned.

- You need to care less what others think of your choices.

- You need to summon the strength of the mad, or wild, woman.

- You are having health issues that require that you request support.

- Your body, mental acuity, or functioning is compromised.

- You are writing your will.

- You are planning your funeral or memorial services.

- You enter into the dying process.

- You hold the process of dying for another.

Some Days Sacred to Antiqua

International Mother Language Day—February 21

Mother Tongue Day was instituted by the United Nations Educational, Scientific and Cultural Organization (UNESCO) in November 1999. It has been celebrated every February since 2000 as an opportunity to promote linguistic and cultural diversity through multilingualism.

World Save a Spider Day—March 15

Spiders are our allies. In the environment they show us where there is less pollution. In the dreamworld, they keep our stories. Celebrate this day in honor of Grandmother Spider.

International Day of Nowruz—March 21

UNESCO—An ancient new year tradition celebrated by many in Western, Central, and Southern Asia, as well as the Caucasus, Balkans, and other regions. This holiday is a celebration of intergeneration connection as well as regeneration. This is a time to recognize and reaffirm solidarity and peace between generations.

World Poetry Day—March 21

UNESCO—A day to celebrate cultural expression in the form of poetry. Poetry is one of the main ways that oral traditions are passed down through the generations.

International Day of Forests—March 21

She lives in the wild places! Celebrate her there.

World Water Day—March 22

If Antiqua is aligned with Water for you (see the section on elemental attributes), this would be a good day to honor her.

World Turtle Day—May 23

Turtle medicine! Turtles live to be very old. They are slow, wise, and vulnerable.

World Oceans Day—June 8

Another Water day.

World Elder Abuse Awareness Day—June 15

A sad one, but worth recognizing as one of her days. Our elders need our care.

International Widows' Day—June 23

Most women outlive their male partners. This is a day of tenderness for all women who have lost a beloved partner. The chances she will be a widow increase the older a woman gets.

Grandparent's Day—Different Day Depending on Country

In the United States, Grandparents Day was founded as an opportunity not only to recognize and celebrate one's own biological grandparents, but all senior citizens. Celebrated the first Sunday after Labor Day, it is an opportunity to recognize the contributions senior citizens have made in history and to celebrate the old people in your life. One of the suggestions is to adopt grandparents not just for the day but for life. The official flower of Grandparents' Day in the US is the forget-me-not. In Italy Grandparents' Day is celebrated on October 2, which is also Guardian Angels' Day in the Roman Catholic Church.

Ancestors' Day—Different Days Depending on Country

Qingming Festival, also known as Tomb Sweeping Day and Ancestor's Day, is a traditional Chinese festival that takes place the fifteenth day after the spring equinox. Haiti holds Ancestors' Day on January 2. Obon is celebrated in Japan different days, depending on region. Chum Bennh is celebrated on October 15 in Cambodia. Common elements are visiting graves of ancestors, calling on the spirits, making prayers, and making offerings.

Halloween—October 31

I'm not talking about Samhain here; Halloween is a holiday that belongs to the Old Witch as much as it belongs to the children and the wee folk. Put up an altar to the Hag, whether your Halloween is an autumnal celebration (Northern Hemisphere) or a vernal one (Southern Hemisphere).

Samhain

The cross-quarter between the autumn equinox and the winter solstice, Samhain is a time when our beloved departed walk in the realm of the living. Welcome her with her own place on the Samhain altar. The third and final harvest celebration, this feast belongs to Creatrix, and also to Antiqua.

Samhain is the red harvest. It is the time of culling herds. Many Witches celebrate Samhain as the Witches' new year. This aligns with Celtic tradition, which says that the day starts with evening, and the year starts with the turning toward darkness.

Many Witches believe that this is the time where the spirits of the dead walk free in the living, waking world. Witches who celebrate may devote time to communion with their beloved dead, burn away mementos of the previous year, and commit to new practices, take on new goals, or begin new magickal workings.

> JOURNAL: What days would you celebrate as sacred
> to Antiqua?
>
> ACTION: Create a Feast Day for Antiqua.

Seasons Sacred to Antiqua

Antiqua's time of year is from the cross-quarter of Samhain to the cross-quarter of Imbolg. She spans the time from death to rebirth. She shares part of her time with Femella, which is well and good, because out of death comes new life. Out of darkness, light.

> JOURNAL: What time of year do you associate with the
> Old Woman?
>
> ACTION: Continue the process of creating your own year
> wheel graphic that incorporates the five faces.

Weather Patterns Associated with Antiqua

The time of the freeze. Winter: Ice, snow. Keening, howling winds. Cold.

Her Time of Day

Antiqua is the dark of night.

Her Colors

Purple, dark blue, black, silver.

Animals Sacred to Antiqua

Wolves, spiders, cats, chickens, crows, turtles, elephants, whales, sharks, sturgeon.

Plants Sacred to Antiqua

Pot herbs; medicinal teas that help with pain, memory, dreams, crossing over. Psilocybin; narcotic flowers, willow bark, valerian, motherwort, vetiver, orchids, wild violet; moss and lichen.

Places Sacred to Her

Graves and graveyards, sick-beds, gardens, deep forests, waterways that open to the sea, the edge of the ocean, great bodies of water, archeological sites, burial sites, compost heaps, bone yards, spider holes, portals, some caves, high deserts, cliff faces where the wind blows.

Suggested Elemental Correspondence for Antiqua

The primary suggested elemental correspondence for Antiqua is the element of water. Some attributes: intuition, change, tides, time, emotion, rolling transformation (like waves), and death. To dare.

Her secondary elemental correspondence is north and earth. Attributes; bones, caves, primordial, ancient, ancestors.

> JOURNAL: How does this elemental correspondence fit with your existing magickal practices?
>
> ACTION: Work on your magickal wheel, starting with placing Antiqua in the west. Or elsewhere if you get different information from Antiqua herself.

An Invocation to Antiqua

Have you seen Antiqua?
She wears night like a cloak,
And guards the Ways between Worlds.

Antiqua, Grandmother
Come sit with me
Tell me the Old Stories

Remind me where I come from
Remind me who we are

Antiqua, Old Hag
Show me your wild fury
Let me learn to wield this power
So that when I am old
I too can stand my ground

Antiqua, Mother Death
Sit with me while I await the transition
Show me the ways of impermanence
Take me to your breast
Hold me near as I let go

Antiqua, Care-Taker of Spirits
Draw back the veil
Bring me to my beloved dead
So we may eat the feast of sorrow together
And dance to your whispered song

Antiqua, She Who Guards the Ways Between Worlds
Help me to know time as it is
Paths that intersect and fold upon themselves
Future and past meeting in this moment
Share your secrets that I may weave a better way

JOURNAL: *How does this invocation affect you?*

ACTION: *Write your own invocation to Antiqua.*

8

Rewilding:
The Path from Here

The Path from Here

The journey has been long in getting here. We walk the paths of our foremothers, taking the work they did and growing it within ourselves to new points of potential and awareness. We are capable of new levels of emancipation. Future generations will be even more ready to shift the patterns that hold them back from transformation; we can see the future evolutions of consciousness already unfolding if we know where to look.

Shrugging off the ill-fitting, restrictive garments of compliance, we stand naked before her. We have nothing to hide, and there is less now holding us back. We are more than ready for this new journey; it has already begun.

We are her faces. Each of us holds the vulnerabilities and strengths of Femella, Potens, Creatrix, Sapientia, and Antiqua. She lives in you. Your heartbeat is her heartbeat; your hands, her hands. She is everywhere. She is the sphere with no center. (Every point is the center.) And no circumference found. (She is limitless.)

She is dancing and fighting and loving and creating and playing and teaching, and new ways are being transmitted to and through us as she does. We are living her through the reclaiming of our languages, our bodies, our identities.

This new aeon, new world, new time we are creating is happening now. There is no more waiting. It is being built, created, envisioned, crafted, and birthed by us.

Hold her magick. It is yours. Know it is blossoming in you. It is finding its way through you, finding purchase in you, with its rhizomatic, multivalent patterns. It is connecting the threads of past and future—collective and singular—and weaving them into healing patterns of liberation.

Go forth. Retreat. She is found and expressed in action and repose. She is the ever-present spiral path, and she is the one upon it. She is the wild, untamed waters, the virgin forests, the untempered fire, the sweet unsullied breeze, and she is the primal heart.

And she is the polluted gulf, the drought-fed wildfires, the toxic fumes, and the broken spirit. Where we are broken, she is broken. Where we are healing, she is healing. (At every point she is whole. She has always been so. At every point we are whole.)

Her body is our body. Her redemption, our redemption. In her liberation is ours. In our liberation, hers.

From here, we take to the beaten, broken paths and make them whole and wild again in her name. Break the concrete and find the soil beneath. We will seed it with ancient and new seeds. We will reintroduce Indigenous rootstock. We will become the rhizome. We will break through the walls together and allow native plants to reclaim her lands.

We are not separate. We are one. We are none. We are life continuous, beyond the geographical and ethnographical histories of humankind, and the geological histories of Earth, and the stories of the goddess. She exists beyond all, and we exist in her.

We do not yet know what is possible. We do not know what she will bring, or what we may bring in her name.

She is revelation, revolution, evolution in action. Acting through us. We are her face, her heart, her being. And she is ours.

Part 2

In This Together: Reweaving Our Magicks

9

It's All About Relationship

The Relational

In this part of the book, our focus is on decolonizing our magicks and finding our way into the relational possibilities of this new wave of radical revisioning. We come to the roots and work them together. We deconstruct and reconstruct and find our way into the not knowing that allows the deeper knowing, the collective knowing, to emerge.

In much of part 2, we will not be focused so much on her five faces as much as we will be focused on seeing each other's faces, and our own faces, and the awareness that she is arising with us, within us, around us. She is arising as us. In you, in me, in the *we* that we are together.

We will be exploring topics of relationality, liberation, collectivism, self-reflection, and magick. We will be tearing apart and sewing back together. We will be entering into relationship with the land where we stand.

The goddess comes back around to us at the end of this section; we will take all that we have learned and create rituals to her in a new way, using new terms, new tools, new ways. That may be the Old Ways. If they are or are not the traditions that were handed down, or the ones that stand unrevealed, hidden in the shadows of time, these ways we are creating now will someday be the Old Ways. In this moment, in these choices, in this process we are dreaming into the future as it exists, nascent and burgeoning, in the now.

We do our part by moving the wheel a turn with as much consciousness as we can draw upon.

Collective Liberation and Personal Responsibility

Many teachers, spiritual guides, and authors have probably told you that your spiritual responsibility begins and ends with doing your own work; that examining your own process, working on yourself, defining and discerning your own bullshit ideologies and beliefs, and addressing them in your own heart and mind is not only enough, but that it is really all you can do to change the world.

In the relational context, I invite you to examine whether this belief sits well in you. Imagine that this highly individualist, self-focused approach were not how we walk into our process of spiritual growth. What if our spiritual realities, beliefs, and ethics contextualized us into spherical, whole-systems, relational structures? What if *your* liberation and *my* liberation were truly experienced and understood as a connected, co-arising state? What if the sovereign rights of earth, water, and nature were part of that co-arising? What if the liberation of all were the liberation of one, and the liberation of one was the liberation of all?

> *If you have come here to help me, you are wasting your time. But if you have come because your liberation is bound up with mine, then let us work together.*
> —Aboriginal activists group, Queensland, 1970s

Yes, our process of liberation begins in our own hearts and minds. Decolonization of our magicks and imaginations and bodies are reliant upon precise, incisive, ongoing self-examination. But in this new aeon standing in the soil of atavistic, nascent, and living Indigenous traditions, and in the rooting and budding and blossoming new traditions, in stardust and grit magicks, this one that calls for guidance from the eternal forces of nature and of the green spark of incipient awareness, we step into alignment with the force of the combined power of our relational liberation.

To think we are each responsible only for our own spiritual well-being is like thinking that making sure your own family has food on the table is enough; what about other hungry families? Is making sure they also have food to eat part of your concern? Are the needs of hungry mamas and babies next door, across town, or on the other side of the planet part of your personal sense of well-being? If not, then perhaps we are not ready for this undertaking. If we are not ready to create relational, rhizomatic connections between our own hearts and the hearts of others, between our own minds and bellies and spirits, and the minds and bellies and spirits of others then perhaps we are not ready to engage in this process of deconstruction and reconstruction and the work of dreaming the new dream and living into it.

Yet perhaps in this moment you are struggling and all you can focus on is the food your family needs. When this is the case in the world we are creating, in the world we are dreaming and breathing and becoming into existence, when you are in need, sisters will come and ask you, "Do you have enough to eat?" They will ask, "Do you have a place to sleep, a place to stand, a place to dance, a place to play, a place to pray in safety?" And they will hold the protective circle so you can make your prayers to your own gods and goddesses in your own way, because we are different from one another, and our differences make us stronger.

An integrated spiritual life exists in the realm of our lived experiences. In the realm of our lived experiences we are coming into the perhaps ancient awareness that we can pool our resources and that when we do, the resources serve more of us, and serve us for longer. We are beginning to know that our shared lack can become our comparable shared wealth. In the process, sharing will bring us closer together.

Yes, your spiritual responsibility begins with your process. But in the context of collective liberation, an integrated spirituality does not end in navel gazing or even in continued pursuit of spiritual materialism. The systems of belief mirrored by the dominant paradigm offer us plenty of opportunity to dive headlong into the self-absorbed blindness of spiritual introspection.

It is a privilege to have the time to pursue spiritual development, especially in the way we think of it in the Western, intellectual, dominant consciousness. In this dominant consciousness, spirituality is the provenance of those who can walk away from their "distractions" and commit to a deeper spiritual calling: the beatniks, sadhus, gurus, and priests. As masculine existence is held as the standard, our woman traditions of finding spirit in the flesh has been framed as a "low" magick. This is all right. We don't mind our feet and hands and asses in the mud. We are digging the roots that will tell us stories of how we came to be. We are shaping clay into serving plates and water jugs. We are birthing babies and worlds from the sacred openings in our bodies. We are pouring out stories and songs and chants of death and of creation.

This spirituality, this magick, this worship is rooted in the grit, grime, and grace of it all: the blood and laughter of it; the chop-wood-carry-water of it; the reaching and offering of a hand to hold or grab; the grasping at straws; the cooking-for-more-than-your-own-because-you-have-more-than-enough of it; the "I can't do it alone because I don't know what I don't know and I need you" as well as the "I got you" of it. It is new eyes looking and new ears hearing it.

Your well-being is my well-being in this world we are creating. My well-being and your well-being are the same. I am weighted down in your suffering. In your liberation I am lifted up.

JOURNAL: *Where does your responsibility begin and end? Give yourself some concrete examples.*

ACTION: *Where might begin the process of increasing space for our shared liberation? What action would you take based in the realization that your liberation is bound up in the liberation of your sisters? Work on something that increases the possibility of liberation for all beings.*

Intention is Not Everything

Not all things are mutable. As it is sold to millions, the law of attraction is a slick package designed to make those with enough resources to simply *attract* more resources into the picture not feel guilty—or more importantly, not feel responsible—when others with less privilege are not able to do the same.

We do not "create reality" in a vacuum; we affect one another. Our choices interact with the needs and desires of others. We exist in a system of complex inter-reactions. Not all resources are unlimited. Not all things are accessible to all people.

Intention is an ill-formed concept. The road to hell is paved with good intentions, as the adage goes. Intention without action is worth little; without engaged action even magickal intention falls short. And, one's intentions may be *good* and still have harmful repercussions.

One of the presuppositions that create the foundation of NLP (Neuro-Linguistic Programming) techniques is the notion that the "meaning of your communication is the response it receives." For a long time the core meaning of that presupposition eluded me. It clicked for me when I applied it to communication with my kids: with my little ones it was easy to see that if they weren't getting what I saying, the best solution was to say it differently; to speak to them where they were.

When we feel into it or think back to an argument we might have had, most of us can see that "I didn't mean it the way you're taking it!" is not an apology. When we feel harmed what we want to hear is more like, "I didn't realize how my actions (or words) would harm you. I didn't intend that harm. I see that was the outcome and I'm sorry. I won't do it that way again. I want you to know that I care for you, and I will shift my awareness in order to embrace the way you experience it too."

A relevant question to ask yourself is this: where do your actions land in consensus reality? How will the outcomes of your intentions and actions affect others? How will they affect other marginalized groups? How will they affect your children? Your future self?

Yes, you can—and automatically do, to some extent—create your reality. Depending upon location and resource availability and opportunity you may choose to create the most amazing reality you can imagine. But without awareness of how your actions affect those around you, you might be creating that reality at the expense of others. Without thinking and feeling through the possible consequences of your intentions, your intentions may bear fruit that is not merely neutral but actually harmful.

We affect one another. And we are affected by one another. Our realities interact and become a larger, shared reality.

The values of the dominant culture tell us that self-involvement and self-investment are the pinnacles of development; rhetoric around self-improvement reflects this. Rhetoric around "limiting beliefs" reinforces it. The mentality behind not talking about, reading, doing, or paying attention to whatever we don't like reinforces it. A dedication to radical self-expression before intersectional awareness forms, informs, and reiterates it.

Regardless of intention, it is time to listen if feedback tells you that your actions have injured another. It is time to allow the pain, the tears, the anger, the frustration to take the space it needs. This is necessary. This is the work of transformation. This is alchemy.

When intention is being used as a magickal tool, it is of utmost importance that the whole be taken into account to whatever extent is possible. And as we find our edges on what parts we are willing to extend our concern toward, stay there and breathe into it. And then when you are able to, expand your attention even further.

JOURNAL: Write about a time when your intention landed in a way that caused injury in some way. How did you react? What did you learn from the experience?

ACTION: Tell someone about the story you just wrote down. Have a conversation about intention and consensus reality.

When coaching clients, one of the techniques I use is an **ecology check**. This technique can be applied when you want to get a feel for what your intentions might bear when put into action. To perform an ecology check:

1. Get present in your body—you can use breath to do this, or just feeling into your muscles, bones, flesh.

2. Imagine taking the intended action. You may run it like a movie in your mind, tell yourself a story about it, or just imagine it.

3. While doing so, stay present in your body, and pay attention to the responses you have as the situation unfolds in your mind. See if you can notice how the actions would land for others, and for yourself.

4. *Feel in your body for any sense of unease, hesitation, or pain. Notice if the outcomes feel integrated for you, or out of integrity. If you feel resistance, enquire into it. Ask the resistance what information it has for you. Ask any pain or stuckness or unease what it has for you.*

5. *Listen to the feedback.*

6. *Recalibrate your outcomes depending on the feedback you get.*

7. *With your recalibrations in place, start the process over.*

8. *If you get lost in the process, start over. If you want to try out other actions, start over.*

The Dangers of a Subtle Sense of Spiritual Superiority

Even in a subtle context there is potential harm in the ideologies of intention as the means and ends; when we believe that anything is possible and it is merely the state of mind that drives and draws what we live, we are a hair's breadth from blaming those who are poor, hungry, ill, homeless, jobless, beaten, or oppressed for their circumstances. We cannot live in the "believe it and it shall be so" and "everything happens for a reason" bubble without casting some blame on those whose cultures are being constricted, starved, contaminated instead of looking at the real perpetrators of the desecration. And yes, many of us are that; many of us are to one extent or another perpetrators.

We cannot make ideologies and structures of belief that are held collectively go away just by a solitary act of deciding not to believe in a thing. We exist in a reality generated together by all of us, and shift needs to happen in the consensus reality in order for a thing to truly cease to be, or come into being.

When one is in a position that allows them to ignore consensus reality, they are almost undoubtedly in a position of comparable privilege. And when that person uses their privileged life as an example of how it is possible to simply *make it so*, to "believe and receive," it is impossible for that person—and for any who support ungrounded prosperity theologies—not to judge and belittle the plight of others who have less access to resources.

Racism could be seen as a "limiting belief," but it's not one held solely (or even primarily) by those it harms the most; it is a systemic belief that has systemic ramifications. One may choose to not believe in racism or may consider themselves "color blind," but that obviously doesn't mean that racism is magically no longer an issue. As much as the well-meaning folks who believe that we live in a post-racial society would like it to, not believing in racism doesn't make racism go away. In fact, it does the opposite. When a white person tells a Person of Color that they don't *see* color, that white person is denying the Person of Color's lived experience.

When we choose to turn away from the truth of a person's existence we deny their personhood. We deny their sovereignty. We deny their souls. We must examine our complicity. If we are not actively lifting one another up, chances are we are unconsciously holding one another down. The system was built this way; when we fight for the crumbs we all go hungry.

We will win our freedom by feeding each other. Imagining that everything happens for a reason allows us to wash our hands of elements of influence we could perhaps have if we cared enough, or felt empowered enough, to try. Instead, "white-lighting" can get the best of our spiritual processes and we can end up allowing our sense of some "divine right" to move us into apathy and a lack of care.

Intention as ideology also primes our consciousness for spiritual bypassing. Many of us are familiar with the fallout of white-light spiritual bypassing. It usually goes something like this: "If this horrible thing is happening for a reason, I don't need to feel the enormity of it. So everything happens for a reason" or "Your thoughts are bringing in the negative. Shift your consciousness! If you didn't focus on racism (sexism, poverty, etc.) it would cease to be an issue. Your negative thoughts are part of the problem," or "Your anger isn't serving you."

Even the most noble of paths' lineages and ideologies may be used to justify staying in the spiritual comfort zone. The "everything is perfect just as it is, because it is as it is," mantra leaves little room for looking at ways we can create a more integrated and compassionate reality.

In many cases spiritual shaming is used to justify tone policing when issues that are core and challenging and heated come forward. When bringing up a difficult topic, you and I have probably both been told—maybe more than once—that what we are saying is too much or that we are saying it in a way that makes it too hard to hear. We are told we're too angry, too intense, too confrontational, or too out of control. You have been told to take up less room, be nicer, more polite, less angry. You have been told to wait your turn—and then your turn never comes. You have been told not to be disruptive. Whether these things have been said out loud or simply inferred, you have received these messages. Even if your parents and community members didn't say it, the dominant culture did. You saw it modeled and reinforced in media, in social interactions, in education, in the work place.

Unfortunately, we have carried that same judgment forward. Each of us has felt discomfort when someone brings up a subject that makes us unsure about things. We have probably asked sisters to tone it down so as not to piss anyone off. We have probably even thought and felt that this was for their benefit.

Returning to intersectionality, it is essential to recognize that silencing doesn't happen equally: the opinions of Women of Color are too often seen as unimportant. When Women of Color do speak up, they are often hypervisible—told they are too angry or too loud. And it is not even only when Black women are *angry* that they are told to decrease their visibility. True story: in August of 2015 as I write this book, a story is being shared about a group of Black women being kicked off a tourist excursion called a wine train here in California…for *laughing* on their book club outing. The women were met in Napa Valley by a police presence. The hashtag *#laughingwhileblack* is trending.

If the question is "aren't there more important things than this topic?" I can emphatically say no, there is nothing more important than the right of Black women to laugh in public. Perhaps there are things equally important, but nothing is *more* important. For their part, People of Color are used to being asked the question of importance. Native American people are asked: "Aren't land rights a more important issue than the names of sports teams or the use of war bonnets as costumes?" Black feminists are asked: "Isn't access to health care more important than cultural appropriation?"

If you are not from the culture that's raising an issue of concern, how would you know what's most important? And why should one topic be addressed to the exclusion of all others? It is likely (catch the sarcasm?) that all the issues that are being brought up matter. Why else would they be brought up?

Feminism has a horrible track record of centering the needs of the dominant agenda and pushing the needs and desires of marginalized groups out of view.

Silencing others when they have a challenging story to share is not a benefit to anyone. More often than anything we silence others not out of concern for them, but out of fear of facing discomfort. Silencing the conversation when difficult things arise is just another way that we keep one another down. And when we silence each other, we are stuffing our own voices too. With every story that we ask not be told, we are making the world less safe for all of us.

We all probably also know how it feels to be the one to speak up with an unpopular point of view. We know the rattling heart, shaking hands, dry mouth of it. We know the sweaty palms and queasy stomach of it. We know the fight, flight, or freeze of it. And still when the moment comes to support or to silence, many of us often opt for enforcement through tone policing, lateral aggression, finger pointing. We have been trained to this. It is time to break the conditioning.

The truth is that when hard truths are told, there is no easy way to do it. And it is not your responsibility to make sure that no one feels uncomfortable when you need to tell a difficult truth. In these times your only responsibility is to stay with your truth. The hard issues need to be addressed, felt, held, and heard. We need to stand beside one another and around one another and hold space sacred for the telling of hard stories; the speaking of difficult words; the sharing of hurt, anger, and fear.

In this space we allow the cleansing fire to burn us clean. Beneath the embers under the soil lies the newly waking seeds.

The solutions will only arise when we can all talk and feel and push and pull and fight and cry and eventually come to terms with it all. We will then be able to form a collective awareness. At that point we may begin seeking into collective solutions, agreements, compacts, conscious and magickal conspiracies.

We need every bit of our personal and collective language and presence and imaginations to be unlocked and potentially available in this dance we are doing toward our collective liberation.

As it stands, the beliefs that hold us away from our anger, fear, shame, and the deep knowing of it all are also cutting us off from our power. Our anger and pleasure and passion are a birthright. Our revolution song is our life song, the song we were born singing. It is that first glorious gasp, or cry, or moan of the first exhalation after the first inhalation. It is the furious dancing heartbeat that brought us into the world.

Our responsibility is our privilege, and our privilege is our responsibility. The occult parts of our minds and spirits and beings are a wellspring of divine desire and transformation.

Face the hidden parts. Communicate with them. Learn from them. And in a conscious and integrated way, take action on your best intentions for the liberation of all.

> JOURNAL: What areas of emotion have you cut yourself off from? What areas have you discouraged others from exploring because of your own limitations of thought?
>
> ACTION: Take a good intention, look at the possible implications, and once you have discerned as well as you can the possible impact of the intention in shared reality, and take right action.

Finding Ourselves at the Center

The dominant paradigm places a lot of stock in ideas of self-sufficiency, independence, and self awareness. It does not place a high premium on the relational, the nonlinear, the fluid and facile.

In our communities, we know that coming together and offering helping hands and listening ears and loving hearts means more love, more joy, and more shoulders to bear the weight of the heavier times.

We don't need to go it alone; it's all right—healthy and good—to seek interaction. Our lives and dreams are nourished and take on new form when we seek out the company of our people. Our woman-story tells us this, and our ways of interacting in shared space echo it, and our very guts know that we need each other's support. And that we need to support one another as part of that reciprocity.

In 2007 I spent time in Palestine. During my time there, I experienced ideologies around identity that were so strikingly different from the cultures I had grown up in. In the communities I visited, an introduction began with the family name before the given name; you are known first as being from your people, then as an individual.

In my interactions and deepening relationships, I got to experience that all actions taken were considered from the perspective of how they would affect or reflect upon the community or family first. And as I became more integrated in the culture, became part of the family I was coming to know as my own, fell in love with the heartbeat of the land beneath my feet, came to know the language of the fig trees and water and dust, I allowed myself to surrender some of what I had thought of as core elements of my self (but were, I came to find, really just elements of my self-expression) to this collectivist way of being.

I began dressing more conservatively. I covered my tattoos. I wore modest shirts with sleeves. I buttoned my blouse up to the topmost button. I wore long slacks. Finally, I began wearing hijab—a traditional item of Muslim religious dress—to cover my hair.

And my behaviors shifted. I socialized with the women at parties even though we barely shared a language. I played and laughed and cuddled with the children in the blessed sanctuary of the women's rooms: the kitchen, bedrooms, and living room. The men would gather in the entry room. At one gathering there was a young woman, Israa, who spoke English well. I asked her to ask the women for me, "Don't you sometimes want to spend time with the men?" They laughed, and responded, "Why would we want to do that? With them, we would be expected to talk about things that concern the men. Here we get to talk about exactly what we want to. We talk about the children, our homes and families, and about our politics. Here we are free to be who we are."

And I thought, yes, that is kind of the same in much of the Western world. When we are with men we are, on some level, expected to play to their needs and desires. The reasons these women spend time in the kitchen and living rooms are the same reasons that we seek women's spaces. When we don't find them, we create them.

I went to mosque to pray with the family's grandmother. I sat with the ancient aunties and uncles at the family dinners. I rarely went out with men, and when I did it was always with my host there as my chivalrous guardian and chaperone. He was also my very beloved friend who trusted and loved me.

I didn't do any of this because I felt pressured. I didn't do it because I felt threatened or endangered when I walked or traveled alone. As a matter of fact, I have rarely felt as safe in any city as I felt in the cities and towns where I spent time in the West Bank. I did it out of respect for the family who was becoming my family. I did it to respect their name and their image and their standing. In a small town (there just like here) people will talk.

I also had another motivation—I wanted to allow myself to experience this other way of thinking and being. In a dream a group of women veiled and beautiful stood on a darkened street, waiting for me. I longed to enter their company.

As I shifted my appearance in order to integrate more fully into the culture I was finding a home in, I thought a lot about cultural and sociological agreements, identity, ethics, and priorities. I noticed deeply how familial identity was both a grounding force and a system that held to enforcement of social norms. The mindset is so different from what we experience in the dominant minority world Western paradigm.

In giving myself over to the ways of this culture that I had before no way of knowing, I got to see ways that feminism works I could never have imagined. I witnessed different ways that feminal strength is expressed and honored. I saw how holding the family and the community at the center can also put women at the center. I saw how women are held and honored in this culture that we in the Western world think of as nothing but oppressive.

And I saw the ways in which collective need being held at the center also increases scrutiny and enforcement. I saw how taking the needs of the collective before oneself can be wearing and tiring and challenging.

Individualism and collectivism have their strengths and their limitations, and we can learn from both. We can open ourselves to our own unknowns, release our ideas of ourselves, women, feminism, and spirituality. We can release attachment to the elements that define us and surrender to the process of dissolution.

When we find the stillness at the center of it all, we can engage, modify, and learn. If we can come to respectfully examine the differences, we may emerge from the process with more grounding and more liberation.

JOURNAL: In what ways has your dedication to self-suffi-
ciency or self-expression kept you apart from others or in
other ways isolated you? In what ways have these same
qualities served you?

ACTION: Examine the ways that your family creates
community, or that your community creates family, or
both. What works to bring you and your loved ones into
greater relationship? Choose to do more of that thing.

10

Magickal Conspiracy

Conspiring Into a New Dream

At the root, to *conspire* means to breath together. In common usage it means planning with others to do something unlawful, but it also means to work toward a common goal. All of these things are elements that may lead to new and vital magickal coalitions.

It is clear that becoming allies to those who have struggles different from your own is not enough. We need to become more to each other; we need to enter into conspiracies together.

Are you ready to put your body on the line in support of the people with whom you consider yourself to be allied? Are you coming to this knowing that these struggles are not someone else's struggles—that these struggles are collectively *our* struggles?

Are you willing to stand in the path of "progress," and take a stance against the ongoing desecration of the Earth? Are you ready to break trespassing laws in order to support Indigenous land claims, and the claims of the Earth herself?

Are you willing to take shifts in the kitchen making food to support those who are on the front lines? Are you ready to loan your voice to a larger cry for justice? Are you ready to be part of the seeking for solutions, collectively?

Are you ready to use your privileges—whatever they are—as a tool for culture disruption? Instead of apologizing for your advantages—or worse, denying them—are you ready to pick them up and use them to actively shift culture in whatever ways you are able?

Are you willing to stand in front of the bulldozers as they destroy homes?

Rachel Corrie was an American activist who was killed in Rafah in the southern part of the Gaza Strip on March 16, 2003. Rachel and a number of other activists were attempting to protect the homes of Palestinians from armored bulldozers being operated in the occupied territories by the Israeli Defense Forces. Rachel stood her ground in a safety-orange jacket and was run over repeatedly by the operator of the bulldozer. She was twenty-three at the time of her death.

Whatever our level of ability and consciousness is, that is where we start. We start by having conversations, by making different purchasing choices, by reaching out into your communities and starting conspiracies of love and magick.

We begin by asking difficult questions of ourselves and our communities; asking who is not present, and asking what we may do to create the openings in ourselves to invite the unknown into our circles in ways that are conscious.

We start by raising the children of our communities with awareness of consent and with strong spirits. By making places for dancing and playing and learning and loving at the center of our revolution.

We must be willing to take fire for our beliefs. We must be willing to go deep and address the root of things. We must be willing to enter into the edges of our own capacity in order to find our way to a shared knowing and doing and being.

JOURNAL: In what ways could you use your privilege to make changes in your community? In the world?

ACTION: Decide upon an action you can take now, and take it. It could be something as simple as writing a letter to a representative. Or you could begin looking at the areas you haven't taken into account before now.

We Don't Need Another Hero

In answering the questions asked above it is also important to ask yourself if you are ready to stand—or sit—in the background, listening and learning, when you come into a new community. Are you ready to bring an open mind instead of a head full of answers?

> *Three ways to successfully **destroy** a budding connection:*
>
> 1. *Be an expert on a topic you haven't lived—also known as mansplaining or whitesplaining.*
>
> 2. *Tell people that they are focused on the wrong thing—also known as derailing.*
>
> 3. *Tell people they're overreacting, or to calm down about an issue they are impassioned about—also known as tone policing.*

What is your motivation in seeking this collaboration? Are you hoping for glory? Are you seeking to assuage your guilt? Are you taking on a struggle because it is something you feel as though you should support? Are you adventuring, spectating, or speculating? It is essential in taking on the work of collaboration and conscious conspiracy that we examine our motivations and look at them in relationship to our concepts of power and authority.

When entering into a movement or an action that has history, it is your responsibility to research it, study it, learn it, and make sure that you know how to enter into collaboration from a place that will be truly helpful and will offer reliable and useful support.

It's simple, but it bears mention: if you're new to a scene remind yourself that it's not yours to take over. Enter in humility. Look to the existing leadership. Learn the ways of the culture or community with whom you are seeking to conspire.

Keep in mind that just because your position or privileges may confer a certain visibility upon you, this does not automatically make you the expert in an action or movement you are working to support.

Systemic racism works this way. Let's say, for example, that you are joining a blockade action against the Keystone XL Pipeline under the leadership of the decentralized, worldwide, grassroots Indigenous movement, Idle No More. And let's say you are white and an environmental scientist by trade. Considering your vocation and training, the media may look to you for a soundbite; you are visible as an expert on the topic at hand after all…and you're white. However, unless you have been charged specifically by the leadership of the blockade to be a spokesperson, you are not the proper representative.

While stopping the progress of the pipeline is the issue visible to you, the legal grounds for the blockade are treaty violations and the issue of tribal sovereignty. If you were to give an interview, your vantage would potentially decenter the claim of the First Nations and Native American people whose campaign you were trying to support.

Entering into a movement or community as a beginner may be challenging. You may have years—or even decades—of experience with political organizing and direct action. You may be a trainer who people hire to come into organizations and share your skills. But if you have not been asked to do so in the setting you have stepped into, then don't. Your way of organizing or style of leadership may not fit there. No one asked you to enter as an expert.

Enter as a warrior, a soldier, a comrade, a healer, a servant to the greater struggle. Do not assume that just because you don't recognize the strategies at play, that there are no strategies. Observe. Respectfully ask questions when you don't understand. Watch. Listen. Learn.

> JOURNAL: Have you ever unconsciously taken over a conversation or interaction? Have you consciously done so? How would you enter into that interaction now?
>
> ACTION: Attend a meeting or event that you did not participate in planning. Observe. Respectfully open yourself to conversation. Respectfully ask questions. Respectfully support the work already being done.

Cocreation, not Coalition

White Feminism is a thing, and if you haven't heard about it, that probably means you need to. It might mean that the feminism that you think of as plain old feminism is actually White Feminism, which is non-intersectional. In White Feminism, the issues, angles, and perspectives of white women are the central focal point.

One of the major failings of White Feminism is that the white feminist movement asks for solidarity from our multiracial feminist and Black womanist sisters, but offers none in return. White Feminism treats white concerns as normative or centrist and the concerns of Women of Color as fringe or marginal.

For instance, White feminism treats the topic of *choice* as if there were only one valid arena to operate that choice within. White Feminism hasn't taken to heart that reproductive justice is a larger topic than access to birth control and the right to abortion. The white feminist movement hasn't joined with our Native American and Black sisters in calling for recognition of the history and ongoing instances of forced sterilization, the taking of infants and children out of their families and cultures, the right to spiritually aligned means for bodily autonomy. White Feminism hasn't looked at this issue from the vantage that makes it clear that prison reform and even the consideration of abolition of the prison industrial complex are reproductive justice issues. It has not acknowledged that profiling and enforcement are issues that tie directly into reproductive justice.

Even though personal freedom—including the freedom to dress as you choose—is considered a central element of the message of the mainstream feminist movement, white feminism hasn't fought at the side of our Muslim sisters against laws that remove their agency by outlawing the wearing of items of religious dress. And even more damning than inaction, you can easily find white feminists who agree with the so-called burqa ban.

Members of the Ukrainian feminist shock group Femen are known for topless protesting. A favored focus of Femen protests is "liberating" women from the coverings that many Muslim women wear; not just the full length burqa but also the headscarf called hijab. Femen members believe they have the right to be topless in public, but do not support the right of Muslim women to wear a scarf over their heads. Is it as ironic as it is offensive, or as offensive as it is ironic? (You decide!)

The idea of liberating women from choice is as ironic as it is offensive.

White feminism still speaks of the wage gap as being 74 cents (give or take) on the male dollar without realizing that this number is *white women* making an average of 74 cents on the *white male* dollar. The wage gap exists as an intersecting grid with more disparity the further to the edges you get.

White feminism holds whiteness at the center. It has moved on to wage-parity while women and girls in the majority world are still struggling to get a basic education and access to health care. White feminism argues about whether it's feminist to wear makeup while Muslim sisters are being told by minority world governments that they cannot wear religious dress and by other majority world governments that they must.

At the same time, the white feminist movement thinks we can tell women of other cultures how to be feminists. White feminism holds that there is one way to be a feminist, and that if you don't believe in the banner issues of mainstream feminism, you are not a feminist. In its restrictive scope, white feminism operates as part of the system of white supremacy.

Something to remember when seeking engagement is that *your* issue is not *the* issue. Your normal is not *the* normal. Your experience is not universal. You are not the only center of the universe; everything is its own center in its own expanding field.

When you invite someone to join your struggle, action, or campaign, you are asking for their support. Instead, what if we built matrices of support that were about relationship, cocreation, and conspiracy? What if we put our efforts on living, dreaming, learning, building a new aeon together? What if our cocreations and collaborations were about finding our way to the sacred ground where we can stand together and know that the differences that make us who we are is the context that lends tensile strength to the process—and ultimate outcome—of our shared liberation?

JOURNAL: In what ways have you proscribed feminism? Are you willing to let go of your definition of feminism in order to make space for addressing our collective struggles?

ACTION: Study a feminism or other movement for equality that you aren't familiar with. Indigenous feminism, post-colonialist feminism, multicultural feminism, Muslim feminism, Black womanism, queer liberation movement. Study with an open heart and mind. Remember that respectful acknowledgment and honoring of our differences makes our movement toward liberation stronger.

*Three Ways to **Grow** Your Loving Community:*

1. *Begin with respect; respect for both differences, and for visions and dreams held in common.*

2. *Tend with love; love is strong, and love is supple. Love is a process, a doing, a being. It is The Work, and the reward.*

3. *Give it time; trust is built through shared experience. Make it through some fun times. Make it through some tough times. Learn how to work and play together.*

Breathing Into It

In seeking to create magickal conspiracies we must stay in our breath, in our hearts, in our beings. Bringing ourselves into harmony with a larger dream will be a long road. It will take many conversations, many arguments, many nights of dancing and lovemaking, many days of planting and harvesting ideas and food and relationship. It will take making art and plans and building families and communities.

In our building we will tie ourselves to the sacred, weaving ourselves through it and into it, hold hands and walk together. We will hold each other in the sacred. We will see the sacred in the faces of our children, our sisters, our daughters, our mothers, our aunties, our grandmothers, our old women. We will see her faces in these faces.

And we will march and dance and hike and walk and move into more and more intricate pathways with each other. With any journey, you can't know the actual terrain ahead of time. Once the journey gets underway, you may find that you don't actually even know the direction you need to go. You may have to toss your map and find your way by relying only upon your senses and help from your sisters who have taken to the road too. Help may come in the form of advice from those who have set up camp, started a village, or found her place in a town or a city.

You may find some evening that you are tired of walking, and you may ask someone if you can sit at her fire for a while. You may share conversation and food. You may dream together under the night sky. And you may become aware in that moment that you have found your way home.

JOURNAL: What maps have you thought were useful, then realized you needed to let go of?

ACTION: Go somewhere you haven't been before. Reach out. Begin seeking new sisterhoods.

11

Decentralizing Your Working Group

Examining Power Structures

As we do the work of deconstructing our relationships with power and solidly claiming sovereignty, we will by necessity begin a process of questioning authority. This deep examination is sure to spill over into relationships, and it will show up if you work in groups. Remember: the more conscious this process is, the less painful it is likely to be.

Power is a thing. It is a thing that some have more of, and others have less of. It is a malleable, shifting, palpable thing. Power is magick. It is held in different ways. Femella holds power differently than Potens, Creatrix, Sapientia, and Antiqua. And in different instances, each of those faces may hold more or less power in relationship to her other faces.

Power can be used for good or ill. Power is not a constant. Power is relative. Power is relational. It is mercurial, but may also be ponderous. It is fluid by nature, but it may appear rigid.

Power is not synonymous with authority, though it is often thought of that way. Power does not exist in one place and not in another; power is everywhere present. In some places it is more concentrated, in others more diffuse.

The examination of power and how it works is a multivalent, complex, ongoing process. For a theory of power to be graceful, it must hold constant across the microcosmic and macrocosmic levels. Our ideas of divinity, ourselves, and relationships with deity, our spiritual circles, associates, bosses, students, parents, children, forebears, descendants, beloveds, and our enemies all hold together on some level.

The more consciousness we generate regarding the shifting tapestry of connections between our concepts of power in the personal sphere, the political, and the spiritual, the more integrated we become. Knowing that linearity doesn't tell the whole story, it becomes clear that we cannot separate the ends and the means; the means is the ends is the means is the ends. The process *is* the product. What we are doing is what we become.

Power is not a constant, but our relationship with it can (perhaps must) have more or less consistent parameters. Regardless of how much power we might be holding in a moment—relative to the power others might hold in that moment or to the power we might have held in another moment—or where the power in an interaction may be weighted, we may create and adhere to negotiated structures, guidelines, agreements about how we choose to interact with power, hold power, and share power.

If you participate in a magickal working group, working with this book is an excellent opportunity to go to the root of your personal and collective power ideologies and agreements, examine them, discuss them, and—where desired—reshape them to fit your shared visions and experiences.

When we look at power in a group context, it is essential to also bring authority into the picture. What gives a person power? Authority? Are they the same thing in some cases, or are they unrelated? Is power assumed, and authority conferred? Or is authority also sometimes assumed?

Many of us have never had an open discussion designed to address how we share power with others. If you are part of an existing group, perhaps when you joined it already had a power structure in place. Or maybe the group was informal, and certain people gravitated toward positions of power and authority, and others allowed them to.

Perhaps the structure of the organization feels static, or perhaps the opposite is true; perhaps the group is losing cohesion because there isn't enough structure.

Different practitioners and groups have different ideas about how power and authority can or should be shared. Some groups have static structures where a single high priestess and/or high priest may lead every ritual. Others have offices such as high priestess but everyone in the group may take turns leading rituals. Other groups still have little to no hierarchical structure or a hierarchical structure that shifts according to need.

> *The Reclaiming Tradition, founded by **Starhawk**, is a contemporary Witchcraft tradition with roots in anarchism, ecofeminism, and Anderson Feri tradition. Reclaiming exists as a decentralized organization. There are regional groups that operate as collectives. Most decision making is done by consensus within groups. There is no central authority that governs all the regional Reclaiming collectives.*

It is important that these—and all—power agreements are negotiated. And in working with the aspects of Femella, Potens, Creatrix, Sapientia, and Antiqua you will find different ways that power plays and lands and molds and dances and shifts and stabilizes and shifts again. You will interact with and see in her and hold in yourself the power of insistence and the power of direction and the power of making and the power of knowledge and the power of duration. You will experience the ways in which power is informed by necessity and the ways in which power becomes expression.

As you do the work of decolonizing your magick, crafting your traditions, creating relationships and dreaming into the new aeon, you will have ample opportunity for reexamination and learning through application.

In addressing issues of agency, sovereignty, feminism, and intersectionality, unexamined assumptions and structures of hierarchy are sure to bubble to the surface. We must question our own inherent biases and our collective defaults. We must examine race, gender, age and the ways in which they intersect.

This is part of the work of decolonizing our minds, bodies, and spirits; we get to— and must—decide which forms of organizational structure work for us and which don't.

Resilient, Evolving, Responsive Structures of Power

For a structure to be resilient, it must be able to withstand disturbance and still function. For a group process to be resilient, it must be able to take a blow and keep thriving. It must be able to lose members—even long-time or founding members—and continue with its work.

In order to continue actively evolving, a system must not get stuck. For a structure to evolve it must adapt to new parameters, let go of parts that are no longer working, allow itself to be shaped by past experience and by current need.

In order to be responsive, a group must be able to absorb new members and adapt to new input. It must be able to sense, listen, and take appropriate action at the right time. Static hierarchies are often poor at evolution and responsiveness. And while decentralized group structures in theory would be resilient, in actuality they are often very vulnerable to destabilization by outside forces and ideas.

There is a middle ground where both hierarchy and decentralization may offer strengths to a group model or process. Collectivism, some forms of anarchism, and cellular organization all employ structure while taking the needs of the whole above the needs of the individual or even the group.

In working with her five faces, we can see different ways that structures of power and authority can be crafted into containers for agreement and relationship. Your group may gravitate to the teachings of Potens, Sapientia, or another face. Your group may have a structure informed by Creatrix and a vision informed by Antiqua or Femella. Or your group may find itself flowing between her different expressions and emanations.

In the end, it is not so much an issue of what model is being used as it is an issue of how that model is being used. There are likely elements from each existing model that can be drawn upon in finding our way to balanced, flexible models that will shift, change, release, and accommodate as needed.

Flexibility is key, as is a central organizing principle. Once we have those dancing at a point of responsive balance, we may flow between different structures and agreements based in our moment-to-moment requirements and desires.

> JOURNAL: What experience do you have with hierarchies? With decentralized structures?
>
> ACTION: Observe how situations around you organize themselves. Does your social group lend itself to hierarchies? Are they static? Or are they fluid? Is your social environment collectivist?

Creating Group Agreements

A collectively agreed upon set of parameters may take some time to create, but if your group is committed to working together, whether working magick or doing work in the world, it will be time well spent. Having thoroughly thought out and constructed agreements will help your circle, family, community, or organization find or build its foundation, and it will make it possible for your group to decide its collective goals and to act in accordance with them.

Doing the work of this is also the larger Work. To create these agreements in a mindful way, we must be continuously doing the work of examination, decolonization, deconstruction, reflection, coming present in our desires—both personal and collective—and reweaving, renewing, rerooting, and creating.

In getting to the heart of the matter, the first thing to discuss will be power itself. Do you, as a group, have an agreement (or agreements) about power? Does that agreement hold consistent with a shared mythology? Is it a political concept? Both? Or are there other elements that stabilize your common agreement?

Who holds the power? How is it held? How are decisions made? Who is empowered to make decisions? How are decisions carried out? What is the purpose of your work together?

If you work through these and whatever other questions come up in the process of the inquiry as a group until you arrive at a core agreement, it may become the beginning of a shared vision statement and a set of guidelines that will allow your group to move into better accord.

It will be helpful to build in agreements about how you intend to handle conflict, how to transfer power and authority as needed, how to create openings for new members, how to accommodate new visions, and how to integrate and accommodate shifts in power distribution.

If you choose to craft agreements together, attempt to build in responsive elements. You may want to include a commitment to review your group agreements on a regular basis. At first it may be monthly, or quarterly, and then perhaps move to biannually or even annually over time.

> *JOURNAL: What are some of the things that you see as being central to the purpose of your group, or to your purpose in the group?*
>
> *ACTION: Research the vision statements of a group you admire.*

Group Ritual Workings

Even if you're not used to conducting your rituals this way, your group may choose to take this as an opportunity to experiment with collaborative group process and ritual development. This means different people may take on different duties or charges for tending your magickal container. These roles or duties may be casting the circle, calling elements, calling a face or the faces of the goddess, and/or any of the other parts of ceremony you choose to draw in. These duties and roles may even land with a different group member each time you circle together.

It may also mean sharing the work and play of creating your physical ritual space and the ritual itself, from concept to manifestation; building altars, bringing offerings, sharing hosting at different homes or taking the crew to favorite out-of-doors spaces to perform rituals, crafting the ritual and performing it.

In group workings, I suggest that each person who feels drawn to take a turn at performing or leading different parts of the ritual have a chance to do so. This creates a more egalitarian, collaborative group and allows each person the opportunity to come into their own power and skill as a ritualist. Being able to perform any and all the steps to creating a strong ritual will make each practitioner a stronger priestess.

In creating ritual together you will also strengthen group cohesion, and have an opportunity to collectively step into application of agreements about power and authority.

If you work with calling in the goddesses, I also suggest that different members try playing with the different energies of her five faces. It's easy to get stuck thinking of someone as holding this or that aspect of her, but at a deeper level we all hold all the aspects. Try working with them and allowing them to work in and through each of you.

> JOURNAL: What pitfalls might your group face in working magick in this more collective way? And what aspects of ritual working are you most excited about trying out?
>
> ACTION: Cocreate a ritual with your magickal working group.

Names Have Power

In revisioning our relationship with power and authority in group practice, it is important to recognize—and change as needed—the places where our shared language anchors us to ideologies we no longer hold.

As a step toward deconstructing magickal and ritual power and authority, I offer a new term: *facilitating priestess.*

The somewhat common term *high priestess* (HP for short), holds a hierarchical implication and is often a static position in a group. For use in an egalitarian, more hierarchically flexible group model, I suggest using the term *facilitating priestess*, or FP.

The FP has the biggest job in any ritual; she makes sure the ritual proceeds apace, makes sure the creation and dissolution of ritual space is done cleanly, and prompts the other participants to take their turns as needed. The FP facilitates the ritual's flow. Like the high priestess would be in many cases, the FP is a director, orchestrator, and energy holder all at once.

In group work the role of FP may be a floating responsibility. In a group that's working for egalitarian structure, taking turns holding the FP energy helps to keep things less static on both the mundane and magickal levels.

JOURNAL: What are some other terms that you use in your magickal work that have subtle, or not so subtle, connotations of hierarchy?

ACTION: Examine hierarchal assumptions in the world around you. Do you call a doctor by her first name? Would you if the doctor were a man? What about teachers? Is your hierarchical thinking prone to gender-based bias? Race-based bias?

12

Building Divine Relationships

Another Magickal Conspiracy

Some will consider the words in this section heresy. I am sure to get parts of it wrong; there are places where you and I will probably disagree. I'm still working to figure it all out, and we as a subculture are doing the same.

While I could perhaps leave this part out or gloss over it, instead I choose to dive in. I believe that as individuals and groups who are seeking greater consciousness, it is incumbent upon us to feel and think our way into—and eventually perhaps through—the sticky territories of belief, spirituality, worship, and religion. So here, as before, my invitation: let's create this together.

What if we came to our relationships with our gods the same way we come to our relationships with our people? What if it was like entering into communion with our spiritual communities, being responsible to our elders and the children of our communities, or like making commitments to our lovers? What if our relationships with our gods were like that?

As radicals and revolutionaries and feminists and activists and anarchists and punk rockers and Witches, it is not a requirement that we check our commitments to non-hierarchical relationships at the figurative temple door. We can—and many of us do—enter into our relationships with our gods as co-conspirators.

In this new dream we are dreaming, I invite you to enter into a divine conspiracy with the gods with whom you are engaged. A new format for relational worship is possible: it is one where we are in service to as much as we are being served, but more than that it is one where we are breathing together.

We are a young spiritual and religious movement, only just now coming into a larger, longer-visioned awareness as a group. We are experiencing the strengths and struggles of intergenerational community. We are looking at how to accommodate our elders, and how to empower our young leaders. We now have perhaps five generations, from Antiqua down to Femella, sometimes all present in one circle.

The process in some manner reflects the process of individuation within family structures. There are the areas of struggle in the vortex of generational values shifts. There are the rigid structures of duration, and the sometimes impatient rush of the new ideas. There are the rifts between motivations based in tradition and innovation.

This is an interesting time for our movement. As I write there is a reformation twisting itself into shape in the contemporary Pagan movement. The umbrella of "Pagan" is becoming too imprecise for some, so the movement is organizing itself out into smaller, more defined subgroups.

There are polytheists, monotheist Pagans, duotheists, atheist Pagans, pantheists, dharma Pagans, Witches, and goddess worshippers, to name a few. Those groups have subgroups within them as well; a polytheist may be a druid, heathen, or Hindu. A polytheist may or may not consider herself a Pagan. A pantheist may consider herself a polytheist or not. An atheist Pagan worships nature and may even have a ritual practice, but does not believe in the gods (nor the Goddess). A monotheist Pagan believes in one god, of which the gods—plural—may emerge as aspects or manifestations.

There are old words for some of these designations too: henotheism—the worship of one god while believing that other gods also exist; pantheism—the belief that everything is god; panentheism—the belief that everything exists within god. Polythesim may exist in any of these frameworks. There is hard polytheism and soft polytheism. There are reconstructionists who are modeling contemporary worship on what can be found of historical records of ancient traditions. And there are deconstructionists who are breaking down concepts, structures, and contexts and finding new inspirations in the space left open.

We all come to the divine in different ways and with different motivations. Some of us worship alone, and some of us come to spirituality and religion for the connection they offer. Some of us are ritualists, and some of us worship organically. Some of us work magick, and some of us do not. Some of us found or operate within groups, circles, covens, kindreds, or communities; others work solely with our gods.

One may believe in the gods as living beings, or one may believe in the energies as archetypes existing in human consciousness. If the gods are living, and if they exist as part of consensus reality, they are capable of—and most likely prone to—growth and evolution.

If everything works in the same way at its core—plants and people and cells and mountains and minerals and stars—then the gods can't help but evolve. Their evolution is ours, and our evolution is theirs. There is no single right way to be Witch, or a goddess worshipper, or a feminist, or a Pagan.

In the framework of the fivefold goddess, the invitation is to cocreate and co-conspire with nature, the forces, and the goddesses themselves; whether we believe in them as beings with their own agency or as manifestations of our own psyches ultimately doesn't matter. In whatever way the goddesses help to liberate you and your relationship with the feminal divine, that is the way to enter into the process. It is the means and the ends.

In forging your relationships with the faces of the fivefold goddess, I invite you to find the space to come together with her in a way that inspires your soul, enriches your dreaming, and delivers us into the new aeon. We are creating a new time; one where we are conscious of the shifting centers of need and desire, where we are checking in with our agreements and being accountable to our selves and our communities. In our coming to the new present in the relational we are liberating the gods, and in them, liberating ourselves.

> *JOURNAL: How do you experience, envision, or conceptualize the gods? And your relationship with them?*
>
> *ACTION: Create or participate in an opportunity to interact with your gods and your community in a relational way.*

Seeking Her Children

In your work here and on your magickal path, you may find yourself encountering a specific goddess. You may fall in love with her. You may find yourself absolutely in her thrall. As with any relationship, if you want it to be long lasting it will be advantageous to meet her people. Yes, she has people. And they exist in a natural reciprocity with her. If she is calling you, you may find that you have a responsibility to her. And if you have a responsibility to a god, you have a responsibility to her people.

We spoke briefly about appropriation in the beginning of this book. Here's some more: not everyone wants to be in a "melting pot." There is a very clear definition we can rely on when wondering if we are appropriating a thing or idea like a goddess, a magickal tool or tradition, or a way of worshipping. Appropriation is about taking. Honoring is about community. Becoming a dedicant or a priest to a goddess is a responsibility and a privilege.

Sometimes her will is a force that is undeniable. If you have given yourself time for self-examination and for communication with the goddess who is calling you and found that your heart is steadfast, it is time to undertake the initiations she offers. Seek out her children; they are your siblings now. Remember to mind your manners, be respectful, and offer your service. You are honoring her by honoring them. And when the time is right and you believe you understand enough about her people to know how to ask them respectfully for guidance, ask them about her. Know that even if you do everything as consciously as you can, her children may reject you. They may not welcome your presence, your questions, or your offerings. And they may not want to share their goddess or their spiritual technologies with you.

If this happens, remember that they owe you nothing.

It's more likely that if you are engaged and enter into community and reciprocity with humility and patience, they may teach you her songs.

If you want to study more deeply into her magicks, her mysteries, and her technologies, find a teacher among her people. Do your research; find out what is customary in compensation and exchange. And then come to the teacher and offer yourself as a student and seeker.

Sometimes a goddess will come to you, and in seeking her people you will find that they are all dead or assimilated. But you must really seek before you know if this is true or not; the dominant paradigm makes a habit out of writing about Indigenous peoples as if they are all dead and gone. It will sometimes appear on paper that her people no longer exist, when in reality they may be alive and actively working to reclaim their traditions.

In the rare case that her people are gone, this goddess perhaps needs your worship in order to stay alive because what is remembered lives. If her people have all been taken or slaughtered or disappeared or scattered, if they have lost her and haven't yet been reunited with her, perhaps you are part of her preservation in the same way she is perhaps part of yours. If her people are gone, it is still important to seek out her old stories. You must look for the threads woven into whatever cultural elements still exist. Seek the folk tales, the songs, and the anthropological studies.

It is also important that you listen to her as she shares her truths with you. Some of these truths will have been lost. Some of them exist in the weave of a basket or the curve of a skin on a ritual drum but are no longer contained or carried in writing or even in spoken language.

Sit with her in the places where she is strongest. Visit the sites she tells you about in dreams and visions. Research the stories she tells you as you hold her in sacred space. If you are patient and engaged and you enter in with humility, perhaps she will teach you her songs.

In showing up with and for her, stay open to her people. Her people of lineage, of spirit, of blood, of remembrance; they need her. And in the time outside of time you are bound to them through her.

> JOURNAL: What stories have you been told by your gods? Did you research them? Were you able to find references to the stories you received in literature or other places?
>
> ACTION: Taking on a relationship with a god is potentially like a marriage; you are gaining a whole new family. Invite members of your new family to dinner, or on a hike, or on some adventure. Offer gifts commensurate in value to that which you are asking for.

Grounding It

In the grounded realm, we ask "how" questions like "How do I create a relationship with a being who does not have a human body—most of the time, at least?"

This conscious building of relationship is something we can use with humans too. The rules are pretty easy:

- Make time for your relationship. Set aside time to sit with your goddess. Create the time for daily check-ins. Take walks with her. Sit in contemplation, supplication, or prayer.

- Make space for the relationships: create altars for her, plant flowers, vegetables, or trees for her; find an open space with flowing water, a stand of strong trees, or a hill of moss-covered rocks, or a secret alleyway, and—if it is in alignment with the desires of the space— invite her to make a home there.

- Perform rituals for and with her. Do it monthly, weekly, or daily. Do it religiously. Light candles to her, make offerings, sit with her.

- Pay attention. Listen for her words in the world around you.

- Dedicate a piece of jewelry or other wearable item to her, and wear it when you want to feel close to her.

While working this book you may choose to give each goddess—Femella, Potens, Creatrix, Sapientia, and Antiqua—a week or a month.

As you begin feeling your way toward creating a deeper relationship with her, you may wish to invoke her into you and learn her ways through direct transmission. You can give her your body. You can take her in. You can merge, two becoming one.

> *JOURNAL: How do you build relationship in your life? How can you map that across and use the same techniques to build your relationship with your goddess?*
>
> *ACTION: What will you do today to foster your relationship with the goddess?*

Spirit Possession

Allowing a god or spirit into your body is a sacred opportunity. You may allow yourself to be possessed body and soul, and you will learn so much. As you are able to contain the experience in a negotiated way, you may even be able to speak from and for her. Allowing a spirit or goddess to take possession of your body is also an excellent way to deepen your relationship with her, and it may help you become a better magick practitioner.

Building a relationship with a deity before you agree to host them in your body is a very good idea. In the previous sections I offered some ideas on how to build that relationship. You may be able to hold her in a ritual container.

In a little bit, I will offer some more ideas on how to create space and protocols for this process. First, here's some basic information on spirit possession in case you are not yet familiar with the practice.

What it is: An altered state where one calls in (invokes) a deity, elemental force, or another being and allows them to temporarily possess, borrow, inhabit, or "ride," the body. Some groups or traditions call this process aspecting, some call it being ridden, some call it channeling, others call it being taken by or caught by or filled with spirit.

What it may be: In some cases, a person who is possessed may experience complete possession where the invoked being is in complete control of the person's faculties. In other cases the being may be partially in control, but the possessed person may also be collaboratively in control with the invoked being.

What it is not: Spirit possession is not play-acting, performing, or pretending.

The group format for the final ritual in this book includes spirit possession: the practice of allowing a goddess or other being or entity to come into your body and use it as their own for the duration of the Working.

JOURNAL: Have you heard about spirit possession before? Do you have opinions on the practice?

ACTION: Research magickal traditions of possession in different cultures.

Preparing for Possession

The steps that follow should make your experience of possession relatively safe and somewhat predictable. This does not mean that your experience will be easy or that it won't shake you up. It may shake you up, and it may be emotionally arduous, regardless of whatever protective measures you have in place. It may also be heartening, exhilarating, and illuminating. It will surely be rewarding. There are some amazing side-benefits to holding a goddess or other being. You will likely find that you learn whole worlds of new information without any effort. She will call up in you awarenesses and levels of consciousness that live in her, and this will be yours to keep even after she leaves.

Allowing the gods or other spirits use of our bodies is a common practice in many spiritual traditions with deep roots. Practices are diverse, yet at the core perhaps more similar than dissimilar.

Depending on your tradition or training, your experiences with spirit possession may be varied. In the process offered here, I invite you to think of it as possession but with agreements. Spirit possession can be an intense experience, and having agreements in place will make it a safer one.

Sometimes, though not often, possession will happen without prior consent or even anticipation. For example, in cases where a goddess really needs a body or when a person is naturally inclined toward being possessed, the possession may occur without preamble or prior negotiation. The occurrence is rare but has been known to happen. The best protection in this case (and many others, of course) is education.

More often than not the process of spirit possession requires willingness and fore-knowledge on part of the one who allows the spirit of the goddess or other being to assume her body. For many it requires a bit of training.

Given the option, it is best to consider and craft agreements with the being or goddess before allowing spirit possession. It's a very good idea for you to put parameters on the ways in which the being may use your body—after all, this loaning out of your body is a real thing.

The being who is borrowing your flesh doesn't have the same considerations you do. Her dietary desires may be very different from your needs. Her physical capabilities may differ greatly from yours. Her sexual choices may lead into areas that are not in alignment with promises you have made to yourself or to others.

Being possessed can have real consequences that follow you after the session of possession is complete. A spirit or goddess doesn't have the same concerns you have for your physical being. Out of sheer exuberance or joy or grief or anger, a being may use your body in ways you would not. But in the space of possession, your body is *theirs*. Sometimes you will not register the pain of the being's actions (which they took in *your* body) until after your body is out of their possession.

All this considered, it would be wise to craft an agreement regarding what kind of treatment your body can participate in, and what condition you need it to be in when you step back into it. In the process of crafting your contract, you will probably want to come up with agreements about your dietary needs, any physical activities your body is not capable of, and sexual boundaries and agreements you need to adhere to.

Another thing to take into account is that these beings exist outside of bodies, and some of them really, really enjoy the opportunities to be in the flesh. It's not all hard work or possible damage; you will feel their joy. You are also likely to feel their sadness as they leave.

Some Protocols to Start Out With:

- *Have a trusted friend be with you while you attempt possession until you feel confident and comfortable.*

- *Negotiate with the being you're working with that they take possession of a scarf, piece of jewelry, or clothing so you can literally put her on and take her off. (Make sure the spirit is on board with this idea so she doesn't feel toyed with. Ask for her consent, then receive her answer.)*

- *Make sure you have grounding items (salt crystals, water, food) near you so you can come out of possession quickly if you feel like you need to.*

- *Make time agreements with the being. Agree to allow possession for ten minutes, five, fifteen, or seven, for example. This may become more flexible over time.*

JOURNAL: What is the most appealing part of magickal possession? And what are the things you would most want to put into a contract?

ACTION: If you feel open to it, connect with a goddess you're building a relationship with—or whom you already have a relationship with—and ask her if she would like to enter into a possession agreement with you.

Divine Contracts

A contract is a formal agreement. It is not an altogether uncommon thing to create a contract if you are going to be in spiritual service; however, there are not many resources offering templates of training within the Pagan and goddess spirituality communities. Perhaps it's because we're a more touchy-feely kind of folk. Whatever the case, learning to negotiate is a great skill to have.

There are two categories of contract we will be addressing. The first is a spirit possession contract. This contract is designed to help you create safe boundary agreements for your work in cases of trance possession. The second is a contract of dedication to a goddess, and is on page 229.

Template Contract for Spirit Possession

- I willingly offer my body into your possession for the duration of this ritual.

- The possession will begin when I put on [item of choice—necklace, crown, cloak, etc.] and will end when it is removed.

- My limits are [your limits here—food choices, sex choices, activities, etc.]. I ask that you honor these.

- I am grateful for your presence, and recognize the value of this experience for me. I am honored to be your vessel.

Your spirit possession contracts will likely change over time as you become more familiar with the process of willing spirit possession, have experiences with hosting more beings, and begin to find your strengths and edges shifting with your process. Once you become clear about your capacities and are more comfortable in your relationships, you may find that your contracts can loosen up or that there are elements you overlooked entirely that you want to pull into the agreement.

Steps to Consensual Spirit Possession

- Build relationship with deity or Being
  - This may happen over a period of seconds, or years.

- Create agreement/contract
  - A very good idea, but not always pragmatic nor desired.

- Invoke the deity or Being into you
  - Alternatively, have the facilitating priestess invoke into you. Or perhaps just allow! In some cases it just comes over you.

- Once done, devoke or release
  - You can also have someone help you devoke. You will want to remove any clothing that belongs to the Being, or put down items that are theirs. (Tips on how to make this part easier are on the previous page.)

- Ground
  - Place salt on your tongue and let it dissolve. Drink water. Eat food. Sit down. Relax. Feel the earth and put your roots down into it.

Now you know the how of it. The *why* is yours alone. Some will never in their whole lives choose to allow a spirit or goddess possession of their bodies—even temporary, negotiated, consensual possession. But for those journeyers, devotees, priestesses, and ritualists who desire to enter deeply into the mystery, spirit possession is an experience of great value.

> *JOURNAL: Have you experienced spirit possession?*
>
> *ACTION: If you feel like you might want to learn how to allow spirit possession, think about what steps here seem the most useful to you.*

~ *13* ~

Decolonizing Our Magicks

Deepening Magickal Practice

Throughout this book we have explored possible elemental, seasonal, and other associations for the five faces of the goddess. Throughout, you have also been reminded how important it is to sink into your own relationship with the faces of the feminal divine and with the forces of nature. As you come to the goddesses in this process, you come into a stronger relationship with your own deepest self.

As you begin trusting your internal process, you will find a new sense of alignment between your magick and your waking life, between your inner and outer worlds, between your values and your practices. As your intuition grows stronger, you will find it more automatic to act in accordance with your internal impulse. And as you begin acting in accordance with your intuition, your intuition will continue to grow stronger.

In this process of organic magick, you have already begun to let go of book learning and memorized correspondence charts, instead feeling your way into a deep reverie and honoring of the relational aspects of the deeper knowing. In your experience of organic magick you are finding the current of strength that pulses within and outside of you. And going deeper, you find that there is no inside and outside: you are the holon within the holon. You are the feminal divine, birthing herself into consciousness.

You are Femella playing with gentle beasts in a shaded glen. You are Potens standing strong on the crest of a hill with the moon above her. You are Creatrix dancing a spiral pattern in a rainstorm. You are Sapientia tending the wild herbs. You are Antiqua sitting on a bluff overlooking the sea.

And you are perhaps something else beyond all that, a thing primal, wordless, resting just beyond the edge of your own ability to perceive. You are that, too. Magick exists in the space beyond words, symbols, concepts. It is the raw and vibrant life force dancing in you, through you, and around you.

> JOURNAL: Can you find your inner knowing now?
>
> ACTION: Sit in a space where you feel safe and comfortable. Now sink more deeply into your awareness. What do you notice? What do you feel connected to? Repelled from? What do you find attractive, and how so? Just notice these things. Notice other things. All of this information appears to you like it appears to no one else.

Coming from the Place Where You Stand

Organic magick is also about becoming from the land where you are. It is about being in relationship with the place where you live, pray, make magick, worship, do ceremony. It is about coming into the awareness that you owe the land you stand on something; you owe it reciprocity.

My friend Corine Pearce is a wisdom holder for her lineage. They are called Pomo by the colonizers, but one of the names her people call themselves is *C'ha ma'aa*, which means "blessed person of the earth where I am."

Corine was at a primitive skills gathering in the region she's from when someone asked her what the descendants of settlers could do to make peace with her people. Corine responded, "Make peace with the land you are standing on."

Corine is not the spokesperson for all Native American people. (Obviously there is no such thing: Native American culture is not monolithic.) But she does speak for or give voice to the land I am living in concert with. When she told me this story, it landed profoundly; I grew up on land that was stolen from Corine's direct antecedents. While my family are not the ones who perpetrated the massacre that put the land into white hands, we and our contemporaries unwittingly continued the injury. Our land association unearthed pieces of Corine's family's history, and to this day it holds those pieces —obsidian blades and arrowheads, grinding stones, pestles—hostage, as if they are in some ways "ours" because we "own" this stolen land.

After a lifetime of awareness that I was living on stolen land that had been bathed in the blood of the land's first people, I was given a key to how to make peace with the rift in my own heart. This land is Corine's family. The plants and animals and stones are her family. This land is living. This land as it exists today is a Being with whom I must work to make peace.

At a festival, at night, under the stars, on the land that is the origin-place of Corine's cousins, Corine and my mother and I were sitting and talking about the impact of the festival on the land. We were talking about how the trees were responding to the noise levels and the lack of regard and connection from the festival goers. Corine had, that day, taught a wild-tending workshop to offer people a chance to create relationship with the place they were standing.

As we sat under the ancient oaks, Corine said, "In our culture we don't own land, but we do own trees and plants. We own them in the way you own your mother."

"Yes," I thought. "*My* mother. Not *a* mother. We own our parents like they own us. We own them because we are bound. We own them because we owe them our lives." And Corine's words again brought me to a deeper alignment with and awareness of relationship with place.

I am learning that becoming from the place where you are standing means coming into relationship with the dirt, plant, animal, rock, and water beings. It means getting to know them, learning how to tend to them, giving at least as much as you take. It means tending the wild and learning from it before you take from it. It means coming to awareness of yourself as dependent upon the land where you are. And that means you owe it your life.

This is not an invitation to recolonize, invade, claim, or reclaim something that is not yours. It is an invitation to come into relationship with the land where you are. It means also coming into relationship with the people of that land. It means seeking out the first people of that place and offering your reciprocity to them as well. It means coming into relationship with those who know this land better than you do, the people who consider themselves to be the children of this place. It means being willing to listen and learn about the ways the land needs to be treated, what it wants from you, and how to care for it. It means listening to the land itself to teach you these things.

It means introducing yourself to the gods and spirits of this land. It means waiting until you understand them and feel understood by them before negotiating the conscious bringing in your own gods. It means making offerings, learning their stories and songs, coming to know them; their dreams and desires and old stories.

It means building reciprocity and standing in humility; stillness at times, action at others. It means creating relationship from and for your own soul. It means not claiming the land, spirits, or people as your own, but allowing them—over time, through conversation and community building and deep listening and offers of invitation and acceptance of offers of hospitality—to claim you.

Once the land and the spirits and the people of the land have claimed you, then you can truly come from where you are.

In finding your way to the core of these teachings, you will find your way to organic magick, a magick that grows from the very ground of being and takes form within you and around you.

> JOURNAL: What is your relationship with the place where you are?
>
> ACTION: Learn something about how the place where you are needs your support—are there environmental degradations going on? Community gathering places threatened by gentrification? Are there wild plants that need to be given care? The answer to at least one of these questions is for sure yes. Find something that needs doing, find out how to do it respectfully, and do it.

Your Voice is a Magickal Tool

As the old ways—the ways of Witches and women—were passed down from generation to generation, from woman to woman, magickal tools as we know them today were in most cases not part of the transfer.

For many of us, herb lore, family recipes, faerie and folk stories, old wives tales, and superstitions were the container that allowed magicks to be handed down through the ages. In times where witchery by necessity went underground, tools were different. The tools passed down were the tools of women; mortar and pestle, mixing bowl, wooden spoons, a broom. As reminders of family lineage; a recitation of names, portraits, pictures, photographs. A locket. A ring. A cradle.

In times of war, bow and arrows, guns, blades, and bludgeons have been tools of women's power. War chants, prayers to the spirits of place. Gospel, whips turned back on the slave owners who held them, prayers to the saints. Secret maps told as whispers in passing and stitched into quilts.

Our work-worn hands, our strong legs, our tree-trunk backs, our throats and mouths speaking spells, singing incantations, and screaming out wardings; our bodies and our stories and our ceaseless working, loving, fighting for remembrance of our past and hope for our future, the safety of our loved ones, the knowledge of our ways; all these have been the true magickal tools of our survival.

We can easily become dissociated from the ways of magick held in our flesh and bones. My invitation is to *remember*. Remember the stories your cells hold for you. Remember the ways in which your body and the bodies of those who walked this path before you, who bore you, held—and hold—the mysteries. Revive the old ways through the living ark of your body. Feel the power beckoned by your blood and bones, by the echoes of the voices of the old ones in your being.

*In **American slavery**, marriage between slaves was not allowed by most slavers. In place of a church wedding, jumping the broom became a common ceremony throughout slave communities. It was recognized as a binding marriage ceremony.*

*Jumping the broom was a tradition carried over from the West African country of **Ghana** during the period of the **Trans-Atlantic slave trade**. In addition to its obvious basic use, in Ghanaian belief the broom carried spiritual importance; it had the power to sweep away past wrongs and to rid a space of evil spirits. Because of this, it was a potent symbol in starting out a marriage together. All past ills were behind the couple as they entered into their marriage.*

In a movement to reclaim their own story, some Black Americans reintroduced the tradition of jumping the broom as a symbolic part of wedding celebrations in the 1970s. This ritual is a potent and bittersweet reminder of the power of self-determination even under the inhumane conditions of slavery. When used, the broom is decorative and becomes a wedding keepsake.

Some Witches also include jumping the broom as part of a handfasting ceremony. Often a handfasting ceremony will end with the handfasted partners jumping over a besom that is often hand-made and artfully decorated.

This tradition in Paganism and Wicca may be rooted in a borrowed (or appropriated) Romani ceremony, or there may be Welsh roots. It is difficult to say exactly where it originates as an American Pagan ceremony.

Regardless of origin, the symbolic meaning of jumping the broom is similar; it offers a clean, new beginning.

Reclaiming Your Instruments

Enter into the natural world with reverence and you will know that a downed branch picked up off the forest floor is a wand already imbued with incredible amounts of power. A fallen branch easily serves as a besom. A found feather calls spirits of air, a running creek is more powerful in its wildness than a chalice could ever be, and green shoots growing out of charred remains of an old growth redwood hold all the associations of fire; passion, transformation, innocence, sensuality, will, desire, power. The Earth hums with a vibrant and primal magick no pentacle can contain.

These do not need to be placed on an altar in order to become your tools; this place *is* your altar, your sacred space. This natural world, teeming with the powers of life and death. To take the raw material and make it into a symbol would be mistaking the finger that points at the moon for the moon itself. You don't *need* representations when you have the actual forces of nature in front of and around you. When you come present to the elements, even calling them into sacred space (a practice common in many contemporary Pagan and Pantheist traditions) becomes an almost moot point. They are present already; you are the one who has wandered. You are the one coming home.

It's when you're away from the raw, growing, dying, regenerating cycles of earth, water, fire, and air that you may want or need symbols to place upon your altar. A shell, a fossil, a stone, a forest wand, that feather, an acorn or other seed, a blade of grass, a flower, a handful of decomposing evergreen needles; all these can be placed upon your altar or in your magickal circle.

JOURNAL: *What are your views of magickal tools?*

ACTION: *Perform a ritual using no tools. See how it feels.*

If You Must Have Tools

Organic magicky dirt-worshipping aside, some Witches love their magickal tools. I wouldn't want to take that from anyone! If you love your formal tools but want to feel more connected to them, I recommend making a set yourself. Tools you make will be bound to you and are made sacred by the intention you put into them through your work. The process of crafting your tools is a magick in itself.

> *The Society for Creative Anachronism, or SCA, is an international living history organization dedicated to recreating the skills, arts, and crafts of pre-seventeenth-century Europe.*

It may not be a project you want to take on alone, but crafting your own blade is a powerful process. There may be shared workshop space in your community where you can find metalworking tools, support, and camaraderie on your quest. Or there may be a blacksmith in your community who would want to help you out. The Society for Creative Anachronism (SCA) can be a valuable resource in finding a smithy, or your local Heathen kindred may also be able and willing to assist you.

If making tools doesn't sound inspiring, maybe you can find them—or let them find you—in perhaps unusual ways; reclaim them, repurpose them, upcycle them. An heirloom teacup passed down from your grandmother might be the perfect chalice. A hunting knife given to you in your youth or a wooden sword you played with as a child may be the perfect athame.

The teachings of some traditions say that you should never use your magickal tools for "mundane" tasks; that your athame shouldn't ever be used for cutting, and your chalice shouldn't be used for drinking outside of ritual space. However, other traditions offer different teachings, and some deities may require that you use your magickal tools as actual tools—in ritual or outside of it, depending—in order for the tools to be imbued with spirit and meaning.

Don't get stuck in dogma. What does the tool itself want? What about the elements associated with it?

Another thing to consider; maybe what you think of as standard tools are not a good fit for you. What if a pen is your athame? What if your chalice is a shell, or a cauldron? What if your disk is a flower pot?

In revisioning and reclaiming your magickal tools, think about the fivefold goddess's faces. Maybe one or more of her aspects have some requests regarding your (or her) tools. You may find that you want to have a different set of magickal tools for each of her aspects.

Ultimately, remember that your true power lies not in your tools but in your body, spirit, and mind. The most essential tools are intention, will, and the love to power them.

> *JOURNAL: What DIY tools do you find the most inspiring?*
>
> *ACTION: Fashion yourself a temporary or permanent-ish tool using something you have near at hand.*

Creating Consensual and Meaningful Rites of Passage

Rites of passage are by nature built around intensely personal (and potentially tumultuous) times. When the rite is addressing changes in the body—as in the case of menarche, for example—the possible tumult may be sizeable, and because the body is involved, the context of sovereignty and agency are immediately relevant.

In the dominant culture many of the rites of passage we undertake as women are already complicated by the complex relationship our cultures have with aging, the female body, and life stages. So if your intention with creating a rite of passage is to create an opportunity for honoring the person undergoing the transition, it is essential to first get her full and enthusiastic consent.

With the fivefold model, there are no externally verifiable markers that decide for us when it is time to step into a rite of passage. And there is no need to create just one rite of passage between any two points in the spectrum from Femella to Antiqua. And even within each stage one may encounter multiple rites of passage.

Where on the spectrum that rite falls for you and your loved ones is up to you. Remember that there is no need to stick to a linear timeline when it comes to rites of initiation. If you see a reason for it, nothing is stopping you from having a rite dedicated to Sapientia for a child, or Femella for an old woman, or Potens, or Creatrix, or Antiqua at any time. There could be a case made for rites of passage dedicated to Potens every time you begin a new venture, or to Creatrix every time you decide to make something new, or have a child, or dream something into being.

Sometimes rites of passage are small and meaningful, and sometimes they are monumental and highly visible. Sometimes they are spontaneous, and sometimes they are planned out for months or even years. Sometimes they are the beginning of a thing, sometimes the end. Most often they are both.

Some rites of passage are nearly unnoticed yet are essential to creating a process of growth. The gift of a first pair of scissors, for example. A first blade for magick or for craft or for hunting. A first job, a driver's license. The first purchase or gift of safer sex supplies or birth control. A first lover. All of these have built in levels of increased responsibility, hand in hand with increased freedom of experience.

Some rites of passage are recognized across cultures; marriages, graduations, moving out of one's home. Some are conscious and recognized and some are silent. Becoming a widow, losing a child, losing your work due to age or illness.

With a mind toward honoring the changes we face we may choose to make even the silent and hidden rites of passage known, seen, acknowledged. We may choose to plan a rite of passage for ourselves, or we may ask our sisters and brothers and siblings to hold it for us.

In any case, we can create and hold these rites together. We can hold them with and for one another.

When considering creating a rite of passage for or with someone, here are some steps to consider:

- *Ask for consent: ask if they want their transition (example; menarche) to be publically recognized and celebrated in your community. If not, you may ask if a more intimate celebration is wanted. For example, with family members, or friends from school, or just you and her.*

- *Seek collaboration: if consent is given, ask for input on how she would like to celebrate her transition.*

- *Ask what would be the most fun, comfortable, sweet, good-feeling way to celebrate the transition. For example; a ceremony or ritual, or a slumber party, or a spa day, or a picnic in the forest or at the beach.*

Ask who they would like to have present at the celebration or ceremony. For example; her spiritual community, family, friends, teachers, mentors, all of those. (If she instead tells you whom she would like to not have there, listen to that feedback too.)

- *Cocreate the Celebration: empower her by letting her know that she gets bottom line veto power on any suggestion made, and then get cocreative!*

Planning a rite of passage with someone you want to honor—especially a young one in your care—may be a far more memorable and formative part of the experience for her (and for you) than the ritual itself is. This process of cocreation is an opportunity for her to learn new skills, and it's an opportunity for the two (or more) of you to learn about each other in new ways and to increase trust and respect in your relationship.

JOURNAL: What rites of passage have you experienced in your life? Were they honored the way you would have liked them to be?

ACTION: If you had rites of passage that were not honored sufficiently, it's not too late! Ask a sister or two to help you plan a rite of passage that you missed out on before. If, on the other hand, all of your rites of passage have been perfect so far, consider planning a rite of passage for another sister, or other sisters. What rite of passage would you most like to share?

🌀 *14* 🌀

Ritual Elements and Templates

Foundations

In this section I offer templates that you can work from to create your own rituals to the goddess's five faces. The templates are scaled down and may be integrated into a more elaborate ritual format if you like, or they can be performed in the stripped-down form found here.

If you are going to integrate into a more formal format, you will most likely want to work within the system you have already developed or committed to. Or, if you have an intuitive feeling for your ritual practice, go with that. If you want to work with the somewhat standard Northern or Southern Hemispheric associations, do that.

In this as in all else, do what fits best for you and your spiritual community. Before we dive into the ritual templates, we will go over some basic elements to keep in mind with ritual practice.

Time

As you ready yourself to engage in solitary or group ritual, I encourage you to allow enough time on the days or evenings you'll be holding your rituals to really get into your work and create the space to experience her. Read through your journaling from her chapter, look at your drawings, look at your magickal wheel, check in energetically.

Taking a bath offers an opportunity for purifying your body, mind, and spirit. Use mineral salts, massage yourself, relax, clear your mind. Use herbs in your bath water for extra-charged cleansing power and to honor the goddess.

You may even want to begin the process of invoking her starting with the bath. Use salts or oils that she would like. Put flower petals in the water. Light candles.

> *Oil* and **water** don't mix! If you want your oils to mix in with your bath water put some milk in a jar and put the oil into the milk. Shake well, and add to your bath. (Bonus: milk is good for your skin.)

You may wish to prepare a special dinner, incorporating foods she would like.

Afford yourself sufficient time to go deep in your ritual space. And afterward, leave time to transition back out of magickal space while retaining the information with which she has gifted you. (See *Ritual Aftercare* for more on this topic.)

If you are working in a group, make sure all time agreements work for all parties.

Another element of time to consider is consciousness in choosing a day or night on which to perform your ritual. Some Witches like to work with lunar cycles, while others find it more satisfying or pragmatic to work with a certain day of the week. There may be magickal correspondences you are pulling into the equation, like using one of the holy days listed in her chapter to honor her, or taking into consideration an astrological alignment, or a day that is emotionally significant to you. There are also traditions that consider each day of the week to be dedicated to a different god or energy.

For some kinds of magick, tying your ritual to certain times or alignments can be very powerful. However, doing magick when it works for you and for her, or for them, is really the essential thing. How exacting you are on magickal timing, correspondences, and associations is up to you.

Possession and Ritual Aftercare

Sometimes rituals are intense. While this is an awesome thing when it happens, it can also be kind of destabilizing if you're not prepared for it. I highly recommend that you build in time to process, reflect, and relax after your rituals.

In a group, this process may be very different from when you practice on your own. Your group may want to create an agreement to not talk about the working just after you perform it, as you each may need time to process on your own. You can also spend time talking about other things.

Or you may agree that it's perfectly okay and right to talk about your experience of her immediately afterward. Again, there is no single right way to do this stuff.

On the whole, for my personal self-care I find drinking some water, eating some food, and sucking on good, clean salt to be good techniques for grounding after encounters with the Divine.

Going for a walk can help, but sometimes lying down may be what's called for. You may want or need to write things down. Or you may want or need to sing, cry, or talk to a friend. Remember that it's all just energy moving, and it will settle when it's time.

With practice you will find the things that work best for you for ritual aftercare. For the time being, just make sure you aren't rushing yourself in coming out of ritual space.

What to Bring to Your Rituals

This is a basic list of things it would be good to have at hand for your fivefold goddess rituals. In the outline for each of the rituals to the five, you will find an additional list that's specific.

*Before using **incense** in ritual, make sure you (and others) can tolerate scents and smoke in an enclosed space. Incense can be overwhelming. It can alter your senses in a good way, as long as it's not triggering an asthma attack or allergies.*

Items

- Your copy of this book.

- Your journal and artistic pieces that you've created during your work. Your journal may also be needed for writing or making art in the ritual.

- A pen, markers, paints, or whatever you like to use to journal/create art.

- Your ritual outline.

- The invocation from the chapter, or your own if you've written one.

- Incense if you want it, and charcoal for the incense if needed.

- Wine, juice, or other sacramental drink if desired.

- Offerings for the goddess (or goddesses) you are working with. (See ritual outlines for details.)

- Water to drink.

- Tissue or a hanky in case of tears.

- Any other specific items mentioned in ritual outlines.

- Don't forget miscellaneous things that may be needed such as matches or a lighter, a bottle opener, or a corkscrew.

Building Your Ritual

In the appendix at the end of this book I've included detailed directions for conducting a modified and at least somewhat decolonized form of the Lesser Banishing Ritual of the Pentagram (LBRP) that I call A Witch's Banishing Ritual of the Pentagram (WBRP), some information on eclectic circle casting, and a few examples of ways to call the elements. If you don't yet have an established way that you do magick, I recommend that you read that section before diving into ritual design.

In the sections that follow, you will find basic outlines for rituals of invocation, initiation, and dedication to each of her five faces. These ritual outlines may be layered into the design elements from the appendix, or added into your existing ritual structures, or performed as they are written here in their stripped-down elegance.

All the templates are swappable. Simply shift the name of the aspect you are honoring and change the altar to reflect the phase you are invoking. The templates include options for solitary or group practice. You may easily adapt it for either by shifting the template.

Each of the levels of ritual—invocation, initiation, and dedication—are offered in succession. These three different types of ritual offer a course of action by which you may increase the depth of your relationship with each of her faces—or with one in particular if you are so called.

Initiations are an experience of transition; to initiate means to begin. The ritual of initiation may be a powerful experience. It may put your spiritual process on fast forward. And sometimes a ritual of initiation can slide

right into a ritual of dedication. Depending on how deep your connec-
tion to your goddess is, or hers to you, you may end up going very deep
with the ritual of initiation. Remember that whatever agreements you
make with her in ritual space are deep commitments that echo outward.
What happens between the worlds changes the worlds.

A ritual of *invocation* calls her into the circle so that you may honor her, or even have a conversation with her. A ritual of *initiation* lets her know that you are ready to experientially take on the trials and ultimately the learnings that will offer you a true understanding of her ways. Finally, a *dedication* ritual is one where you dedicate yourself to serving her. Dedication to a deity is a deep process and commitment, akin to marriage. It's not to be taken lightly, and you will know if it's the right thing for you.

There is one template for the invocation and initiation rituals, with only the visualization element being different. (The dedication ritual template is different from the first two.) Both visualization scripts are included. The template is also swappable for all the goddesses; just use the name of the aspect you are honoring and change the altar to reflect the phase you are invoking. The templates include options for solitary or group practice. You may easily adapt it for either by shifting the template.

Performing the rituals of invocation and initiation before you do a ritual of dedication will allow you to meet her, interact with her, and learn from her before deciding whether you are ready to bind yourself to her as a faithful co-conspirator. If you progress in the manner outlined here, you will know more of who she is, what she may want from you, and how to offer yourself to her.

All that said, she may demand a dedication ritual from you immediately. If this happens, I highly recommend that you do at least take time to create a starting point for contract negotiation before stepping into that ritual. Directions on how to do this are in the section just before the dedication ritual template.

The templates section culminates in a group working, an opportunity to offer worship and commune with all five of her faces in one ritual.

Rituals of Invocation and Rituals of Initiation

Invocation rituals offer you the opportunity to get to know the goddess with whom you are working. In this simple format you'll have a chance to honor her, and to ask her to teach your something about her. Initiation rituals offer you the opportunity to have the goddess you're working with take you through an initiation into her ways. You will have a chance to honor her, journey to her, receive instructions from her regarding a task, and then pledge to do work in her name.

Template

Preparation

- Make sure you have all of your ritual items with you before you begin.
  - In addition to the list of items you've already read, you will also want to gather specific items for the aspect you are working with during this ritual. This will include an altar cloth of the color you associate with this aspect and any offerings for her. (See the appropriate chapter for offering suggestions).

- Clear ritual space.

- Create altar or altars, including offerings of food and drink.

- Add in formal ritual elements here if desired; or use this basic outline as it appears:

Ritual

1. Light incense if you wish. You may instead asperge the space with water—flower water, herb water, salt water, or fresh water. Or you can clear the space with a tree branch, feathers, or other clearing tool.

2. Bring yourself present in the space. Use your breath, listen to your heartbeat. Feel your body. Embody yourself. Come into your skin, and into the present moment.

3. Light a candle for her.

4. Set out your offerings for her. In addition to food and drink and other items for her altar, you may include artwork you have created during the time you have been working with her. It may include your journal or other memory-collecting projects—which you will also be using after the visualization to record your experience.

5. Read or recite her invocation—as written in her chapter or in your own words.

6. Honor her with favorite foods and wine/juice/water (communion)— you get to eat some, but be sure to leave the sweetest, best, most generous treats for her. In a group working the following may be read aloud by the FP prior to feasting—if working solo, you may recite it:

   [NAME OF HER ASPECT HERE], look what I have brought you! I have brought the foods you love to eat, and the libations you love to drink. I have brought your favorite gifts. Please look upon me with favor, and know that I come before you to offer myself in witnessing and service to YOU.

6.5 You may also want to offer her your works of art or other items here. This is an opportunity to consecrate the items in her honor, and to dedicate them to her.

7. GUIDED VISUALIZATION
   In preparation for the guided visualization, you will want to make yourself comfortable. You may want to sit or lie down, though doing a visualization while standing works just as well for many. You will probably want to close your eyes so you can turn your focus toward your inner sight.

   With visualization, you may not actually *see* everything offered in the visualization. That's okay! You will notice what you notice. Some people feel visualizations, or hearing the words may be the magick in itself. Don't get stuck on the *shoulds*. Stay present in the *is*.

This visualization also may be read aloud by the FP. If working solo, you may record it for yourself or visit jailbreakingthegoddess .com to find a recording in the author's voice. It's a longer piece, and you need to be able to give yourself to the experience of it, so find a way you can listen to it:

GUIDED VIZUALIZATION FOR *INVOCATION RITUAL:*

Imagine, or visualize, yourself moving toward [NAME ASPECT]. You may see her in the distance, or perhaps she is right in front of you.

You may feel her presence, or you may even see her. She may reveal herself through sound, or feel, scent, or even taste. She may reveal herself to you in all of these ways. Or in a different manner entirely.

How [NAME OF ASPECT] reveals herself to you is of little consequence; she is everywhere, and she is in all things!

Take her in. What do you notice about her?

Whatever the way [NAME OF ASPECT] reveals herself, allow yourself to fully encounter her. Enter into her presence.

She has a gift for you. She may offer it through her gaze, or through words, or a scent that reminds you of a truth that you have known since time immemorial.

She may offer you an actual item.

Allow the importance of this gift to come into you. Accept what she has to offer with gratitude.

Thank [NAME OF ASPECT] for the gift, and for all of her gifts.

And now, it is time to leave this space, but know that [NAME OF ASPECT] is always here, because she is everywhere. When you need her, you can find her.

And she can find you, too.

For now release her, and slowly find your way back to this time and space. Follow your heartbeat. Become aware of your breathing. Find your way home to your blood and bones and flesh.

Feel yourself rising to the surface of your consciousness.

When you are ready, open your eyes, and write or draw, or in some way capture your experience with [NAME OF ASPECT].

GUIDED VIZUALIZATION FOR *INITIATION RITUAL:*

Imagine, or visualize, yourself moving toward [NAME OF ASPECT]. She may reveal herself through sound, or feel, scent, or even taste. She may reveal herself to you in all these ways, or in another way.

Feel her near you.

Whatever the way [NAME OF ASPECT] reveals herself, allow yourself to encounter her with love and honor.

Enter into her presence.

Let [NAME OF ASPECT] know that you are ready and willing to learn her ways. To learn what she has to teach you. That you are ready to enter onto the path of her teachings.

Ask [NAME OF ASPECT] if she has a task she wants you to perform. This task may be performed right now, or it may be carried out of this ritual and into the world.

If you don't understand what it is that [NAME OF ASPECT] is asking from you, ask if she can offer more clarity.

Once [NAME OF ASPECT] has clearly let you know what she would like from you, consider deeply whether it is something you are capable of offering. If it is not, offer [NAME OF ASPECT] something of similar intent, but which is within your capacity.

Once you are done with your negotiations, let [NAME OF ASPECT] know that you are honored to carry her work into the world in this way.

Then thank her for the charge she has set upon you.

It is now time to leave this space, but know that [NAME OF ASPECT] is always here, because she is everywhere. When you need her, you can find her. And she will find you as she desires as well.

For now, release her.

And slowly find your way back to this time and space. Back to your heartbeat, your blood and bones and flesh.

Open your eyes, and write or draw about your experience with [NAME OF ASPECT].

8. Write, draw, or otherwise commit to memory what she has offered you.

9. If in a group space, share your experience if desired. If so, you may also share food and drink in a sacred way.

10. Thank and release any energies that have attended the ritual.

11. Extinguish candle.

12. Breathe, center, release the space.

13. Add in formal ritual elements as desired to end the ritual here.

Rituals of Dedication

In preparation for a ritual of dedication, there are some steps that I encouraged you to take. One is to really enquire into your calling to become dedicated to a deity. Another is to consider whether this is something that feels aligned, sustainable, and of benefit to you. And if so, does it feel aligned and sustainable for your family? Your community? The world?

To that end, here are some things dedication to a deity means and does not mean:

Dedicating yourself to a deity means that you are committing to working with that deity, to being a co-conspirator with her, to staying in good communication with her, to doing as she requests in cases where it is also in alignment for you, and all-in-all to staying in integrity in your relationship with her.

It does *not* mean that you can't have relationships with other deities, unless that is something she is requiring of you or something you feel is essential to your bond with her. It doesn't mean you have no say in how you serve her. And just so both you and the deity can stay clear on exactly what the fine points are, it's a good idea to create a contract before performing a ritual of dedication.

Contract of Dedication

This contract is about long-term agreements with the deity who has chosen you and whom you have chosen. This contract outlines your commitments to your goddess and also covers the limits to your agreement.

When entering into a long-term relationship with a deity, having agreements in place will make the relationship more consensual, navigable, and sustainable.

One of the things to know as you enter into an ongoing relationship with your goddess is that her needs may be great at times. She may want or need you to do things for her—you're offering to be her hands in the mundane world, after all. She may need your attention, intention, voice, or even your body. That said, you will be getting so much from this relationship that it will be worthwhile exchange. And if you aren't sure that's true, perhaps you should reconsider the dedication.

Your contract of dedication may be adapted as your relationship with your goddess deepens and shifts. It is wise to build into your contract a provision that the contract be reviewed, updated, and renewed at regular intervals. At first you may want that interval to be short; perhaps every full moon, or new moon, or gibbous moon, every month for a run of thirteen cycles—which would be approximately a year. After that, perhaps it would be every sabbat, or quarterly on the equinoxes, solstices, or cross quarters. Then perhaps you will move to yearly—or if you like, every year and a day.

The template that follows is just that—a template. I encourage you to come up with your own sections, vows, and words. The best vows come from your own being, emerging as expressions of the love and connection you feel.

In crafting the physical contract, think about whether you would like it to be framed and hung on a wall, kept on your altar, or secured under lock and key. Whatever your choice, you will perhaps want to make it beautiful. The crafting of this item is in itself a magickal act.

Template for Contract of Dedication

- *Preamble*

  - *I am dedicating myself to you, [NAME OF HER ASPECT HERE], because I see myself in you, and I see the me I want to become. I see your works, and I see how to carry them into the world. I love you. You are my heart. It is my True Will and life work to know your ways, to learn and teach through you and for you. Together we will create the world we know is possible.*

- *Vows of Fealty*

  - *I am yours. Together we will dream new dreams and old dreams, and live them into the waking world. I offer myself as your willing vessel and vassal, your beloved, your co-conspirator.*

- *Limits*

  - *I will take your will as my own when you need me to or want me to. I ask that this relationship always be a conversation; that together we decide the best courses of action, or inaction.*

  - *I offer my body for your use as agent of your Will in the world, and I ask that you take into account my humanity, the comparable frailty and transitory nature of this body. I will need to sleep when it is time and eat when it is time. When you are feeling impatient, please remember that feeding and tending this body is in your honor. Taking care of this vessel is in our shared highest good.*

- *Vows of Service*

  - *My hands are yours, my body is yours, my heart is yours, my mind is yours, my spirit is yours. I offer all of these into your service.*

  - *My Works are your Works, your Works are mine. In our cocreation, we will together manifest the most powerful offerings and most needed services in our shared nature.*

Your Ritual of Dedication

You may choose to perform this ritual as an experience you want to share only with your goddess. Or, you may choose to perform it with your circle siblings. Your ritual of dedication is a ceremony of commitment, and it's sweet and also important for many of us to have those witnessed. It is also a celebration of your love and dedication to her, and this may be something you want to share with your circle, your family, your community.

If it feels right to perform this ritual with your magickal family, perhaps you will want to have the facilitating priestess role be taken on by someone other than you, so that you can give yourself completely to the experience of taking your vows and making your dedication.

Note: In addition to the role of FP, I've added another for this ritual: dedicant. That's YOU!

Template

- Make sure you have all of your ritual items with you before you begin.
  - In addition to your usual lists, this ritual requires that you have your contract of dedication. If you want to sign the contract in ritual space (in addition to speaking it) bring a pen as well.
  - In addition to your usual offerings, you will also need an item you have already consecrated to her that you can use as your symbol of dedication. A wearable item is a good idea. Like a wedding band, this will be an external reminder of the vows you have made. It may be a ring, a necklace, a bracelet. It should be something that is easy to wear and durable. You might even end up getting a tattoo as part of your dedication. (It's been known to happen!)
  - You may want to bring flowers or other items to really make the space beautiful. Remember: it's like a wedding!
- Clear ritual space.
- Create altar or altars, including offerings of food and drink. And flowers (if desired).

- Set out your offerings for her: food, drink, and other offerings; any artwork or other items you've created that you want to have present for the dedication. Your journal or other memory-collecting.

- Add in formal ritual elements here if desired, as well as at the end of the following outline. Or you can use this basic outline as it stands:

Ritual

1. Light incense if you wish. You may instead asperge the space with water—flower water, herb water, salt water, or fresh water. Or clear the space with a tree branch, feathers, or other clearing tool.

2. Bring yourself present in the space. Use your breath, listen to your heartbeat. Feel your body. Embody yourself. Come into your skin, and into the present moment.

3. Light a candle for her.

4. FP says to those gathered:

   We are here to honor and celebrate [DEDICANT'S NAME]'s commitment to the goddess she has chosen to dedicate herself to. Each of us will stand as sacred witness to the vows that are taken. In the days to come, we will each have opportunity to be part of the fabric that holds the container for this relationship. We will have opportunities to become co-conspirators. This is an honor, and it is a responsibility. At this time, we ask you to close your eyes and breathe together with us.

   Let this be the sign of our consent.

5. DEDICANT reads or recites her invocation, as written in her chapters, or in your own words

6. DEDICANT SAYS:

   [NAME OF ASPECT], I have brought the foods you love to eat, and the libations you love to drink. I have brought your favorite gifts.

And today I bring myself as an offering on your altar; come to me now, that I may give my heart, my mind, my body, and my soul to you as well.

DEDICANT honors her with offerings of favorite foods and wine/juice/water.

7. Taking of Vows

    a. If working in a group: FP calls DEDICANT forward and SAYS:

    You have told us, your community, that you are ready to take vows of dedication to this goddess, [NAME OF ASPECT]. What are the vows that you will now take?

    DEDICANT reads vows from contract.

    When Dedicant is finished, FP asks the group to give assent of support

    b. Or, if solitary: DEDICANT opens contract, and reads vows aloud.

8. Taking on the Symbol of Dedication

    a. If working in group, FP SAYS: *What item do you choose to invest with these promises you have made? As you are ready, put on the (ring, necklace, etc.) and affirm your vows.*

    b. OR, solitary: DEDICANT takes symbol of dedication and places it on her body.

9. Time for reflection:

    a. Group: FP SAYS: *This is a big magick. A big offering. An offering of love and dedication. [NAME OF ASPECT] is among us. Perhaps we all feel her or hear her. Now we will all take some moments for contemplation.*

       i. After some moments of silence, the FP invites participants to share some of what the goddess is telling them in this sacred time.

    b. Or solitary: DEDICANT takes time for contemplation, listening for anything the goddess has to tell her new dedicant.

    i. After contemplation, write, draw, or otherwise commit to memory what she has spoken or otherwise brought.

10. Sacrament of food and drink

    a. If in group ritual, time for offerings to the dedicant. All circle siblings give words of congratulations, encouragement, or words they have received from her, or even other gifts if they have brought them.

    b. If solitary, eating and drinking in contemplation and celebration.

11. Release of the Goddess

    a. FP SAYS: *Thank you ALL for being here. And now, it is time to prepare to go. We will go knowing that [NAME OF ASPECT] is always here, because She is everywhere. When you need Her, you can find Her. And She will find you as She desires as well.*
        For now we release Her, with love and gratitude.

    b. OR, solitary: DEDICANT releases Goddess.

12. Release any other energies that have attended the ritual.

13. Extinguish candle.

14. Breathe, center, release the space.

15. Add in ritual elements as desired to end the ritual here.

You may want to follow this ritual with a celebration, or with quiet contemplation. This is a choice best left up to the dedicant and her goddess.

The Ritual of Five Faces

This is an opportunity to honor the five aspects, and to learn from them. This is designed as a group working. It is not readily adaptable for solitary performance.

In this outline we work from the primary set of elemental correspondences offered in the chapters; Femella at center, Potens at fire, Creatrix at earth, Sapientia at air, Antiqua at water. However, if you prefer you may shift the format to align with the secondary associations: Femella with air, Potens with fire, Creatrix with water, Sapientia with earth, and Antiqua at center. Depending on your tradition, and your feelings about the elemental associations, this overlay may work better for you. It does align more easily with the sunwise circle casting and invocation format, but it's all a matter of desire. The former pattern is graceful in its complexity, and I encourage you to stretch yourself in ways that shake you free from old, stuck forms.

This ritual includes the practice of spirit possession as part of the working, so please feel grounded and secure in your capabilities and the capabilities of your working group before deciding to perform this ritual.

In this outline I use the term *spirit priestesses*, or SPs, for those who will be vessels for her five faces. These priestesses should for sure do some homework (and homeplay!) with their aspect in anticipation. Each priestess should have a solid relationship with her aspect already in place, and ideally, should have already created her contract of spirit possession.

Preparation

Build four elemental altars, and five goddess altars, one altar for each of the five. Alternatively, these altars may be combined; Potens with fire, Creatrix with earth, Sapientia with air, Antiqua with water, and Femella at the center altar. (Or in another configuration if you choose that.)

The term I'm using for those who are calling an element is *elemental guardians*, or EG. The elemental guardians may want to take responsibility for building the altar for their element, and the spirit priestesses may want to take responsibility for creating the altar for their deity.

Those who are offering themselves in the role of spirit priestesses are responsible also for making sure they have appropriate offerings for their goddess. These items will go on her altar; some before the ritual starts, and some during the ritual.

If others in the group have items to add to any altar as an offering, that's a great way to encourage group cohesion, and to make the spirits feel really welcome.

Make sure there are seats available in the circle for those who need them. Antiqua will likely be one of them! Regardless of how youthful or able-bodied her priestess is, Antiqua may want or need to be seated.

Also, always make sure there is water for staying hydrated.

Assign/Assume Roles

Guardians of the circle: one or two people who can asperge with sacred water, and/or use smoke (sage, copal, sweetgrass, or other) to cleanse those who are entering into the circle.

Facilitating Priestess (FP): casts circle, and tends to flow of energy. If you are a small group, she may also call elements.

Elemental Guardians: call air, fire, water, earth. May be conducted by one person if your group is small. Or, may be called by those spirit priestessing, as detailed below.

Spirit Priestess of Femella: aspect

Spirit Priestess of Potens (may also call fire)

Spirit Priestess of Creatrix (may also call earth)

Spirit Priestess of Sapientia (may also call air)

Spirit Priestess of Antiqua (may also call water)

All spirit priestesses should take time as they build their altars to connect with the aspects of her that they will be holding.

A final word: the wording in this outline is suggested wording. If it doesn't feel right, say it differently. If it comes out differently in ritual, it's okay! For example, I've put the word *love* in this outline. If someone doesn't feel inspired to say love, they shouldn't say it.

Staying true to the heart of it is, in my opinion, always more important than saying a specific word. I also know that this is not a common opinion among some magick workers. I'm not saying that anyone is wrong—do what's most right for you.

And begin!

············

GUARDIANS cleanse and bless those entering circle

FP conducts banishing (optional).

FP casts circle.

Elemental Priestess/es call air, fire, water, earth.

FP, calling Femella, SAYS: *At the center stands Femella, Divine Child.*

FP offers items of food, drink, perhaps toys or other items to *Spirit Priestess of Femella.*

FP SAYS: *Femella, I invite you to come into this priestess before you. She is willing to be your servant in this rite. Let her body be your body in this circle. We welcome you.* (or other words the *FP* has chosen)

FP Reads or ideally, recites an invocation to Femella. (The one in her chapter or a different one.)

Spirit Priestess of Femella allows the goddess to come into her, and SAYS whatever *Femella* has to say at the moment. It may be nothing at all! She may smile and offer hugs to those around. Her priestess allows this process and gives herself over to her. (LEAVE TIME AND SPACE HERE.)

FP interacts with Femella. SAYS: *Welcome, sweet one. Would you like to sit here, or would you like to walk with me as I call upon your sisters?*

Femella does as she will.

············

FP turns and SAYS: *With the Fire stands Potens, Brave and Wild!*

FP walks forward, and offers items of food, drink, or other items to *Spirit Priestess of Potens.*

FP SAYS: *Potens, I invite you to come into this priestess before you. She is willing to be your servant in this rite. Let her body be your body in this circle. We welcome you.* (or other words the *FP* has chosen)

FP reads, or ideally recites, an invocation to Potens. (The one in her chapter, or a different one.)

Spirit Priestess of Potens allows the goddess to come into her, and SAYS whatever *Potens* has to say at the moment. Her priestess allows this process and gives herself over to Her. (LEAVE TIME AND SPACE HERE.)

FP interacts with Potens. SAYS: *Welcome, sweet one. Would you like to sit here, or would you like to walk with me as I call upon your sisters?*

Potens does as she will.

. . . .

FP turns and SAYS: *With the Earth stands Creatrix, Creator Divine!*

FP walks forward, and offers items of food, drink, or other items to *Spirit Priestess of Creatrix.*

FP SAYS: *Creatrix, I invite you to come into this priestess before you. She is willing to be your servant in this Rite. Let her body be Your body in this circle. We welcome you.* (or other words the *FP* has chosen)

FP reads, or ideally recites, an invocation to Creatrix. (The one in her chapter or a different one.)

Spirit Priestess of Creatrix allows the goddess to come into her, and SAYS whatever *Creatrix* has to say at the moment. Her priestess allows this process and gives herself over to Her. (LEAVE TIME AND SPACE HERE.)

FP interacts with Creatrix. SAYS: *Welcome, sweet one. Would you like to sit here, or would you like to walk with me as I call upon your sisters?*

Creatrix does as she will.

. . . .

FP turns and SAYS: *With the Air stands Sapientia, Woman of Knowing, Woman of Art!*

FP walks forward, and offers items of food, drink, or other items to *Spirit Priestess of Sapientia.*

FP SAYS: *Sapientia, I invite you to come into this priestess before you. She is willing to be your servant in this rite. Let her body be your body in this circle. We welcome you.* (or other words the *FP* has chosen)

FP reads, or ideally recites, an invocation to Sapientia. (The one in her chapter, or a different one.)

Spirit Priestess of Sapientia allows the goddess to come into her, and SAYS whatever *Sapientia* has to say at the moment. Her priestess allows this process and gives herself over to her. (LEAVE TIME AND SPACE HERE.)

FP interacts with Sapientia. SAYS: *Welcome, sweet one. Would you like to sit here, or would you like to walk with me as I call upon your sisters?*

Sapientia does as She will.

. . . .

FP turns and SAYS: *With the Water stands Antiqua, Ancient One!*

FP walks forward, and offers items of food, drink, or other items to *Spirit Priestess of Antiqua.*

FP SAYS: *Antiqua, I invite you to come into this priestess before you. She is willing to be your servant in this rite. Let her body be your body in this circle. We welcome you.* (or other words the *FP* has chosen)

FP reads, or ideally recites, an invocation to Antiqua. (The one in her chapter, or a different one.)

Spirit Priestess of Antiqua allows the goddess to come into her, and SAYS whatever *Antiqua* has to say at the moment. Her priestess allows this process and gives herself over to her. (LEAVE TIME AND SPACE HERE.)

FP interacts with *Antiqua.* SAYS: *Welcome, sweet one. We are blessed by your presence.*

With all Five Goddesses present:

FP SAYS: *Welcome, great goddesses. We are honored to have you present in our circle. We offer you our hospitality. Please stay for a while. Let us eat these fine foods together, and drink these delightful drinks, and talk of the things we women must talk about. (Or other words as the FP feels best.)*

At this point, any of *the Five* may offer words. Or *the Five* may interact with each other, or with the group as a whole. (LEAVE TIME AND SPACE HERE.)

FP SAYS: *Dear goddesses, would you be willing to offer your insight? There are those among us who may have questions for you. We would be grateful for your council, and as you speak to any of us, we know you are speaking to all of us.*

Note: If the group is very large, you will want to limit questions or be prepared to sit in circle for a long time. Since you have food and drink this should be fine, but FP must stay attentive to the circle and make sure that everyone is taking care of themselves and one another.

With this in mind, those in the circle who have questions for the goddesses may ask.

FP SAYS: *I invite you all to make yourselves comfortable, as we listen to the council these goddesses offer.*

FP facilitates as questions are asked and answered.

Once this—which is truly the main part of this working—has been given time and comes to a natural conclusion:

FP SAYS: *Great goddesses, we thank you for your attendance, your attention, your wisdom, and your teachings. We will carry your offerings with us into our lives. We will plant these thoughts like seeds so your wisdom and compassion will grow within the people.*

And now, we know it is time for us to go our way and you to go yours. We know that you are not truly leaving us; we will watch for you in the seasons, the cycles. We will recognize you in the faces of our sisters, mothers, daughters, friends, and lovers.

And we are not truly leaving you; we will come back to your altar again and again. We will make offerings and invite you into our hearts, our minds, our work, and play. We will keep your rites, and we will honor you in the work we do.

ALL sing a song—of your choosing. (Some suggestions: *River of Birds* by Libana, *We Are a Circle* by Rick Hamouris, *Circle Round for Freedom* by Alice DiMicele.)

FP walks to Antiqua. If they are not at her *altar*, they go there together.

FP SAYS: *Antiqua, thank you for your gifts. We are grateful. We will keep your words in our hearts and hold them safe. Now we will let you rest. We invite you to return to the time outside of time and space outside of space where you exists always. We ask that you return the body of (NAME), your faithful priestess to her now.*

ALLOW SOME TIME AND SPACE for the release. Then,

FP greets spirit priestess by her name and offers her water.

FP SAYS: *(Name), we thank you for your service, and are happy to have you back! We know that some of her memories are yours now, and we will honor you when she speaks through you. For now, welcome home. We love you.*

Spirit priestess SAYS: *Thank you. I'm honored. And I love you all.*

. . . .

FP walks to *Sapientia.* If they are not at her *altar,* they go there together.

FP SAYS: *Sapientia, thank you for your gifts. We are grateful. We will keep your words in our hearts and hold them safe. Now we will let you rest. We invite you to return to the time outside of time and space outside of space where you exists always. We ask that you return the body of (NAME), your faithful priestess to her now."*

ALLOW SOME TIME AND SPACE for the release. Then,

FP greets spirit priestess by her name and offers her water.

FP SAYS: *(Name), we thank you for your service, and are happy to have you back! We know that some of her memories are yours now, and we will honor you when she speaks through you. For now, welcome home. We love you.*

Spirit priestess SAYS: *Thank you. I'm honored. And I love you all.*

. . . .

FP walks to *Creatrix.* If they are not at her *altar,* they go there together.

FP SAYS: *Creatrix, thank you for your gifts. We are grateful. We will keep your words in our hearts and hold them safe. Now we will let you rest. We invite you to return to the time outside of time and space outside of space where you exists always. We ask that you return the body of (NAME), your faithful priestess to her now.*

ALLOW SOME TIME AND SPACE for the release. Then,

FP greets spirit priestess by her name and offers her water.

FP SAYS: *(Name), we thank you for your service, and are happy to have you back! We know that some of her memories are yours now, and we will honor you when she speaks through you. For now, welcome home. We love you.*

Spirit priestess SAYS: *Thank you. I'm honored. And I love you all.*

. . . .

FP walks to *Potens.* If they are not at her *altar,* they go there together.

FP SAYS: *Potens, thank you for your gifts. We are grateful. We will keep your words in our hearts and hold them safe. Now we will let you rest. We invite you to return to the time outside of time and space outside of space where you exists always. We ask that you return the body of (NAME), your faithful priestess to her now.*

ALLOW SOME TIME AND SPACE for the release. Then,

FP greets spirit priestess by her name and offers her water.

FP SAYS: *(Name), we thank you for your service, and are happy to have you back! We know that some of her memories are yours now, and we will honor you when she speaks through you. For now, welcome home. We love you.*

Spirit priestess SAYS: *Thank you. I'm honored. And I love you all.*

. . . .

FP walks to *Femella.* If they are not at her *altar,* they go there together.

FP SAYS: *Femella, thank you for your gifts. We are grateful. We will keep your words in our hearts and hold them safe. Now we will let you rest. We invite you to return to the time outside of time and space outside of space where you exist always. We ask that you return the body of (NAME), your faithful priestess to her now.*

ALLOW SOME TIME AND SPACE for the release. Then,

FP greets spirit priestess by her name and offers her water.

FP SAYS: *(Name), we thank you for your service, and are happy to have you back! We know that some of her memories are yours now, and we will honor you when she speaks through you. For now, welcome home. We love you.*

Spirit Priestess SAYS: *Thank you. I'm honored. And I love you all.*

Elemental Priestesses release elements in the opposite order of invoking.

FP releases circle.

FP performs banishing in reverse order.

REMEMBER to build in time for aftercare. Be especially mindful to take care of the facilitating priestess, and the spirit priestesses. These are intense roles to take on, and those holding them may feel depleted, raw, or energized, or ungrounded. Make sure that these members are allowed to go "off-duty" once the circle is released.

Other group members may want to offer them food or water, help in taking down altars if they want it, or other support as needed.

In clearing off the altars, find a creative way to release whatever offerings made to the goddesses that still remain. Put them somewhere they will find and enjoy them. At the same time, be conscious of the dietary needs of the wildlife and domesticated animals where you are among other environmental considerations.

Appendix
— Magickal and Ritual Considerations for a New Practitioner —

If you are just starting out as a ritualist or worker of magick, this section is for you. We will go over altar building, magickal dress, some magickal techniques, and some ritual design and templates.

Many opportunities for intuitive training are offered here, and there is a lot you can learn throughout the book in this regard. There are strengths to formal, structured, and performance-based practice. If a formal ceremonial format appeals to you, take what I offer here, adapt it, infuse it with your own spirit, and make it yours.

Altars

If you have an altar set up in your home you can dedicate to the goddess, you may do so by adapting the altar to her needs and desires. In this case, you will bring your rituals to the altar. If you have never built an altar, start with this section.

You can build your altar on any surface that makes sense to you. You may leave your altar up all the time or build it for rituals and take it down after you are finished. How "out" you are able to be about your practices will play a part in choosing the best option.

If you're planning on leaving your altar up, do you want it to be in a more public and visible part of your home (or yard) or do you want it in a more private or secluded space? You may build your altar on a countertop, the top of a dresser in your bedroom, a table set up for this purpose, or outside on a stump, rock, log, or even on the ground.

If you're creating a mobile altar that you can build and take down and rebuild for a specific ritual, you may find a milk crate or wooden or molded plastic box to serve the purpose well; you can store and carry all your altar pieces in the box, and then turn it upside down to use as your altar surface. If you use a milk crate, a cardboard, plastic, or wooden top will be needed to create a stable, solid surface.

*Interesting things Witches use as **traveling altar boxes**:*

- *Upcycled ammunition boxes*
- *Lunch boxes*
- *First-aid boxes*
- *Suitcases*
- *Hat boxes*
- *Cases that once held a musical instrument*

To create your altar, you may want to place a cloth of an appropriate color on the altar surface. This color may be chosen from the correspondences offered in the chapters on the five faces, or you can simply intuit a color and go with that.

Next, place any tools and items you regularly use to create ritual space, such as candles, an incense censer or essential oil diffuser, and your magickal tools if you use them. If you like to make an offering or take a sacrament of wine, spirits, or juice in addition to water, make sure you have two chalices. Or you could use a shot glass and a chalice, depending on who you're working with.

Place the parts that go into creating the altar specific to the ritual you are working, including your offerings to the aspect of her you are working with. Again, if you aren't sure what these might be, look in the chapter of the face of the five you are working with.

Ritual Wear

When performing ritual alone I'm more likely to be skyclad (Witchy code for naked) than wearing ornate robes, but that's mostly because I prefer being naked to being clothed.

Even in group ritual I am not likely to be wearing fancy dress. The only time I can be relied upon to show up in ritual dress is when it is required such as in a performance-based ritual or when it has been commanded to me by the deity herself. When a goddess I'm working with requires costumery herself, of course I do as she requests. This is a phenomenon far from unheard of. Just like she will tell you what she wants on her altar, if you listen she may tell you what she wants you to wear to her ritual.

Generally, wear whatever makes you feel best. Whether you dress for comfort, for fashion, for devotion, or for fun, make sure you feel good. That's really the only essential part. If you like wearing finery for ritual, do it up. If you want to be naked, do that!

Some Traditional Magickal Tools

There is very little standardization on tools and associations. As you will see, some items show up in more than one elemental category. Also, I have added some you won't find in other lists of association. At risk of sounding like a broken record, do as you feel aligned to.

Air: blade/athame, pen, sword, feather, censer/incense, staff, wand, broom.

Gemstone: amethyst, fluorite, angelite.

Fire: wand, flame of any sort, blade/athame, staff.

Gemstone: tiger's eye, tiger iron, carnelian, red jasper, fire opal, smoky quartz, obsidian.

Water: chalice, shell, cauldron, ocean glass.

Gemstone: pearl, blue calcite, sodalite, aventurine.

Earth: pentagram, disk, cauldron, mortar and pestle, salt, compass, rocks, lodestone.

Gemstone: crystals, hematite, jaspers, and all gemstones.

Center: bonfire, cauldron, altar, scrying mirror, lodestone, compass, candles, athame/blade, bell, pentagram.

Gemstone: crystals, lapis lazuli, gold, silver.

Broom: clearing space, warding. Also a fertility symbol.

Bell or singing bowl: to clear the space energetically, to call the spirits or quarters.

Tool Consecration

There are many ways to consecrate tools. Here is a very simple formula. There are two basic parts to consecrating: cleansing and charging. An optional third is dedicating. Again that main tool in consecration is your intention, so if that is in good working order, everything else is secondary.

Cleansing can be done with salt water or pure water if an item can take damp (some can't, so use your good judgment), smoke (incense, wood fire, candle), air exposure, moonlight, sunlight, or soil.

If an item may rust or disintegrate, don't use the water or soil options. If an item can take exposure to damp, burial for a time is a good way to let it discharge any negative energies it may be holding. Direct exposure to salt can also work, but iron combined with salt and dampness will get you rust, so be careful.

If you have a stone, gem, or crystal that you want to cleanse be sure to first research the care and feeding of your particular stone. Some stones cannot be soaked, but can be washed. Some, like pearls, are very absorbent; exposure to oils or solvents can discolor or degrade them.

Charging can be done using the same elements, but if you are using a tool for a connection to a particular element, it makes the most sense to use that element to charge the item. For example, if you're going to use a wand to interact with fire you will want to charge the wand with fire; a candle is easy, and an outdoor bonfire—especially a dedicated festival fire—would be fantastic.

Dedication of your tools to one of her faces may be done in one of her rituals.

Magickal Timing

Moon cycles

Dark moon: the actual moment of the monthly Solar/Lunar conjunction, when the moon is not visible from Earth.

New moon: the point where the moon moves through the conjunction and is visible as a sliver crescent.

Quarter or gibbous moon: When the moon appears as a half-moon. The point between new and full, and between full and new.

Waxing: Increasing, or growing, from new to full.

Waning: Decreasing from full to dark.

Moon cycles are often employed in magick. The new to full and back to new cycle of the moon is used as a measure of magickal time, and different points in the lunar cycle offer different kinds of energy to power magick. Some practitioners begin spell workings on the full moon and work the spell though the following moon cycle back to full. Others start a spell at the new moon and work the spell through to the next dark moon. Some start, perform, or complete different kinds of magicks at different times of the moon.

Spells for growing, developing, bringing in, and increasing are often performed during the waxing phase as the moon grows larger, while spells for releasing, diminishing, letting go, or banishing are often performed during the waning phase between full and dark.

Year and a day
A year and a day is the amount of time many Wiccan and Neo-Pagan groups expect one to be in a group or coven before becoming an initiate, and sometimes between degrees. In some traditions, a year and a day is also a common "trial" hand-fasting period.

Elements of Ritual
There are as many ways to create and conduct rituals as there are ritualists to design them. Some people like grand, dramatic, scripted ritual. Some like simple, short, no-frills ritual. Some don't mind reading out the spoken parts of ritual, the evocations and the invocations. Some would rather memorize it all before embarking on a ritual. Others prefer to make it up as they go along.

I deeply believe that there is no single "right" way to do ritual. The outlines, ideas, structures, and even invocations I offer here are suggestions. Even more shockingly, I will posit that *every* system of magick, ceremony, and ritual was made up by someone at some point along the way. Keep this in mind, and let it liberate you as you embrace magick in your own way.

Magickal consciousness is highly intuitive. As you feel ready to step more and more solidly into your relationship with magick, you will become a stronger and stronger ritualist. Trust yourself to come to the right words, the right movements. Trust your own voice, body, senses. Create your own invocations, castings, clearings.

I offered full and adaptable ritual outlines earlier in the book, as well as a more stripped down model in the actual ritual formats in previous chapters designed for her five faces. There's something to be said for rituals that are simple enough to remember without a script.

Ritual, ceremony, and magick are very much about consciousness. There are many different ways to create one desired outcome.

Invocation and Evocation

Some use these terms interchangeably. Others don't. For those who don't, to evoke means to call, or invite, a being (goddess, element, entity) into the circle. Some just call evoking "calling in."

To invoke means to call a being (goddess, element, entity) into and through, you. Or you may invoke a deity into another person who is prepared to take on that role for the ritual. See the section on spirit possession in chapter 12 for more.

Clearing Your Magickal Space

If you want to create a protected or sterile ritual space, but performing a banishing doesn't feel authentic to you, you may instead want to smudge with sage, palo santo, copal, or other cleansing smoke.

If you don't tolerate smoke, you may use salt traps to pull away negative energies. You may also draw your circle in salt to keep negative energies out. Or you can asperge the area with salt water.

You may also (or instead) mentally clear the area before you begin. This can be done by creating a simple banishing phrase and saying it out loud or silently. This phrase might be something like, "I now clear this space of all negative energies. This space is safe and protected."

If you take any of these measures, your ritual space will be clear and protected. Some methods are likely to feel more solid or complete for you than others. Feel into it, and arrive at the one that best fits your sense of magick, aesthetic, style, and process.

Using Visualization in Ritual

Another word for *visualization* is *imagining*, so if visualizing is a stretch, try imagining on for size. Visualization, or imagining, can be used in place of movement or speaking in cases where moving or speaking aloud is not realistic. You can actually conduct a whole ritual in your mind through visualization or imagining. You simply imagine you are doing each thing. This is a great magickal skill to have, as sometimes doing a banishing ritual in the privacy of your mind is one of the most powerful things you can do to clear your space of negative energy or protect yourself.

There are traditions that use this method primarily for learning ritual. In some traditions you don't do a ritual with voice and movement until you can do the whole thing without interruption in your mind.

Another use of visualization is to journey and find new information on spiritual levels. The journey may take you deeper into your own process, into other spiritual worlds, into contact with deities, spirits, angels, or other beings. Often journeying is a guided process either with a live guide or a recorded guided visualization.

Sometimes the process of journeying is aided by the use of sound, such as drumming or other music, in addition to voice. Journeying can also be intensified by use of incense, teas, scents, or any variety of plant medicines.

At its most basic level, just remember that visualizing can be as easy as imagining.

Scaling Things Down

The sections here are designed as large, ceremonial rituals that can be performed by one person, or can be adapted to be performed by a group as was outlined above. When there is space to perform a ritual in this manner it can be very powerful.

However, these steps can all be adapted to take up less space. If you don't have room for four elemental altars, you can create a single altar and build in spaces to honor each of the elements on that altar, along with the goddess or aspect you are honoring. You may mark out these spaces with candles, herbs, gemstones, tools, goddess statuettes, or in any way that feels right.

A Witch's Banishing Ritual of the Pentagram, Modified from the Lesser Banishing Ritual of the Pentagram

In addition to being its own elegant little ritual, the Lesser Banishing Ritual of the Pentagram (also known as LBRP) is a simple and profoundly effective way to clear ritual space, cast the circle and call on the guardians of the gates all in one fell swoop. It's a beautiful ritual when executed well, and can be modified to encompass your orientation. I call the modification I offer here A Witch's Banishing Ritual of the Pentagram (WBRP). While retaining much of the structure of the LBRP, the WBRP encourages self-examination and personalization.

This ritual format originates in the Western ceremonial systems of magick, and therefore uses the directions in accordance with the assumptions held in those systems. You may switch the elements around as desired.

In the section titled "The Pentagram" below, you will be using words to clear and charge the quarters. The word will carry the intent of bringing the guardian, entity, or energy present. This can be done by assigning a goddess from a pantheon you work with to each quarter.

You may call upon goddesses for this work. For example, if you work the Roman pantheon you might call Aurora for air, Caia Caecilia for fire, Juturna for water, and Tellus for earth. If you work with the Orishas, is might be Ayao for air, Oya for fire, Oshun or Yemeya for water, Aja for earth. If you work with Feri Tradition Witchcraft, Arida for air, Tana for fire, Tiamat for water, and Belili for earth.

(I will stress that I am using these as examples of pantheons you may already work with, not suggesting these as goddesses to borrow without first creating a relationship.)

Since we are working with the fivefold goddess you may choose to use her names; perhaps Sapientia in the east, Potens in the south, Antiqua in the west, and Creatrix in the north. You may envision them all holding the circle with Femella in the center. Alternatively, you may say the name of the associated element according to your tradition or belief. You could work with what the elemental association represents; perhaps air as inspiration, fire as passion, water as regeneration, earth as wisdom.

Finally, you may use any of the words that have been used by any of the ceremonial magickians, including the names of the archangels—which you may potentially adjust to align with Vodou, Candomble, or Santería as well.

There are many formulas and phrases to use or modify, and you can easily find them by doing a web search on the Lesser Banishing Ritual of the Pentagram, or LBRP.

1. Enter circle.

2. At the center of your circle stand and face AIR, and perform The Witch's Tree of Life:

   a. Point index and middle fingers of your dominant hand, folding other fingers.

   b. Touch forehead with the extended fingers, and say, "I am I."

   c. Point to the sky and say "In harmony with the heavens,"

   d. Point to the ground and say " … with the Earth,"

   e. Touch the front of your right shoulder and say " … with the Sun." (Adapt to left shoulder in the Southern Hemisphere if desired).

   f. Circle in front of chest to touch front of left shoulder and say " … and with the Moon." (Adapt to right shoulder in the Southern Hemisphere if desired).

   g. Bring hands to prayer position (hands facing each other in front of your chest) and say, "Forever and ever,"

   h. Lay left hand palm down on top of right hand palm up, in front of your solar plexus, and say, " … so it is."

3. The Pentagrams

   a. Walk to the AIR edge of the circle. (In Western ceremonial traditions, this is east.) Stand with your feet shoulder-width apart, facing the altar or direction. Raise your dominant hand, and starting at the left lower corner trace a pentagram in the air with your finger, wand, or athame. You will use the earth-banishing pentagram for all quarters. (Note: If it works for you, visualize the pentagram in glowing light as you draw it. This may add impact.)

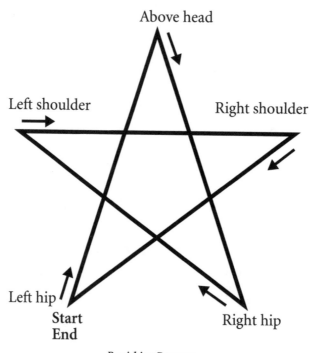

Banishing Pentagram

   i. Pointing toward the ground in front of your left foot, draw a line in front of you on the diagonal to up above your head.

  ii. From the apex, draw the line down toward your right foot.

 iii. Continue the line from your right foot toward your left shoulder.

 iv. Then from left to right in front of you, crossing at chest level.

v. Then go from the right extension back to the left in front of your toe.

vi. This completes the drawing of the pentagram. (You will do this four times—one for each of the directions.)

b. Bring your hands back to your sides.

c. Arms relaxed at your sides, slowly raise them to shoulder level, while you focus intently on the pentagram you've drawn and the word you will use to charge the direction in your mind.

d. Once your arms are stretching out from your shoulders parallel to the ground (your body shaped kind of like a five pointed star), bring your hands to the sides of your face, palms facing back.

e. Step forward strongly with your right foot into a shallow lunge while with both hands forcefully thrusting the energy forward, and say with intention the word you have chosen to charge this direction. With your intention you are energetically and magickally clearing your magickal and psychic space, and setting (or requesting, or calling to attention) a guardian in the direction you are facing.

f. Step forward with your left foot to meet your right. Once standing fully erect, weight distributed on both feet, arms relaxed at your sides, bring your index and middle fingers of your right hand to your lips in the sign of silence—like you're saying, "Shhh." (This is the sign of the initiate.)

g. Next, walk sunwise toward the next direction, while drawing an arc from one elemental point to the next. (This is the circle you are inscribing.)

h. Standing facing the next elemental quarter, again draw the pentagram, and follow the same steps as above, using the word you have chosen for this element.

i. Continue through the four directions in a sunwise progression, drawing an earth-invoking pentagram at each, and tracing an arc in the space between.

j. Complete the arc back to AIR, having inscribed the whole circle and charged each of the directions.

k. Turn sunwise to face the center of the circle again, and walk into the center of the circle.

4. Invocation of the forces of nature

a. Standing in the center of the circle, turn sunwise until you again face AIR.

b. Center, and then stretch your arms out at your sides until parallel to the ground, palms facing up.

c. SAY: "Before me the rushing wind, behind me the raging sea, to my right hand the leaping fire, and to my left hand the cool and trembling Earth. For about me is the omnipresence of her body, and within me is the consciousness of the continuity of existence." (Adjust for different elemental/directional correspondences as desired.)

5. Back to the Tree

a. The practitioner performs the Witch's Tree of Life again as in step 2.

Circle Casting and Opening

Depending on your magickal orientation, you may perform only this circle casting, and then move on to the rituals as I have written them for this book, for which you saw templates in chapter 14. Or, you may perform the circle casting and the calling of the elements (see below), and then the ritual. Or you may perform the WBRP banishing, then the circle casting, and calling the quarters—and deities, if you like, and then the body of the ritual.

> In some traditions it is common practice to cast the magickal circle walking **sunwise**, and to open (remove, dissolve) the circle walking the opposite direction.

You may choose to do none of the above, and use the simple format of the ritual templates as offered in chapter 14, or something else entirely. I will continue reminding you that you get to design your rituals in the ways that make the most sense to you.

To cast a circle is to create a bubble or sphere of sacred space. Many practitioners use an athame or a wand to cast and release the circle. With a blade (or a hand used with intention), it becomes the "cutting" of a circle. You are cutting yourself out of the mundane world, and into a space that is amplified, protected, and sanctified.

Casting and opening a circle, as any magickal act, must be done with intention more than anything. Adding actual function of movement may intensify. As you cast and then open the circle, visualize these things occurring. As you cast, envision the circle becoming a protective sphere. As you open, envision the sphere of sacred space dissolving into nothing.

Some Witches use the "Rule of Three" as a basis for ritual and magick. To cast a circle in the tradition I come from, you walk the perimeter of the circle three times sunwise to cast and three times opposite sunwise to open or release the circle. Like unwinding the magick. Depending on your tradition, you may have different assignations for the three times around, or walk the circle once to cast and once to open.

As you cast the circle you may voice an incantation (which you can write yourself, or find on websites or in any number of books), or you can do the casting and opening in silence. Whichever route you take, employ the energy of visualization in the casting and opening. You can lend your energy to the casting and opening without even saying a word.

Calling (aka Evoking) Elements and Spiritual Entities

The calling of quarters, also known as the elements, is a widespread Wiccan and Neo-Pagan practice. It is also employed in ceremonial, Feri, and many other traditions. Calling the quarters is asking the elements (or "guardians of the watchtowers" if you are ceremonially inclined) to be present in your working. Calling the elements is performed as an aspect of the WBRP, but if you choose to not perform the banishing, calling the elements may be done in concert with circle casting. Even if you do the WBRP, you may be inspired to call upon the elements in this more conversational manner.

You may call the four elements (air, fire, water, earth), or five (the four elements and center which is often associated with spirit, or with the ancients and future beings), or seven (the five already listed, plus above and below). You may also invoke Goddess and God if you desire.

Instead of any of these options, you may call each of the five as guardians (or servants) of the elements. You may do this with one each assigned to the element you associate with her.

Calling the elements and deities or energy forms can be done a lot of different ways. Many traditions have their own scripts for callings. Another way to do it is just to focus on the representations that the entities hold for you, the practitioner.

With all callings, it is traditional to close with the whole group saying a statement such as "So it is!" or "So mote it be" or "Air (or earth, fire, water, or she, or he) is here," or "Hail, and welcome!"

Working in an intuitive manner, callings might go something like this:

For AIR: "Spirits of air, I call upon you. Please bring clarity, inspiration, and ease of communication to this circle. I call the spirits of dawn, new ideas, and freedom of thought. Please be present here, and bring your blessings to this circle. So it is." And then ALL say, "So it is!"

For FIRE: "Spirits of fire, I call on you. Please bring passion, warmth, and transformation. I call on fire to warm and transform this sacred space. Bring your heat, desire, and light. Burn bright in this circle. So it is." And then ALL say, "So it is!"

For WATER: "Spirits of water, I call on you. Please bring us sweet healing waters, tears of joy, and tears of loss. Bring to us the life, death, and regeneration all held in the watery womb. Please be present here, and bring your blessings to this circle. So it is." And then ALL say, "So it is!"

For EARTH: "Spirits of earth, I call on you. Please bring wisdom, stability, creation, growth. I call on earth to bring us present to the very soil we stand upon, our feet growing roots like trees. Please be present here, and bring your blessings to this circle. So it is." And then ALL say, "So it is!"

Continue, with whatever energies/entities you choose to call.

You may also wish to light candles at each elemental altar or on your central altar as part of the calling. The elements are most often called in a sunwise progression like the casting, usually starting with air, which in many cases is associated with the east, though some traditions start with earth.

Again, you get to decide. It's your magick; do what feels right to you.

The Body of the Ritual

Believe it or not, all you have seen so far is preamble to the main body of the ritual, although it is quite important! The body of the ritual, where you do the working, comes next. In chapter 14 you saw ritual templates that could be plugged into this space depending on which aspect of her you are working with and what level of ritual (invocation, initiation, or dedication) you are performing.

This part is where you will make your offerings, and in group working where you will witness and be witnessed in your magickal work and commitments.

Releasing Quarters and Spiritual Entities

At the end of a ritual, entities and quarters that have been called must be released. Releasing goes in the opposite order of calling, starting with the last entity or quarter called, working back to the first. It can be very simply stated, such as "Spirits of Earth, thank you for your presence and your blessings on this circle" or as flowery as you like.

In the tradition I grew up in, we would end the releasing with the statement "Go if you must, stay if you will. Hail, and farewell." Use whatever wording feels right.

Some concepts to work with:

- Gratitude to the entities who attend.

- Permission for them to move on if they must.

- Recognition that they are ever-present, and that it is our attention that leaves them.

Again, in group ritual, a group refrain is a useful piece of ceremonial technology. The phrase, "Hail, and farewell" works, as do many others.

A Comprehensive, Eclectic Ritual Outline

If you want to include all of the steps offered in your ritual outline, here's a template of how it might look:

1. Perform WBRP.

2. Cast the circle by circumambulating three times sunwise.

3. Call elements in a sunwise progression, and call center.

4. Call deity/deities.

5. The central working of the ritual (healing, devotion, observation of sabbat).

6. Opening or ending the circle: at the end, everything is undone in the opposite order of how it was done, last to first. It's like you're walking back out to the world and you want to retrace your steps. Starting with the last invocation, release each deity, guardian, and/or entity you called. The releasing will move around the circle counter-sunwise.

7. Release deity/deities.

8. Release each element counter-sunwise.

9. Open the circle by circumambulating counter-sunwise three times.

10. Perform banishing counter-sunwise.

So Many Options!

You might be experiencing a bit of ritual design overload about now, and that's okay! You've just consumed a huge amount of information. Take some time to let it settle. Try things on for size. Imagine yourself performing different sections that feel compelling to you. Feel into correspondences. Orient yourself to the space, or spaces, you will be performing your rituals in.

Over time you will find what works best for you, adapting and fine-tuning these elements to fit you and your relationship with your goddesses and gods even better. You will come into a fluidity with your invocations and other ritual language whether memorized or made up on the spot. You will become more and more comfortable in your capacity for design, and in your ritual facilitation.

As you work toward this, just remember you can use as many or as few of these elements as you like. The most important thing is that you build a ritual design that feels aligned and integrated for you, your gods, and whomever you practice with.

Further Reading

Books

An Aesthetic Education in the Era of Globalization, Gayatri Chakravorty Spivak, Harvard University Press, 2012.

Bringing Race to the Table: Exploring Racism in the Pagan Community, Crystal Blanton et al., Immanion Press, 2015.

Ceremony, Leslie Marmon Silko, Penguin Books, 1977.

The Fifth Sacred Thing, Starhawk, Bantam, 1994.

For Indigenous Eyes Only: A Decolonization Handbook (Native America Sereie), Waziyatawin Angela Wilson and Michael Yellow Bird, et al., School of American Research Press, 2005

Gender and Transgender in Modern Paganism, Sarah Thompson, Gina Pond et al., Circle of Cerridwen Press, 2012.

Genocide of the Mind, Vine Deloria, Jr., Paula Gunn Allen, Leslie Marmon Silko et al., Nation Books, 2003.

God is Red, Vine Deloria Jr., Fulcrum Publishing, 1972.

Kissing the Hag, Emma Restall Orr, John Hunt Publishing Limited, 2009.

Power, Linda Hogan, Norton Paperback Fiction, 1999.

Shades of Faith, Crystal Blanton et al., Megalithica Books, 2011.

Sovereign Bones, Eric Gansworth et al., Nation Books, 2007.

The Spiral Dance, Starhawk, HarperOne, 1989.

Woman, Native, Other: Writing Postcoloniality and Feminism, Trinh T. Minh-Ha, Indiana University Press, 2009.

Electronic Media

Awakening the Horse People, www.awakeningthehorse.wordpress.com

Black Girl Dangerous, www.blackgirldangerous.org

Unsettling America, www.unsettlingamerica.wordpress.com

Acknowledgments

My first thank you goes to my kids, Sol and Aurora. I love you both with everything I am. I am so blessed to be your mama.

Aurora, sorry I was writing while you were getting ready to move out! Maybe I should have waited until after you left for UCSC to take on this project. However, the book has of course been informed by our conversations on the topics at hand, so I'm actually really glad you were here while I wrote it. You're amazing. Though I will greatly miss you living under the same roof with me, I'm sweetly anticipating the process of watching how the next chapters in your life emerge.

And to my kid Sol; thank you for helping me unlearn gender. And, thank you for being so understanding and supportive. You really know how to check in and be present with me, and I'm so grateful for that. Your hugs and laughs and our walks are a delight. You are an outstandingly compassionate person. I deeply love and appreciate you.

Huge gratitude to my husband, Robert Allen. You have supported me every step of the way. Thank you for all you do and all you are. Thanks for feeding me—literally. And for reading, again and again. And for talking it out with me. For the debates. For holding space for my crazy. And for loving me even when I mess up. I love you. Por vida.

And to my mom, Marylyn Motherbear Scott. Thank you for everything, but especially for sticking with it. I know it's not easy, but we do it. Thank you for teaching me and for raising me to be a rebel, and especially for loving me even when I'm challenging. I love you.

Corine Pearce, my gratitude for you goes far beyond what I can say in these pages. Thank you for being my co-conspirator, my friend, my sister. If I have to be in the trenches (and I do), I want to be in them with you. Thank you for being a sounding board. And more than anything, thank you for sharing your heart with me.

Deep thanks to Jenya Turner Beachy for loving me. I love our deep, strong, complicated, wonderful love. Thank you for those sweet opportunities to rest in our shared sense of what it is to be magick workers in this world. Our shared magick feeds me in a way nothing else does.

Mai'a Williams: woman, you went above and beyond! You read, offered feedback, had convos with me at all hours of the night, and brainstormed with me when I felt stuck. Wow, mama! I love you. I can only hope to be as helpful to you when you're ready for me to return the favor.

Rosa De Anda: you have been a tireless champion, offering amazing feedback and inspiration. My deep love, admiration, and gratitude go out to you. I am honored to feel that you consider my work to be in some manner part of your legacy.

Jade Karyn Dietz Dance: you have been a tireless support, an excellent proofreader, and a source of much needed comic relief. Thanks for the Easter eggs in the edits.

To my advisors and sounding boards: Aaminah Shakur, Sarah Clark, Kanyon Sayers-Roods, Michaela Spangenburg, Soror Sovran, Elena Rose, Christopher Bradford, Crystal Blanton, Heidi Marian, Alley Valkyrie, Kirsten Johnson, Nico Gamache. Robert, Corine, Motherbear, Mai'a, and Jenya also fall into this category. Some of you served in this capacity throughout, and some were there for just a moment, at just the *right* moment. Thank you.

And thank you to all my test readers and editors! Elinor Prędota, Jackie Chuculate, Áine Anderson, Kat Phillpotts, Sage Fae Wolf, Katie Kaput, Teresa Rosetta, Syren Nagakyrie, Chris McBride, Alan Young, Cat Crawford, Tanisha Rose Jolie, Jaron Smith, Mary-Charles Rasbach, Sherry Glaser, Laurie Sagewoman, Amy Blackthorn, Della Hillman, Sunny Logsdon, Bobcat Gwin, Morganne Baum, Durga Fuller, Jenna Buckmaster, Ioana Tchoukleva, Dee Schull, Gina Pond, Christy Meyer, Breezy Barcelo, Dani Leis, Jonathan Korman, Gina Pond, Ariel Gore, and the crew in Ariel's Literary Kitchen.

I'm sure I left a few names out because I'm nearly done and am pretty addled, but I am deeply grateful to every person who took the time to read and to offer feedback.

Thanks also to my sister, Patience Foster, and to Jonna Weidaw, and Tori Perreault. George Villaluz, Junior. Kahlid Arar Shawabka. Nicholas Yardley. And Josh King. And to

Michele Marlene York, Jessica Blank, Daniel del Vecchio, and Gwion Raven for interceding on my behalf.

And to my funders on my Fundrazr campaigns.

And of course, thank you to my publisher, and especially to my editor, Elysia Gallo. Without your encouragement *Jailbreaking the Goddess* would not have happened.

Also, thanks to the artists I had playing on repeat while I was writing: Lindsey Stirling, A Tribe Called Red, Vitamin String Quartet, Break of Reality, and Steve Jablonsky.

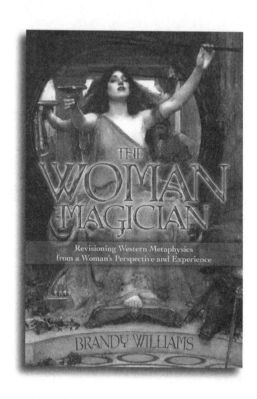

THE WOMAN MAGICIAN

Revisioning Western Metaphysics
from a Woman's Perspective and Experience

BRANDY WILLIAMS

The Woman Magician
Revisioning Western Metaphysics from a Woman's Perspective and Experience
BRANDY WILLIAMS

The Woman Magician is a thought-provoking and bold exploration of the Western magical tradition from a female perspective, celebrating the power of women's spirituality and their vital role in the magical community.

Drawing on thirty years of study and personal experience, Brandy Williams reframes magic around women, examining and challenging traditional Western notions of women's bodies, energies, and spiritual needs. She discusses women's roles throughout magic's history, gender issues, and honoring the voice within to live authentically as women and magicians.

Part two features personal and group initiatory rituals based on Egyptian cosmology, created by the Sisters of Seshat, the first all-female magical order since the French Revolution.

978-0-7387-2724-0 , 384 pp., 6 x 9   **$19.95**
